CHRIST

The Self-Emptying of God

by

Lucien Richard, O.M.I.

Paulist Press

New York / Mahwah, N.J.

Acknowledgments: I am especially grateful to Ellie Clarke for typing the first manuscript, to Brian M. Doyle for the typing and research for various drafts of this book, and to Alice Goodman for her editorial help.

Cover design by Tom Dove, C.S.P.

Book design by Kathleen Doyle

Library of Congress Cataloging-in-Publication Data

Richard, Lucien.
   Christ : the self-emptying of God / by Lucien Richard.
     p. cm.
   Includes bibliographical references and index.
   ISBN 0-8091-3668-6 (alk. paper)
    1. Incarnation. 2. Jesus Christ—Person and offices. I. Title.
BT220.R53 1996
232'.1—dc20   96-32526
                                                       CIP

Published by Paulist Press
997 Macarthur Boulevard
Mahwah, New Jersey 07430

Printed and bound in the
United States of America

CONTENTS

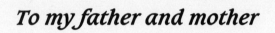

To my father and mother

Introduction

Christology has never been a peaceful possession for the church. The bitter controversies of the first seven centuries of the church's existence bear witness to that. Today every step of the Christological task is questioned. What may have appeared in the past as a satisfactory answer no longer seems so. This is true of the early church dogmas concerning the incarnation.[1] To Jesus' question "Who do you say I am?" there is today a variety of contradictory answers. Christology is the area where all contemporary theological battles seem to be waged. As soon as we enter the area of Christology, fundamental issues of faith emerge. Reductionism and fundamentalism become tempting possibilities.

> What many Christians both past and present have regarded as orthodox Christology may be regarded (not altogether unfairly) as a curious amalgam of different elements taken from different parts of first century Christianity—personal pre-existence from John, virgin birth from Matthew, the miracle worker from the so-called "divine man" Christology prevalent among some Hellenistic Christians, his death as atonement from Paul, the character of his resurrection from Luke, his present role from Hebrews and the hope of his parousia from the earlier decades.[2]

As much as Christology is still a debated area and the Christian faith is still moving through a variety of critical phases, Christ's question attracts responses today. As Hans Küng remarked: "The Christological debate that has persisted since the dawn of the modern age has not yet been resolved."[3]

> When he came to the territory of Caesarea Philippi, Jesus asked his disciples: "Who do men say that the Son of Man is?" They answered, "Some say John the Baptist, others Elijah, others Jeremiah or one of the prophets." "And you," he asked, "who do you say that I am?" (Mt 16:13-15; cf. Mk 8:27).

Jesus put his question to his disciples shortly before he went to Jerusalem

1

to suffer his passion. Two thousand years later, we are being asked the same question and, just as then, being given a variety of answers.

While the answers are of interest, what is most important to the student of Christology is the manner in which the question has been posed through two thousand years of Christianity. Initially, it was a two-part question: It was asked about the people—"Who do they say the Son of Man is?"—and it was asked directly of the disciples—"Who do you say that I am?" Today the question is asked of believers and of those outside the circle of faith. While their answers are not and need not be the same, they cannot be unrelated and in contradiction.

From within the circle of faith it is Christology's task to show what is really meant by the profession that Jesus is the Christ. Christology must establish the intrinsic foundation of that profession in the person of Jesus. It must attempt to answer how, why, and with what justice Jesus the proclaimer became Christ the proclaimed. And it must attempt to answer how that historically unique Jesus of Nazareth relates to universal claims about the Christ. For the title *Christ* has always been the expression used by faith to speak of Jesus' universal significance while, at the same time, identifying him in his own person. It is only through such an investigation that we can exclude a unilateral kerygmatic and dogmatic Christology and a Christology directed solely to the historical Jesus.

There is a twofold hermeneutic operative here: one that concerns the origins and foundations of Christianity's proclamation that Jesus is the Christ, and another that concerns the consequences of such a proclamation. Both interpretations must be made from within the circle of living faith. The contemporary Christian must have an answer to Jesus' question. But a simple recitation of what others have said in response is not sufficient. Today's Christian must be concerned with the here and now—"Who do you say I am?" Today.

Christology must be an attempt to trace the way from Jesus of Nazareth to the Christ of Christian belief. Since the theologian has to tell a story that is not only his or her story but also the story of Jesus of Nazareth, the story must be told in a different way for each generation. Retracing the way from Jesus of Nazareth to our proclaimed and confessed Christ can only be accomplished in the contemporaneity of faith.

In retracing this path a proper relationship must be maintained between the present Christ and the historical Jesus. Christology must constantly and simultaneously move in both directions. It is necessarily both critical and practical. This is possible only if we take part in the past event. We must understand more clearly than ever that the message of the New Testament is a legacy, a text to be interpreted. And we must bridge the distance in time between the past event of revelation and the present reality of our own faith, for the truth of the Christian message is rooted in the historical nature of our relationship to primitive Christianity. We cannot understand the life, death, and resurrection of Jesus the Christ without involving our lives in those mysteries we seek to understand.

Early Christianity understood the Christ event as the encounter between the human and the divine: Jesus is truly divine, truly human, truly one. At Chalcedon that belief was expressed in incarnational language. Such language, often metaphysical in nature, could not in any way take away the mystery present as the ground of the Christ-event. Every attempt to determine more specifically the idea that Jesus was both God and man has broken down. While much of Christology has been couched in metaphysical language, there is consensus today that when it comes to the Christ-event we are deep in the realm of symbols. In the 1973 Christmas issue of *Commonweal*, Avery Dulles wrote: "In some sense the Incarnation is a myth. Like other myths, it is a tale that holds us in its grip because in some strange way its symbolism casts light upon the riddles of our life and enables us to deal creatively with forces that threaten to destroy us."[4]

The point is that Christology must be concerned with human destiny, with meaningfulness. Christianity claims that in the person of Jesus Christ we are given not only a revelation of who God is but also a revelation of what it means to be human. Vatican II, in its Pastoral Constitution on the Church in the Modern World *(Gaudium et Spes)*, constantly affirmed that in the person of Christ the true answer to the mystery that is the human can be found.[5] The key sentence here is the opening one: "The truth is that only in the mystery of the incarnate Word does the mystery of man take on light." For Vatican II, Christ is the key to the human riddle. "Christ the Lord, Christ the new Adam, in the very revelation of the mystery of the Father and of His love, fully reveals man to himself and brings to light his most high calling."[6] Christology, a word about Christ, is understood as the summation of all anthropology. In truth, the mystery of Christ and the mystery of humankind are one and the same mystery.

Although at Vatican II the focus of attention moved from Jesus' divinity to his humanity, his divinity is not and cannot be forgotten: Jesus is the one who is truly divine, truly human, and truly one. In the mystery of the incarnation the God who is revealed is a God for and with men and women. Theology is truly anthropology. The trajectory of anthropology is the discovery of meaning. Each person at different times bears witness to the questions: Who am I? Why am I? Where have I come from? What am I to become? What does it mean for me to be human, to be forgiven? Why suffering? Why death? Christianity, in communion with all religions, is concerned with these questions. Meaning-making is a central human activity and the central function of a religion. According to George

Lindbeck, "Religions are seen as comprehensive interpretive schemes, usually embodied in myths or narratives and heavily ritualized, which structure human experience and understanding of self and world."[7] Central to religion's function is the question of meaning, of ultimate meaning; the greatest threat to religion is that of meaninglessness.

The centrality of meaningfulness is the reason for the church's efforts to understand "the joys and the hopes, the griefs and the anxieties of the men of this age." The church's mission is to answer "in language intelligible to every generation...the perennial questions which men ask about present life and the life to come and about the relationship of the one to the other."[8] At Vatican II the Council thus affirms its fundamental mission: Relying on the inspiration of Christ, it "wishes to speak to all men in order to illuminate the mystery of man and cooperate in finding the solution to the outstanding problems of our day."[9]

Christianity offers to the world a vision, an ideal of humanness, and a promise of salvation. It offers these in a complex of stories, symbols, metaphors, and rituals. This complex of symbols is known as the paschal mystery, the center of which is the person of Jesus Christ. The paschal mystery as a complex of symbols is Christianity's response to humanity's search for meaning. The paschal mystery emerges out of a series of particular historical events and interpretations. It functions for Christianity as an interpretative framework.

Christology can be defined initially as a critical reflection on the meaning and truth of the paschal mystery from within a specific cultural situation. The basic contemporary method in Christology is that of correlation. The process of correlation attempts to harmonize the past tradition and the present situation. In Christology it is necessary to correlate the paschal mystery and present-day experience. Christology seeks to explain the meaning of the complex of symbols that make up the paschal mystery and its truth for our time and culture. The world of experience expressed in the paschal mystery is made to resonate with our own human experience. It is my contention that the experience most in need of elucidation is the experience of suffering.

Christology is always about humanity and God, and the most important question about God is whether God makes a difference in our lives in the world. The greatest obstacle to the answering of this question is the existence of suffering among the innocent, which can only be perceived as evil. The greatest argument against the existence of an omnipotent and all-loving God is the existence of evil; there can be no escape from theodicy. No word about God is ultimately valid that cannot be offered in the presence of innocent suffering. The issue of meaningless suffering in the world appears to be the test for the Christian faith and especially for Christology.

Suffering is a universal experience for human beings. No one escapes it, and therefore suffering functions as a common factor. As common as suffering is, it is also the one experience that is most personal and existential. Suffering leads to the fundamental questions about the self: Why me? Why do things always go wrong in my life? Why live? Common and universal as it is, suffering causes a sense of isolation in the sufferer. The personal and existential nature of suffering expresses itself as victimization. Suffering also has a historical objectivity which characterizes human life on such a massive scale that it often defies thought.

While suffering in all of its forms is present in the human condition, the real anguish of suffering is found in its perceived meaninglessness. More than twenty-five hundred years ago a man named Job stood under the curse of meaninglessness. He could not find a reason or a purpose for his suffering. The suffering of children is a particularly painful expression of meaninglessness. Humanity cries out for it to end. Suffering is at once so pervasive, so personal, so unwarranted, so shocking, and so meaningless that it eludes interpretation. History presents itself to us as a mixture of meaning and meaninglessness, of sorrow and happiness. Such a mixture raises the question as to whether, in the last resort, we can trust life at all. The quest to find meaning in our life is a primary motivational force.

Meaning-making is also the central function of a culture, for culture can be viewed as "the structures of meaning through which men give shape to their experience."[10] Thus religion may be understood to function as a cultural system. Religion is "a system of symbols which acts to establish powerful, pervasive and long-lasting moods and motivations in men by formulating conceptions or a central order of existence and clothing these conceptions with such an aura of factuality that the moods and motivations seem uniquely realistic."[11]

It is therefore not accidental that the common address to suffering has been religious. All religious traditions have attempted in various ways to wrestle with the fact of suffering, and most religious traditions are rooted in the belief and the fundamental trust that life is good and meaningful despite the suffering it entails. Religion constantly must ask if life has some ultimate meaning despite the suffering and the succession of frustrations and tragedies it brings.

All revealed religions are concerned with the agonizing questions that humankind confronts in the encounter with suffering and death: Does life have meaning? Is wholeness possible? Why suffering? Each religion offers a vision of reality where such questions are answered. At the heart of these various religions a rich complex of symbols, stories, and rituals is found that attempts to interpret and illuminate experiences of loss and suffering. Such narratives and symbols have a unique educative power; they appeal to the whole person. Symbols and narratives are offered by revealed religions to help humankind identify suffering, name it, and overcome it. Religious narratives and symbols create a world of habitation where individuals can somehow feel at home. Such narratives enable the human community to live amid cosmic, social, and historical tensions; that is, they have life-affirming qualities.

Christianity as a religious tradition does not argue against suffering or proffer a solution; it tells a story about Jesus, the crucified and risen Lord. Christians from the very beginning have claimed that the life, ministry, death, and resurrection of Jesus have made a radical difference to human life and death. The paschal mystery as a complex of symbols is Christianity's fundamental response to humanity's ineluctable involvement in suffering, evil, and death. The paschal mystery emerges out of a series of particular historical events; as a complex of symbols, the paschal mystery is the expression of the experiences of a particular historical community. Our experience of suffering or hostility recalls the symbolic events of Jesus' life, death, and resurrection, and so becomes the means of comfort and understanding.

The Christian tradition correlates the paschal mystery and present-day human experience. Christology seeks to explain the meaning of the complex of symbols that makes up the paschal mystery and its truth to any given age, and thus to demonstrate its universal relevance. The world of experience described in the paschal mystery is made to resonate with the condition of our fundamental human experience. Christology draws on what these symbols have meant in the past in order to explicate what they mean for us today. Bonhoeffer's question must be that of every generation: "What is bothering me incessantly is the question what Christianity really is, or indeed who Christ really is for us today?"[12]

Jesus Christ was experienced as disclosive of ultimacy within the realm of history. The paschal mystery in all its symbolic dimensions is an attempt to express this disclosure. As symbol, the paschal mystery has been interpreted by successive generations as illuminating and explicating ordinary existence in the world. Conversely, the paschal mystery is not encountered by an unilluminated and unexplicated human experience. Even common human experience possesses an initial horizon that focuses concerns and quests and heightens sensitivities to certain meanings. The paschal mystery further enlarges and transforms these initial horizons; they themselves give meaning to the paschal mystery as it encounters us individually. What is essential in this encounter is a personal willingness to accept interpretation by the paschal mystery. As in all authentic encounters, critical freedom and receptivity are of equal importance. This is especially true in the encounter of the self with the paschal mystery. The disclosure of God in Jesus Christ is also a disclosure of the self. For Christology, the fundamental question concerns the adequacy of the symbolic dimension of the paschal mystery to express the disclosure of God and, further, the adequacy of the contemporary expression of that same mystery. Since the encounter is of ultimate concern, the adequacy of symbol and of contemporary expression can only be relative. The paschal mystery as symbol sought to bring to expression the manifestation of God in Jesus Christ. It did not originate or speak in a situational vacuum. Hence the symbol itself is relative, all the more so because of the reality expressed, God in our midst, and the particular situation out of which it originates.

Form criticism and redaction criticism have underlined the amazing diversity in the understanding of the paschal mystery. Both methods recognize that in the New Testament there are a number of Christological traditions, each with a different point of departure (early Palestinian, Judeo-Hellenistic, Gentile, Markan, Pauline, Johannine, etc.) and a different emphasis. The same diversity is true of our own situations, of our experiences, questions, meanings.

The Christology developed at Chalcedon is characterized by abstractness. It lacks powerful imagery through which to appeal to devotional and spiritual life. Yet Christianity has given us in the cross a most powerful symbol. The incarnation of God reached its true meaning and purpose on the cross. It is there that God's self-giving love is embodied in its most radical form. The cross provides Christianity with enduring imagery and symbolism. In the Pauline letters that message of the crucified Christ emerges as the essential point. The crucified Jesus is presented by Paul within the framework of a kenotic Christology. Kenotic Christology, present in the gospel of Mark and developed in the nineteenth and twentieth centuries, is a Christology centered on the cross, on the mystery of the suffering humanity of Jesus. Its characteristics are well expressed by Karl Barth:

> We are confronted with the revelation of what is and will always be to all other ways of looking and thinking a mystery, and indeed a mystery which offends. The mystery reveals to us that for God it is just as natural to be lowly as it is to be high, to be near as it is to be far, to be little as it is to be great, to be abroad as to be home. Thus that when in the presence and action of Jesus Christ in the world created by Him and characterized *in malam partem* by the sin of man He

chooses to go into the far country, to conceal His form of lordship in the form of this world and therefore in the form of a
servant, He is not untrue to Himself but genuinely true to
Himself, to the freedom which is that of His love.[13]

The strength of kenotic Christology is both intellectual and symbolic; its
imagery of the self-emptying of God revealed in the person of Jesus is
one that resonates with the deepest elements of our human nature. This
Christology addresses the issue of human suffering in stark and challenging terms, and it provides Christians today with a fundamental
understanding of the transformative power of love that always entails
vulnerability.

It is my contention that the kenotic interpretation of the paschal
mystery in the gospel of Mark and in the writings of Paul and the fundamental question of power can lead us to an acceptable model of what it is
to be human. It can provide our contemporary culture with a model of
human and theological anthropology that is capable of entering into the
most desolate reaches of negation, a theology that will not cause us to
retreat from negation and evil, those deep threats to individuals and society. I am proposing a kenotic Christology as an attempt to enlighten, the-
matize and make intelligible the common experience of human
suffering. I also contend that there is a transcendent dimension to
human suffering that gives meaning to the Christ-event today.

According to St. Paul, the preaching of the kenotic Christ is a folly
for the world; it does not correspond to experience. It appears as an erup-
tion into our culture from the transcendently other. However, it does correspond to one facet of the human experience: our own experience of
suffering. And it is this experience that provides the ground for a preaching of the kenotic Christ.

A kenotic Christology is necessarily a transformative Christology.
The attempt to correlate human experience and religious symbols must
be made within a context in which one understands that all meaning and
knowledge are acquired in action, that ultimately all meaningful action is
for the sake of human solidarity, which, in most cases, is emancipatory
solidarity. Essential to the meaning of the major religious symbols is
their embodiment in action. As Gilkey writes,

Christian proclamation does not enter this quest (man's
search for himself) only to make itself understandable and to
adjust its own tradition to the present. It enters it for the sake
of liberation...Hermeneutic is then not simply the "art of
understanding" written expressions of life, but of under-

standing all historical expressions of life within this political context.[14]

Religious symbols such as the cross and the resurrection are intrinsically related to the specific dimensions of our concrete existence and the various aspects of our action. Gilkey writes of religious symbols that

> they promise illumination, a new understanding, they challenge the way we concretely are, they call for a new way of being, a new attitude to ourselves and to others, new forms of our actual relations in community, a new kind of action in the world...Every fundamental theological symbol means a critical stance toward past and present forms of existence and order in the social world, and the call to historical and social action on behalf of a new earth.[15]

In any valid Christology what is needed first, before reflection takes place, is contact with the reality. In a sense, it is following Jesus that permits us to know the reality of Jesus. A kenotic Christology is credible and viable only if it does not remain simply a theory. In fact, the theory itself is only possible if it emerges out of a practice.

CHAPTER ONE

Kenosis: The Cultural Context

Each generation has attempted, from within the context of its own concerns and anxieties, to retrace the way from Jesus to the Christ. Contemporary Christology can only discover its own truth in dialogue with its cultural setting. It is part of our task to discern the distinctive concerns of our contemporary situation.

The major task of Christology becomes one of translation. This culture, like other cultures, has certain basic characteristics; it has a mood or a mind. To speak about the "mood" or "mind" of our culture is, Gilkey suggests, to "refer to that deep, preconceptual attitude toward an understanding of existence which dominates and forms the cultural life of any epoch, the way people of a given time characteristically apprehend the world they live in and their place within it; their fundamental self-understanding of their being in the world."[1] Christology must translate into this culture's mind without capitulating to it. While modernity is the norm, it is not necessary and it may not even be possible to translate the Christian tradition in conformity to it. Theology must interpret and communicate the Christian message to people of a specific time and place. There is no a priori guarantee that such an interpretation is possible or that it will succeed. The spirit and mind of a culture can be so totally in contradiction to the Christian message that there is no point of insertion or contact. In this event theology can be but a proclamation, an attempt at counterculture.

To characterize the mood and spirit of a specific culture does not imply that every participant is determined by such characteristics. Yet, since the culture generally operates at a preconceptual level, its characteristics determine the general background of most human creations of an era. These characteristics determine the fundamental attitude of a whole group toward reality, truth, and values, and therefore toward religion.

Modern culture is wholly concerned with "the making of the human." With the continual debate about humanization and dehumanization, modern men and women are searching for a new image of humanity. At the most fundamental level what is humanity? How should men and women imagine themselves? All are seeking an image of authentic personal existence.

The problem of humanization, always a central concern, has now taken on the character of an inescapable preoccupation. Dehumanization is not only a real possibility, it is a historical fact. It is not surprising, therefore, that dehumanization should be a central concern of our culture.

The general consensus today is that "the secular spirit" represents the "mind" of our culture.[2] Secularization, Peter Berger claims, is a process wherein large sectors of society and culture are no longer dominated by religious symbols or institutions. The process is not only a social structural process; it also affects the consciousness of individuals.[3] The major characteristic of secularity as it relates to religion is the absence of any reference to transcendence. Berger also claims that "the reality of ordinary life is increasingly posited as the only reality. Or, if you will, the common sense world becomes a world without windows."[4] Secularity involves a qualitative change in human consciousness, particularly with regard to self-knowledge and the nature of relationships. It leads to a radical change in the understanding of what it means to be human.

Technology and the Technological Mind

Gilkey has underlined four major characteristics of secularity: contingency, relativity, temporality, and autonomy.[5] He sees the last as the most important. Tillich has identified a fundamental relationship between secularity and the industrial society.[6] According to Berger, the transformation brought about by technology, the predominant force in industrial society, "has had economic, social and political dimensions, all immense in scope. It has also brought on a revolution on the level of human consciousness, fundamentally uprooting beliefs, values and even the emotional texture of life."[7]

Tillich posits two primary elements within technology:

> The first...is the concentration of man's activities upon the methodical investigation and technical transformation of his world, including himself, and the consequent loss of the dimension of depth in his encounter with reality. Reality has lost its inner transcendence...God has become superfluous and the universe left to man as its master.[8]

The second characteristic of industrial man in the industrial society is that

> in order to fulfill his destiny, [he] must be in possession of creative powers, analogous to those previously attributed to God...The conflict between what man essentially is and what he actually is, his estrangement, or in traditional terms his

fallen state, is disregarded...He is pictured in a position of progressive fulfillment of his potentialities.[9]

Tillich sees technology as a thrust toward the transformation of the world and of self through the progressive acquisition of power. This process of transformation is accompanied by the belief in continuous upward progress. There is an inherent goal-less trajectory in technology, because it is its natural tendency not merely to fit means to ends but to bring about new ends. There can be indefinite progress because there is always something new and better to find.

Among the many definitions of a technological mentality Nisbet's is to the point: "What is central to technology is the application of rational principles to the control or reordering of space, matter and human beings."[10] Technology is the rational ordering of processes in view of definite goals. Reality is reduced to a calculable quantity, to units. All units are subjected to predesigned control. The power of technology is established in its capacity to extend the horizon of calculability. The reduction of reality to calculable quantity is given credence by a new materialism, "which asserts that man is in fact part of nature rather than something apart from it."[11]

Nature is considered not as rigid and determined but as a dynamic process, a constant becoming, for the technological mind assumes the interconnection of all realities. Reality is consequently understood in terms of componentiality; its components are self-contained though interdependent units apprehended and manipulated atomistically. None is meaningful without the whole and none can be defined or understood save in relation to the whole.

The operations model of technology, Ellul tells us, is extended to every field of human endeavor.

> Techniques in the translation into action of man's concern to master things by means of reason, to account for what is subconscious, make quantitative what is qualitative, make clear and precise the outlines of nature, take hold of chaos and put order into it.[12]

The human faculty of knowledge is an instrument of power. It annexes reality; everything becomes predictable and attainable. As possessor of knowledge, humanity is deemed capable of projecting its world; its orientation is to action, change, and control. Hannah Arendt predicts that technological man will not accept that life is a given but will grasp existence as "something he has made for himself."[13] "The image of *Homo faber*," it has been said, "is the key to contemporary identity."[14]

Elevating *Homo faber* to the essential characteristic of being human also implies elevating power to the position of a dominant and intermediate goal. "To become ever more masters of the world, to advance from power to power, even if only collectively and perhaps no longer by choice, can now be seen to be the chief vocation of mankind."[15] The will to power can be seen at work within the framework of Kant's revolutionary discovery of the phenomenon of subjectivity. According to Kant, the human subject is an active generator of the universe of meaning. It is not imposed upon the subject. Kant's series of a priori categories was postulated in order to ground this subjectivity. These a priori categories are present to the mind before any experience has occurred; they account for experience itself. Kant's epistemological model led to a specific cognitive mode: autonomous rationality. This model emphasizes the independence of the subject in constituting a personal universe of meaning. The Kantian person is in charge of his or her own destiny and constructs his or her reality. For Kant this reality was primarily the inner self; in our technological age this reality is also the external world.

Nietzsche proclaimed the will to power as the key to human behavior.[16] In *The Birth of Tragedy and the Genealogy of Morals* (1887) he developed the theme that all that which proceeds from power is good and all that springs from weakness is bad.[17] Nietzsche's anticipated "superman" is *Homo faber* par excellence. Both Marcuse and Heidegger subsequently affirmed that the "logic" of technology is that of domination. In Heidegger's mind there is a fateful metaphysical decision of the will for boundless power over the world of things. Rudolf Bultmann, commenting on Heidegger's affirmation that the twentieth century is centered on subjectivity, writes about our age as "the era in which the world conceived as object is subjected to the planning which is controlled by the values which man himself establishes."[18]

Gilkey describes autonomy as man's "innate capacity to know his own truth, to decide upon his own existence, to create his own meaning, and to establish his own values."[19] This concept of autonomy is forcefully perceived and expressed in Sartre's *Being and Nothingness*. For Sartre, the human person is being-for-itself, "in which consciousness and freedom are totally independent and completely autonomous. Every person is a law unto himself."[20] Technology enhances this sense of autonomy. The individual who experiences technological might feels equipped with power and influence enough to conquer even the biological conditions of existence. To be master of all is the goal of the technological mind.

Autonomy and the Will to Power

The essence of technology is a will to power that is never satisfied. Technological developments have progressed to a point where it is possible to control our environment sufficiently to meet human needs. But the will to power drives individuals far beyond the point where any alleviation is effected. Paradoxically, freedom over destiny accompanied by the power of technology often leads to the destruction of autonomy and freedom. Technology demonstrates a tendency to dominate and violate reality, to master other people and nature.

When B. F. Skinner announced that we could no longer afford freedom for the human race, he merely drew attention to what was implicit in technology itself. In *Beyond Freedom and Dignity* he advocates the delegation and control of the population to specialists. Skinner believes that freedom and dignity are harmful ideas, which have created all kinds of social problems. Skinner's approach is utopian, and he believes fully in human perfectibility.[21] He writes, "Almost all the best changes in our culture which we now regard as worthwhile can be traced to perfectionistic philosophies."[22] Men and women can, through science, control their world, and in so doing, they have the opportunity to achieve control of themselves. Skinner has boundless confidence in science. He believes in the human ability to unlock the mysteries of the universe. His intention is to place human beings in their true relation to the rest of nature, even at the risk of removing them from the center of the universe.

Skinner, in the opinion of C. E. Wollner has "pressed a soaring optimism for the prospects of modern man in that he is confident that the ascendancy of science and technology so far from besetting, if not overwhelming man, as more than one humanist has suggested it has done, is an occasion for rejoicing."[23] Wollner considers that for Skinner "the modern movement of the proliferation of technology based on science, therefore, portends not disaster, but hope, as man at last possesses in science the optimal vehicle, the most efficacious tool for logical, quick and resourceful change."[24] Skinner's doctrine calls for the wholesale manipulation of human beings for their own good, or rather for the survival of the species. Skinner believed that the science of behaviorism had exploded the notion that a human being is the initiator of his or her own behavior. His design for a new culture is founded in an empiricism so absolute that it absolutely excludes the possibility of explanation beyond material reality.

Behavioral technology has been defined as a "developing science that aims to change the environment rather than people, that seeks to alter actions rather than feelings, and that shifts the customary psychological emphasis on the world inside men to the world outside them."[25] Skinner conceives of culture as a social environment that patterns the behavior of its constituents. Insofar as the environment, both physical and cultural, is a human construct, it can be altered to serve men and women.[26] But the form of control Skinner advocates is a form of manipulation. *Manipulation* can denote the most beneficial achievements of human skill and power; it can also indicate the use of the most debasing and insidious means for the degradation of life and the overpowering of one's fellows.[27] *Manipulation* can refer to an acceptable and beneficial change of nature. In the process of education toward liberty, for example, some forms of conditioning or manipulation are necessary. The question is always whether these forms in practical terms will eliminate the exercise of freedom.[28] The fields of behavior modification and genetic engineering are not grounded in any theory of essential human values. Inexorably driven by a desire for success, they ask only whether "it works."[29]

There is no doubt that Skinner was, in a certain sense, a humanist. He believed that the progress of science allows humankind to abandon most aversive conditioning, whether it works or not. Conditioning can remain unknown to the persons being manipulated. The manipulator knows what kind of conditioning will be effective, and the manipulator alone decides what kind of behavior is to be produced or reinforced. Justification is grounded in humanitarian values: animals and persons are to be conditioned by reinforcers in a way that fosters the species' survival. Skinner was the perfect apologist for technological man. In his work we see the characteristics of technology, its ambiguities and contradictions.

There is a presupposition at the heart of our culture that technology is ideologically neutral. It is assumed that the crisis of technology lies within the realities—social, political, or economic—that use or exploit it. Change the political, economic, or social system and there would be no crisis. It is the contention of many that technology is only a tool to be used for good or for ill by whoever possesses it. But with technology we are no longer speaking about tools or automation or new discoveries. We are dealing with a methodology, a vision of the human being and the world, with a culture. Technology embodies a particular cognitive style and this cognitive style is transferable to other areas of life. It is possible for individuals to look upon their own psychological life with the same attitude with which an engineer contemplates the workings of a machine.

There seems to be an independent dynamism inherent to technology. Technology possesses its own autonomy and has its own distinctive world view, its own ideological system. It is not neutral. By its very nature technology leads to domination. According to certain authors, science and technology have helped to create the present system of social domination. Marcuse writes:

> Today, domination perpetuates and extends itself not only through technology but *as* technology, and the latter provides

the great legitimation of the expanding political power, which absorbs all spheres of culture.[30]

Domination is not easily democratized. There is endemic to it the important question of who dominates and who is dominated, who is powerful and who is powerless. Perfection lies in domination. Technological men and women are independent, completely in control of their lives. Nietzsche wrote about those who command and rule: "They are unaccountable: they are like destiny, without rhyme or reason, ruthless, bare of pretext, being natural organizers. These men know nothing of guilt, responsibility, consideration."[31]

Christopher Lasch writes, "Every society reproduces its culture—its norms, its underlying assumptions, its modes of organizing experience—in the individual, in the form of personality."[32] Technological culture has given rise to the narcissistic personality. Narcissism has even been recognized as an important element in contemporary character disorders. So the age of technology has developed its own peculiar form of pathology. Lasch writes, "Modern capitalist society not only elevates narcissists to prominence, it elicits and reinforces narcissistic traits in everyone."[33]

Autonomy and Narcissism

Narcissism, as Lasch recognizes, is not simply cultural.[34] Ernest Becker claims that narcissism is inescapable, because it has a biological basis in human nature.[35] The human organism has an inherent tendency to incorporate and expand and protect itself against the world. Sociobiology does not suggest that we are genetically selfish. The sociobiologists assert that we are genetically predisposed to be kind to people in proportion to how closely related to us they are. In biology altruism exists solely as a factor for reproductive success. The crux of evolution is not the good of the species but the good of the individual gene. Dawkins writes, "The predominant quality to be expected in a successful gene is ruthless selfishness. This gene selfishness will usually give rise to selfishness in individual behavior."[36] The author warns his reader that in the building of a society "in which individuals cooperate generously and unselfishly toward a common good, you can expect little help from biological nature. Let us try to *teach* generosity and altruism, because we are born selfish. Let us understand what our own selfish genes are up to, because we may then at least have the chance to upset their designs, something which no other species has ever aspired to."[37] Sociobiology suggests that much of our behavior has a calculated, selfish, deceitful quality. Elaborate religious, social, and linguistic networks are erected to mark underlying manipulative motivations.

The dominant modern psychologies explain human behavior in terms of individual pleasure and pain, individual positive and negative valence, individual needs and drives.[38] In social psychology social interaction is analyzed exclusively in terms of the self.[39] Psychologists and psychiatrists almost invariably side with self-gratification over traditional restraint.[40] Phillip Rieff underlines the fact that contemporary culture proposes an ethic of self-realization for which the well-being of the individual is of the highest value.[41]

Many Western philosophies have seen "the other" not in its full otherness but as an occasion for self-discovery or self-realization. "The other" is accounted for as a valuable investment, which will pay off eventually in the dividend of one's own self-realization. Erich Fromm, who has emphasized the importance of "the other," still defines the relation between self and other in terms of self-realization. For him, the goal is "any aim which furthers the growth, freedom and happiness of the self." He writes:

> The character structure of the mature and integrated personality, the productive character, constitutes the source and the basis of virtue..."Vice," in the last analysis, is indifference to one's own self and self-mutilation. Not self-renunciation nor selfishness but self-love, not the negation of the individual but the affirmation of his truly human self, are the supreme values of humanistic ethics. If man is to have confidence in values, he must know himself and the capacity of his nature for goodness and productiveness.[42]

Fromm makes self-realization the end purpose of any growth, and relation to others simply the means to that end.

The social sciences not only describe people as selfishly motivated but teach that they ought to be so. Sociobiology holds repression and inhibition of individual impulse to be undesirable; it considers all guilt to be dysfunctional neurosis created by cruel child rearing and a repressive society. The contemporary climate is therapeutic. People identify personal salvation with the feeling of personal well-being, health, and psychic security they crave. In this context love and meaning are defined as the fulfillment of the patient's emotional appetites. The self-sacrifice and self-abasement of the old concept of love are seen as oppressive—offensive to common sense and bad for the health. The liberation of humanity from such outdated ideas as love and duty has become the mission of the converts and popularizers of the post-Freudian therapies, for whom mental health means the overthrow of inhibitions and the resultant elevation of the self.

It is not surprising, then, that a retreat to purely personal satisfaction is one of the main themes of our culture. There has been yet another revival of the cults of expanded consciousness, health, and personal growth. To live for oneself in the moment is the prevailing code. Survival has become the catchword of the nineties and a resentful, attenuated narcissism the dominant disposition.[43] What is being cultivated is a transcendental self-attention.

Contemporary Culture and the Experience of Negativity

Over the past two and a half decades there has been a proliferation of books concerning the promotion of the individual.[44] While these books differ in the various kinds of self-love they appeal to, they share certain values; that is, the principal concern and objective in life is the happiness of the individual. Guilt is always subjective and always bad. The dominant influence in these books is assertiveness therapy, which contends that since people are likely to be trying to push you around, you should push them first. Self-interest is the supreme value.

While technology makes life more interdependent, it alienates us by objectifying and controlling us in our relationships to one another and to nature. The alienating character of technology lies precisely in its persistent inclination to reduce realities to calculable quantities. Human beings resent being reduced to units. But the dream of being independent and masters of our lives has been shattered by the traumatic recognition that, through technology, our thoughts, feelings, and talents are being manipulated. We cannot avoid the radical experience of alienation and hopelessness. Alienation springs from the reaction to finding ourselves reduced to calculable entities; hopelessness from the anonymity of the manipulators.[45] As Ruben Alves puts it:

> One can change at will those who seem to be in power and shift from one party to another. It makes no difference. Because those who seem to be in charge are not really in charge. They are nothing more than transistors in a network of power, executives plugged into a system. And ultimately it is the system that programs the course of operations. Individuals are expendable, disposable.[46]

People become increasingly helpless and desperate as they perceive their lives to be dominated by anonymous powers. Hope needs to be associated with names, not numbers. Helplessness increases in direct proportion to numbering mechanisms. Men and women feel helpless before a fluid, inhuman, incommunicable force. As Paul Tillich writes:

The protest is directed against the position of man in the system of production and consumption of our society. Man is supposed to be master of his world and of himself. But actually he has become a part of the reality he has created...a cog within a universal machine to which he must adapt himself in order not to be smashed by it. But this adaptation makes him a means for ends which are means themselves, and in which an ultimate end is lacking. Out of this predicament of man in the industrial society, the experience of emptiness and meaninglessness, of dehumanization and estrangements has resulted. Man has ceased to encounter reality as meaningful.[47]

From alienation and despair to rage and violent self-assertion is a small step. The rebellion of individuals against the "system" is not simply a revolt against the anonymity of a technological society; it is also deeply rooted in the autonomy, subjectivity, and narcissism that characterize that society.

The age's optimistic technological mentality must be qualified in the context of this turn toward the self and its realization in an atmosphere of selfishness. There should be no illusion that we might discover an easy way to achieve a harmony between self-interest and the welfare of others. Consistent optimism in this area leads to false security and the underestimation of the powers of anarchy and enslavement. There can no longer be any illusions about conflict that exists between self-interest and the public good. Marx's dream of harmony between individual and society was another mirage. As Niebuhr writes, "The error is partly the consequence of the Marxist belief that the tendency toward domination is caused by the class structure of human society and will disappear with the revolution which destroys the class system."[48]

The optimism of our technological society has not been without opposition. Existentialism in its various forms, by underlining the finitude of humans and the ultimacy of death, has challenged quite radically the spirit of our culture.[49] It sees anxiety as a basic and irremovable ingredient of personal existence. Indeed, anarchy belongs to existence itself, rather than to the personal. Existence is not a positive state, not even simply neutral, but a state that negates possibilities. Ultimately, existence is for death. While suffering is inherent to human existence, it consists in more than poverty, war, violence, illness; it occurs in the depths of the human spirit. According to Becker:

Once admit that you are a defecating creature and you invite the primeval ocean of creature anxiety to flood over you. But it is more than creature anxiety, it is also man's anxiety, the anxiety that results from the human paradox that man is an animal who is conscious of his animal limitation. Anxiety is the result of the perception of the truth of one's condition. What does it mean to be a *self-conscious animal*? The idea is ludicrous, if it is not monstrous. It means to know that one is food for worms. This is the terror: to have emerged from nothing, to have a name, consciousness of self, deep inner feelings, an excruciating inner yearning for life and self-expression—and with all this yet to die.[50]

One dimension of sin is the refusal on the part of men and women to accept their own identity as living creatures. Human creatures belong to the biosphere; they participate in the same necessities and possibilities as all other creatures. In sin, we reject this condition by identifying our essence as that in which we have least in common with nature. Human persons cannot evolve beyond their character and limits. Becker asks how self-conscious creatures could change their dilemma of existence. It is impossible to transcend the psychological limits of the human condition.[51]

Creation is a nightmare spectacular taking place on a planet that has been soaked for hundreds of millions of years in the blood of all its creatures. The soberest conclusion that we could make about what has actually been taking place on the planet for about three billion years is that it is being turned into a vast pit of fertilizer.[52]

In some of its forms existentialism has been known to lead to the perception that existence is merely absurd.[53] If existence has neither meaning nor value, its ultimate goal and relief are extinction. Sartre's philosophical writings lay out the basis for his nihilism. Although the individual stands alone as a moral universe, no matter what action he or she takes the result is uselessness and hopelessness. Consensus and commitment become impossible. People tend to act to get whatever they can for themselves.

Existentialism in its various forms offers little hope, but it at least gives an honest appraisal of our situation. Douglas John Hall puts it aptly, "The only physician who can be trusted to heal is one who has been thorough and honest in his diagnosis."[54] Existentialism, while not providing us with easy answers, has done us the service of warning against them. Realism is necessary; whatever technology will achieve for humanity, it must be done, as Becker says, in the "lived truth of creation, of the grotesque, of the rumble of panic underneath everything. Otherwise it is false."[55] Too much energy and effort have been given to the task of keeping from ourselves the truth of our condition.

While our technological culture has led to an overwhelmingly positive expectation, our experiences have been predominantly negative. The events of this century have overwhelmed our means of comprehending them. Reinhold Niebuhr writes, "The history of mankind exhibits no more ironic experiences than the contrast between the sanguine hopes of recent centuries and the bitter experience of modern man."[56] This contrast is revealed in its starkest form on the North American continent where, as George Grant observes, "North Americans have no history before the denial of progress."[57] To repress the experience of negation, to deny it, is to assimilate and be assimilated by it. This way of coming to terms with negation is no way to deal with evil. What ways are there for us to face our negative experience without falling into an enervating despair? They must provide, without losing hope, a frame of reference where negation can be affirmed and not repressed.

Our technological world is a windowless house; there is no opening through which we can find a perspective for our increasingly negative experiences. No frame of reference, no mythos exists within the culture for the experience of negation. To challenge the premise of our technological society is to find oneself shut out; the perspective is gained at the cost of isolation. Thus Grant remarks: "So pervasive and deep-rooted is the faith that all human problems will be solved by unlimited technological development that it is a terrible moment for the individual when he crosses the Rubicon and puts that faith into question...One can thereafter only approach modern society with fear and perhaps trembling and, above all, caution."[58]

Christianity and the Experience of Negativity

The question to be asked is how may human freedom prevail against the determinism we have created for ourselves? What chance does unselfish insight have in the arena of selfish, self-seeking power? Are we to let a technocratic judgment govern our future, or have we a credible appeal against it? In what way can we establish a frame of reference to comprehend the experience of negation in an officially optimistic society?

Has Christianity a role to play in the answering of these questions? Can it provide contemporary culture with an anthropological model willing to enter into the bleakest and most empty reaches of negation, a Christology that comes face to face with the evils that threaten individuals and society?[59] Christianity proclaims that it has in Jesus Christ a model of the human, an image of the human. Does it also possess a frame of reference for the experience of negation?

Christianity in North America has preoccupied itself with the negative, but in the context of Christianity's transformative power. The ultimate aim of North American Christianity is the rendering positive of life's negatives. Even the reality of the cross is superseded through a false emphasis on the resurrection. The resurrection is understood as a once-and-for-all conquest; the cross simply becomes an event of the past, the symbol of an evil that has no longer any power over us, that no longer needs to be taken seriously. The force of the "already here" has dulled the edge of the "not yet."

Within the context of the Christian faith, there has been a persistent tendency to see the gospel from a triumphalistic perspective, to give the Christian message the last word. The gospel, despite its own modesty, the constancy of its "not yet," is presented as the source of the solution to every human problem. Christianity in North America replaces the gospel's perspective with a straightforward "already." It has been observed, "It produces a gospel that consists primarily in the overcoming of the experience of evil and negation, a gospel where 'yes' disqualifies the 'no' of human existence."[60] In this context, evil is already overcome, history trivialized and human responsibility for the future set aside.

The Christian vision, which is part of our American heritage, is fundamentally positive. This vision has not prepared us to encounter the negative dimension of our existence, which becomes apparent to progressively larger numbers of persons. Christianity has been "so thoroughly identified with the official optimism of the culture that it is constitutionally incapable of entertaining the affliction with which man in our time is really afflicted."[61] Christianity, for some, wards off the full effect of the experience of evil in our world. It serves as a haven from the darkness of this experience. And on this it has seemed only too successful in explaining away negation, evil, death. Christianity in our culture does not descend to the dead.

Kenosis and Contemporary Culture

But while the gospel presents the activity of God in Jesus as creating a new reality and making the fullness of life available to humans, he accomplishes this in kenosis, a self-emptying. The hymn in Philippians presents Jesus as recognizing that being equal with God means most profoundly to be "not grasping." The self-emptying of Jesus unto death—and death on the cross—is the revelation that to be God is to be unselfishness itself. Hans Urs von Balthasar underlined this when he wrote, "It is precisely in the kenosis of Christ (and nowhere else) that the inner majesty of God's love appears, of God who 'is love' (1 Jn 4:8) and a 'trinity.'"[62]

A theology based on kenosis will be a theology from below, rooted in the suffering humanity of Jesus. It will not hesitate to affirm the passion of

God, God's entering into the depths of human reality. Its image of the human will counterpose the contemporary definition of the human as dominant. It will underline poverty and receptivity, challenging our culture based on power and acquisition with the hope of transformation, an understanding of human nature based on self-emptying.

Such a theology will focus on the cross. A theology of the cross proceeds from the fundamental assumption that any authentic optimism has limits. In Hall's words, "The gospel of the cross tries to interpret the meaning of the experience of limits, and to seek through that experience the possibilities that may be inherent in it, or may emerge out of it."[63]

The cross cannot be the last word; Jesus was raised by God from the dead. But neither is the resurrection the last word on history. In his victory Christ remains with us in the agony and failure of our humanity. The resurrection cannot become the primary theological foundation for unqualified optimism or for the negation of negativity. The salvation effected in the death and resurrection of Jesus is something other than the contradiction of our experience of negation.

When we reform the image of humankind in terms of the theology of the cross, it is necessary that we say something about what is embodied in the person and life of Jesus Christ. Christology is the key to understanding the true humanity essential to contemporary culture. This Christology needs to be directly and compellingly explicated in the context of our multiple experiences of negation.

The world does not desire this theology, but any other would be a deception. This theology is based on a view of human nature that many will consider unrealistic. Yet if one considers the facts, an image of humanity based on self-limitation and self-emptying may be thoroughly realistic. It is becoming more evident from day to day that we are not the masters of creation. The question is, What does it mean to be realistic today? Paul Ehrlich writes:

> Perhaps the major necessary ingredient that has been missing from a solution to the problem of both the United States and the rest of the world is a goal, a vision of the kind of Spaceship Earth that ought to be and the kind of crew that should man her. Society has always had its visionaries who talked of love, beauty, peace and plenty. But somehow the "practical" men have always been there just to praise the smog as a sign of progress, to preach "just" wars, and to restrict love while giving hate free rein. It must be one of the greatest ironies of the history of *Homo sapiens* that the only salvation for the practical men now lies in what they think of

as the dreams of idealists. The question now is: can the "realists" be persuaded to face reality in time?[64]

The need for a profound change emerges as a condition for the survival of the human race, and some "realists" are facing facts: E. F. Schumacher, an economist and a humanist, has demanded that we acknowledge that small is beautiful,[65] and Erich Fromm calls for a radical change in the human heart.[66]

Within the past few years many books have been written pleading for the subordination of economy to the real needs of people. Their authors are in agreement that increase in material consumption does not necessarily result in an increase in well-being. A new attitude toward nature is required and restraint in the use of technology, its subordination to actual human needs. These authors have understood the need for characterological and spiritual changes in order for social changes to occur.[67]

Materialism, which seeks fulfillment in the pursuit of wealth, does not contain within itself a limiting principle. But the earth does. Schumacher writes that the idea of "unlimited economic growth,...until everybody is saturated with wealth, needs to be seriously questioned on at least two counts: the availability of basic resources and additionally the capacity of the environment to cope with the degree of interference implied."[68] Furthermore, "If human vices such as greed and envy are systematically cultivated, the inevitable result is nothing less than a collapse of intelligence. A man driven by greed and envy loses the power of seeing things as they really are."[69]

The principle of unlimited consumption as the goal of living can only lead to disharmony and ultimately war. In a limited world unlimited consumption implies the deprivation of some through the unlimited egotism of others. In the words of Hall:

> What chiefly fires this epochal transformation is the awareness that in the last analysis the civilization the modern era wanted to bequeath is dangerous and destructive. It is no civilization in fact. There is a growing recognition that the image of man elaborated by the greatest minds in the past three or four centuries, man as master, is ultimately annihilating. The mastery of nature must inevitably mean the mastery of human nature, the subjugation of man's own being, to the manipulative technique he has applied to everything else.[70]

The image of man as Master is irredeemable; the "logic" of mastery leads directly to the death of the spirit, the death of man. I again refer to Hall, "Unless man turns from mastering to servicing, from grasping to receiving, from independence to interdependence, we will simply not last very long on the face of the earth."[71] There is evidence, as in these words of Richard Falk, of a desire for change:

> The human species may be better prepared for transition to a new system of world order than is generally evident, especially to those accustomed to thinking about change in the short time horizons of power wielders. Teilhard de Chardin and Sri Aurobindo, among others, have discerned a shift in human sentiment toward solidarity and altruism, and we believe that this shift is one significant feature of our generally bleak modern situation. Just as the collapse of colonialism was comprehensible only after it happened, so might the collapse of or displacement of the state system become visible only when we get a chance to look backward. The call for a world order more responsive to bioethical requirements—species survival, including habitability of the planet—represents a new impulse in human history, itself a hopeful sign.[72]

But the technocrat's image of the human is not only embodied in our institutions, values, and goals, it is also embedded deeply in our minds, in our ways of thinking and doing. Even as we attempt to change our understanding we are still influenced by it in the very depths of our spirits. Only by a radical conversion of the spirit can change be effected. Economic and political changes are possible only if there are fundamental changes in the individual values and attitudes. According to Erich Fromm, "A new society is possible only if, in the process of developing it, a new human being also develops, or in more modest terms, if a fundamental change occurs in contemporary Man's character structure."[73]

Self-emptying presents a clear alternative to narcissism. It is as different from the religion of the non-self as it is from the self-realization of contemporary Western culture. According to Heidegger, in order to counteract the effects of our technological culture, there must occur a "relinquishment" (*gelassenheit:* a term Heidegger borrowed from Meister Eckhart) of the human being from the will to power. Such a "relinquishment" would make it possible to live in this world not as master but as servant—a servant who simply accepts created reality in its manifold expressions. Freedom from the will to power can be known only if reality is no longer perceived as something to be controlled. Freedom in this sense means submitting in attentive awareness to the given reality.

This is the freedom the gospels advocate. It is a freedom based on self-emptying. Self-emptying is neither self-effacement nor servility but letting go.[74] It does not mean withdrawing from "the other" or using "the other," but giving oneself up to "the other." This is not a way of life likely to win much approval.

We are faced with the necessary acceptance of our limits. No triumphalistic theology is capable of addressing this problem. But the theology of the cross is explicitly directed to it. It is at its most basic level a theology of limits. What it rejects above all is that anthropology which thrives upon the delusion of mastery. We are not masters but beggars. The theology of the cross does not rejoice in limits; it does not counsel us to seek suffering, whether for ourselves or for others. In the midst of limits and suffering the theology of the cross strives to discern the presence of meaning. It tries to interpret the experiential meaning of these limits and to reveal their inherent possibilities. Even though our instinct may be to shy away from the negative aspects of life, we must present the paschal mystery in all its dimensions, with the cross at its center.

Amid the wide variety of models that proliferate in our culture, when the most thoughtful secular intellectuals propose their images of authentic humanity, it is noteworthy that they are in surprising agreement and that the paradigm of human excellence is predominantly that of free self-determination from within, motivated and shaped by love for others. This is the affirmation of the gospels, which a kenotic Christology maintains. It is in the outgoing love for others that human nature fulfills itself. We find ourselves when, like Christ, we lose ourselves for others. It is the Lord on the cross who gives to the world that put him there the only model for its own fulfillment. If we are Christians, the Lord on the cross becomes our Lord, and we seek to incarnate his freedom, his poverty, his availability for others. Our culture, like other cultures in the past, needs to be encountered by the person of Jesus Christ. This encounter cannot occur without Christology.

CHAPTER TWO

Jesus: The Way to Salvation

Christology is about Jesus of Nazareth, whom we profess to be our Christ. Christology is not a problem to be solved; rather, it is fundamentally a journey of discovery, of getting to know, to name, and to love God in and through the person of Jesus. For us, as for the first disciples, it is most often a journey of rediscovery and of renaming. Christology is the fundamental and ongoing attempt to say who Jesus is and what he means for each of us; it is not primarily an attempt to sum up what is most important in the mediation of his life, death, and resurrection through the Christian tradition. What influences our life today is what we have heard of Jesus. Paul outlines the basic process that governs access to Jesus Christ: "Everyone who invokes the name of the Lord will be saved. How could they invoke one in whom they had no faith? And how could they have faith in one they had never heard of? And how hear without someone to spread the news?" (Rom 10:13-15). Faith in Christ is inseparable from hearing about Christ; faith in Christ is essentially ecclesial. As David Tracy writes: "It is the tradition of the church that it is our central mediation of the actual Jesus—the Jesus remembered by the church; it is our present experience of that mediated Christ-event which impels our belief in Jesus Christ."[1] Our Christ is the preached Christ.

Christology: The Story of Emmaus

I understand Christology as a journey for a variety of reasons. In the gospel of Luke the story of the disciples of Emmaus is the story of a journey; it is the affirmation of a Christology. In the gospel of Mark Christology is revealed in the journey to Jerusalem. In fact, the journey is a symbol deeply embedded in history.[2] It emphasizes process, movement; it makes us aware of the historical and deeply social nature of our faith in Jesus Christ, and of our Christology as being on the way, characterized more deeply by the "not yet" than by the "already." As a journey Christology is always deeply eschatological. Finally, the symbol of the journey embodies an aspect of our relationship to God that is of greatest importance: invitation. We are called to a journey, a journey we are free to undertake or forgo.

The story of Emmaus is peculiar to the gospel of Luke and probably expresses Luke's own story.[3] Its literary form is found in the Old Testament, where strangers are messengers of God to those who extend hospitality. The other strand in the story is the New Testament tradition of the risen Jesus as the first evangelizer. Jesus' actions in the Emmaus story recall the ministry he exercised in Galilee: compassion and forgiveness. The Emmaus disciples lost faith in Jesus upon his crucifixion and gave up their discipleship, and yet Jesus pursues them like the shepherd in search of lost sheep (Lk 15:3-7).

The point of this story for our own Christological journey is that the disciples had abandoned discipleship because of the cross. Initially Jesus' death on the cross was not luminous with meaning for his disciples; in fact, it represented the end of all meaning. The death of Jesus was the death of a criminal; those who died crucified died outside the covenant. It was impossible to expect a messianic figure to die in such a way. Cleopas expressed the fundamental reason he had become Jesus' disciple: Jesus was a prophet, mighty in word and deed. Cleopas spoke of Jesus' ministry of powerful deeds and persuasive preaching (Lk 24:19). What place does such a Christology leave for the cross? So the risen Jesus teaches the disciples his own Christology: Christ must suffer. The substance of Jesus' Easter message lies in the demand that his rejection and death be understood as part of God's salvific will. "The Son of Man *must* suffer many trials..." (Lk 9:22). This understanding is repeated in the preaching of the apostles: "This Jesus, delivered up according to the definite plan and foreknowledge of God..." (Lk 2:23). Yet what the risen Jesus tells these two disciples is no more than what the earthly Jesus constantly preached. In the story of Emmaus Jesus' suffering is no obstacle to the claim that he is God's beloved Christ; nor should it be an obstacle to discipleship. For Luke, the suffering of God's Messiah is no argument against his legitimacy but the proof of his confirmation as Messiah. It is the essence of the scriptures that the Christ must suffer and so be exalted. What opened the eyes of the disciples is their understanding of the reason for the cross. They recognized Jesus in the breaking of the bread.

Christology and the Cross

The cross becomes the path demanded of Jesus' disciples. Disciples following their master are those who take up the cross (Lk 9:23; 14:37) and lose their life in order to save it (Lk 9:24; 17:33), who humble themselves and are exalted (Lk 11; 18:14) "O foolish men...was it not necessary that the Christ should suffer these things and enter into his glory?" (Lk 24:25). This is the mystery that is disclosed at Emmaus. The risen

Christ is the one who suffered, and the risen Christ is not recognized until the disciples are willing to enter into this mystery.

When we look at the historical life and death of Jesus we discover that the story of the disciples of Emmaus, while clearly of Luke's own construing, expresses the very essence of what Jesus was about. When we probe Jesus' life and ministry of compassion, we find that it is animated by the paradox of finding life through death, of losing one's life and thereby saving it. "Whoever would save his life will lose it and whoever loses his life for my sake will save it" (Mt 16:25).[4] This particular saying is repeated in other gospel accounts (Mk 8:35; Lk 5:24; Mt 10:39; Lk 17:33; Jn 22:25); the paradox emerges as Jesus realizes the growing opposition to his ministry.

The paradox that permeates Jesus' ministry is consummated in his death and resurrection. The paschal mystery represents the fundamental pattern of Jesus' life. Christian faith claims that Jesus is unconditionally grounded in God. This unconditional grounding must be revealed in Jesus' life and death. The question then arises, In what way is the transcendent grounding of Jesus' human life manifested? What does this mean for Jesus' mode of being human? The other question that needs to be asked is, What does Jesus' humanity reveal about God's being as God?

Christology and the Paschal Mystery

The core of the early church's kerygma is the paschal mystery, "that Christ died for our sins in accordance with the Scripture, that he was raised on the third day" (1 Cor 15:3-5). The paschal mystery is also the core of a kenotic Christology. The term *pascho,* from which the word *paschal* originates, means basically to experience something "which comes from without and which has to be suffered."[5] In the gospels we find two kinds of reference to *pascho* as regards Christ: one to the death of Jesus (Lk 22:15; 24; 26; 46), and the other to his suffering in general, though not exclusive of death.

It is interesting to note that out of the thirteen usages of the word *pascho* or *pathein* in the synoptic gospels, seven are found in the three predictions of the passion and resurrection. These words are interpretations of the meaning of the passion for Jesus and his disciples. The paschal mystery is one of life, death, and resurrection; its emphasis is on the crucified Jesus.

Paul, in the last two chapters of 1 Corinthians, argues that the cross cannot be understood as one theologumenon among others that can be leveled into a chain of saving events, but is known, rather, as the center and horizon of theology as a whole: "I decided to know nothing among you except Jesus Christ and him crucified" (1 Cor 2:2). To understand the primacy of the cross in the paschal mystery it is important to realize that after the initial theology of the resurrection and the experience of the Spirit, the early church returned to the earthly Jesus and his death on the cross. According to Moltmann, it was this reaching back that gave rise "to the new literary category of a gospel, in the synoptic sense."[6]

The Paschal Mystery and the Centrality of the Cross

Coming to terms with the cross was a question of life and death for the early church. Virtually from the beginning, the church tried to proclaim the scandalous cross as God's will and God's deed. It first did so by way of scriptural proof—"in accordance with the scriptures" (Mk 14:21). The cross is not an absurdity but God's decree and will. God's command of events is stressed, and the cross is felt as an enigmatic and harsh necessity. The first prophecy in Mark (8:27) speaks of a "must" *(dei)* in relation to the passion of Jesus. "The Son of Man must suffer many things and be rejected." The verb *dei* expresses a necessity an event possesses, without, however, specifying the reason for it. The reason can be inferred only from the relation this event has with the power that lies behind the necessity. In the synoptics, especially in Luke, the term *dei* tends to be used to express the will of God. This will is a salvific will; in this context, the passion and death of Christ are seen as having their basis and origin in the saving will and plan of God.

The New Testament underlines the voluntary dimension of Jesus' death, his self-surrender (1 Thes 5:10; Col 2:20; Mt 20:28). The epistle to the Hebrews presents Jesus as pleading to be spared death (5:7), but his voluntary acceptance of it was included in his career, as fidelity to God the Father. Jesus' death is represented by the authors of the New Testament as the action where he comes to the uttermost limits of his obedience to his vocation. According to Piet Schoonenberg:

> Only when the opposition grows and these opponents develop a truly deadly hatred of him, there dawns upon him the significance of the violent death which awaits him. Now he recognizes from these circumstances that his Father's will for him is to fulfill the function of the Servant of Yahweh to the end, to die in order to bring the many to righteousness. Thus his horizon broadens out from the lost sheep of Israel to Jew and Gentile, and his mission develops from that of a prophet proclaiming salvation to that of victim bringing salvation.[7]

While there are certain affirmations that could be challenged here, the fact that Jesus realized his mission, faced it, and accepted it is what the New Testament writers witness to. Jesus' death is not the surprise ending but the capstone of a career. In his own career, in his fidelity to the Father, his voluntary acceptance of the cross is included.

We must not view Jesus' death on the cross as something that overtakes him extrinsically, either at the hands of men or by the hand of God. Jesus' death was necessary but not as having been chosen by God as one of several options for our redemption. In his message and in his very person Jesus was a threat to both the Jewish leaders and the Roman authorities. Jesus' death was necessary because his life was one of complete dedication to the Father and to the oppressed. As Dorothy Soelle puts it, "It is not that love requires the cross, but *de facto,* it ends up on the cross."[8] It is not that the Father needs the suffering of Jesus; the cross is above all a symbol of reality. In this world, it is the necessary end to a life of free, total self-abandonment to God in the love of humankind.

The Cross and Jesus' Ministry

In the past there has been an ongoing tendency to isolate the cross from the rest of Jesus' ministry.[9] This isolation can be traced to the interpretation of Jesus' death as a foreordained event and to an overemphasis on its nature as a necessary vicarious sacrifice for sin. But the cross cannot be understood except in connection with Jesus' earthly ministry. The cross can be rightly interpreted only in the context of all that Jesus said and did before his death. The saving significance of this particular death arises from the significance of the particular life that preceded it and of which it is the final act; it can be rightly interpreted only in the context of the total event of Jesus' history. Jesus' whole life is the interpretation of his death. That death was the end-product of the radicalization of his message and the actuality of his living—his being-for-the-other and his unconditional obedience to God's will.

The radical aspect of Jesus' message is emphasized by the formula "blessed are you." All worldly blessing and values are to be considered of little worth in comparison to the blessings of the Kingdom of God. But the nature of the blessings involves a total reversal of values, expressed in relation to their recipients. The blessings are not for virtuous people, but for the poor, the hungry, and the sorrowful, the outcasts, and the powerless.

In his inaugural sermon in Nazareth Jesus can take up a saying of the prophet Isaiah (61:1) and proclaim that he has been sent to preach the good news to the poor, to announce the acceptable year of the Lord (Lk 4:18-19). The goodness of God passing all understanding means joy and gladness for the poor. They have received redress, before which all other values fade (Mt 13:44-46). They experience more than they have hoped for; God accepts them and, although they are empty-handed, Jesus himself rejoices with them.

Who are the poor to whom the Kingdom of God is promised? Poor is taken in a very broad sense; it includes the helpless, those without resources, those who suffer on account of their discipleship (Lk 6:22-23). Jesus' poor are those who have nothing to expect from the world, but who expect everything from God. They are the ones who have been driven up against the limits of the world and its possibilities. They are beggars before God; only from God can they expect help.

The poor are the ones with whom Jesus associates—tax collectors, harlots, shepherds (Mt 21:32), or sinners (Mk 21:17), that is, the godless. The godless numbered people who ignored the commandments of God and were held up to contempt. The whole lot were lumped together as *am ha'aretz*—the poor, uneducated people who either did not know the complicated provisions of the Law or, if they did, could not keep them and were consequently despised by the pious. They were considered to be like Gentiles. While God's fatherhood extended to the Jewish people even when they were sinners, the same was not true for the Gentiles, who were sinners almost by definition. Gentiles lived apart from the Law. Jews who sinned could hope for mercy from their heavenly Father, but Gentiles could not count God as their Father.

Against this background we may appreciate the radical nature of Jesus' proclamation of the forgiveness of sins as expressed in the parable of the Prodigal Son. By becoming a swineherd, the son had made himself like a Gentile. Any Jewish father listening to Jesus' parable would have considered this son as dead. Yet in the parable the father forgives in an extravagant way. Here was a reversal, a situation in which God's love was being revealed in a new way. God is the compassionate one, and salvation is available to the most abandoned. The Kingdom of God cannot be contained by existing structures and institutions. God's holiness transcends "clean" and "unclean," "Jew" and "Gentile" (or "Jew who has made himself a Gentile").[10] Jesus' table-fellowship with sinners and the abandoned bears witness to the fact that Jesus, through his actions, carried his proclamation into effect.

To understand what Jesus was doing in eating with sinners, it is important to realize that in the East, even today, to invite a man to a meal is an honor. It is an offer of peace, trust, brotherhood, and forgiveness; in short, sharing a table means sharing a life. In Judaism, in particular, table-fellowship means fellowship before God; breaking bread shows that all who share the meal also have a share in the blessing the master of the house has spoken over the bread. Thus Jesus' meals with the publicans and sinners were not only events on a social level, an expression of his unusual humanity and social generosity, but they expressed his mission and message. The inclusion of sinners in the community of salvation, achieved in table-fellowship, is the most meaningful expression of the message of the redeeming love of God.

The Paschal Mystery and the Forgiveness of Sins

Jesus said again and again that salvation was for sinners, not for the righteous. God opens the Kingdom to children and to those who can say "Abba" like a child (Mt 18:3): "I tell you this: unless you turn round and become like children, you will never enter the kingdom of Heaven." Our response to God's activity must contain the ready trust and instinctive obedience of a child. Only in this way are we truly able to enter into the depth of the experience. To experience God's activity as king requires a new attitude to life in the world—a radical reorientation. To accept it "like a child" means to accept it immediately, without any calculation. The prodigal son received a wholly undeserved grace; his older brother's mistake was to count on a reward. This forgiveness, as characteristic of the Kingdom, bursts the old wineskins. To accept Jesus' message demands a radical conversion from the old ways of perceiving reality. God's Kingdom as forgiveness of sin is a challenge, for it demands a new relationship with God and with our neighbor.

There is an important correlative to the redeeming love of God. While experiencing God's love means experiencing that we have been unreservedly accepted, approved, and infinitely loved, it also means that we must do the same for one another. If God remits an enormous debt of ours, we, too, must be prepared to release our fellows from their petty debts to us (Mt 18:23-24). God's forgiveness gives us the capacity for limitless forgiveness (Lk 17:3-4).

The forgiveness of sins is a gift that God gives totally, unconditionally, and with absolute generosity. The father's reception of the prodigal son was unconditional. The son's repentance was simply his willingness to set aside his pride and accept his father's graciousness. But because of the nature of the gift, we cannot keep it and simply enjoy it for ourselves; it will be wasted if we do not forgive our brothers and sisters from the heart (Mt 18:35). To be forgiven means to forgive "seventy times seven," that is, without limits. "As we also forgive" indicates that the experience of God's activity is linked to a proper response. In the context of God's forgiveness, we learn to forgive and thus to enter ever more deeply into an experience of the divine forgiveness. The all-surpassing love of God makes itself felt in our acceptance by one another.

Jesus' proclamation of the Kingdom of God demands a radical decision in favor of our neighbor. His proclamation is related to the *shema,* with its dual command of God and the neighbor: "Hear, O Israel: the Lord is our God, one Lord: and you must love the Lord your God with all your heart and soul and strength" (Dt 6:4-6). For Jesus, the key phrase is

"with all your soul," and it is encountered in the demand that we be prepared to sacrifice life itself: "If any man would come after me, let him
deny himself and take up his cross and follow me." Everything that Jesus
said concerning our relationship to our neighbor is determined by the
demand that we should be of help. Nothing may be allowed to stand in
the way of care for the neighbor. Jesus' criticism of the scribes and
Pharisees belongs to this context: "They make up heavy packs and pile
them on men's shoulders, but will not raise a finger to lift the load themselves" (Mt 23:4-5). Religious obligations have no priority here, not even
the rules concerning the Sabbath. For Jesus, the Sabbath is for the sake
of the people, and to serve God is to serve the people in their need.

Although everything in Jesus' proclamation centers around the
Kingdom of God, God is not to be loved simply in liturgy and ritual but in
care for our neighbor. The grace of God is compared to the gifts given by
human beings. A man gets up in the middle of the night in order to give
the help that has been requested (Lk 11:5-8). Jesus concludes: "How
much more will your heavenly Father give good things to those who ask
him?" (Mt 7:11).

The parable of the Good Samaritan underlines the same point about
the reality of the Kingdom of God, for it is given in the context of a question about eternal life. It leads away from questions about personal salvation to questions about "the other." Eternal life is in our midst as
compassion.

In Luke, "neighbor" shifts from being the object of compassion
(v. 24) to being the person who shows compassion (v. 36). But the
Samaritan's compassion in no way springs from faith in Jesus. He does
not act religiously. In Jesus' teaching, love of neighbor is not simply a
means to the love of God, for this would not really be love. In the parable
of the Good Samaritan, the help given to the one who has fallen among
the thieves is given strictly in response to his needs.

In this context the compelling question is, "Who is our neighbor?" In
the story of the Good Samaritan, the scribe poses his question at a distance, as a theoretical problem, in the abstract. But such a question cannot
be put in the abstract, because the neighbor cannot be put at a distance.

The neighbor, then, is not simply a friend. It is anyone, friend or
enemy. The love of Jesus invites his listener to break through all boundaries established by religion or nationality. God does not differentiate
between friend and foe: "Only so can you be children of your heavenly
Father, who makes his sun rise on good and bad alike, and sends the rain
on the honest and dishonest" (Mt 5:45-46).

The parable of the Good Samaritan teaches a radically new concept
of neighborliness, one defined in terms of need rather than common

membership in a racial or religious group. The Kingdom of God is in our midst. It manifests itself when compassion and forgiveness are offered to the one in need. Through the coming of the Kingdom of God everyone can now know that love is the ultimate, that what is done out of love will endure forever.

The link between the Kingdom of God and the reception of this Kingdom in our lives is compassionate dedication to those in need. The *metanoia* demanded by the coming of the Kingdom of God takes concrete form in compassion. God's compassion and forgiveness precede and form the ground and source of our compassion to others. We are urged to be compassionate as God is compassionate, for God's mercy is expressed here on earth in our mercy just as God's compassion was demonstrated concretely in Jesus' compassion for the oppressed.

Jesus' Life and Jesus' Death

Jesus' life was one of radical dedication to the neighbor and to God. His life was one of complete self-giving; his death was the definitive act of this self-giving. Christ in freedom poured himself out in loving surrender to the Father and in solidarity with outcasts, even to death on the cross. Jesus was among his disciples as one who serves. Love of neighbor and enemy, living for others, was the way Jesus preached and lived. Such a life is a life of radical poverty; it involves being prepared for anything and demands leaving everything, even one's own life.

Jesus' death, whether political or religious, is not at all in contradiction to the rest of his life, to what we can discern from that life, or from his message. Unless we are willing to separate radically the order of acting from that of knowing, we somehow must affirm that Jesus accepted his own death knowingly, not necessarily as universally redemptive but as essentially in accord with his mission and total dedication to the Father. It is not a question of having Jesus seek his own death as a violent death; accepting his death was simply another form of self-surrender, self-gift.

In the synoptics, Jesus' obedience to God and responsibility for the world are co-constitutive themes. While the word *responsibility* is not used in the gospels, the gospels do make use of a similar comment to characterize the action of Jesus—"to have compassion," which is to be understood as a stronger phrase than "to love," and more commonly associated with Jesus. To have compassion means to be moved from the viscera as from the heart. In Karl Barth's words, "The expression is a strong one which defies adequate translation. Jesus was not only affected to the heart by the misery which surrounded him, but it went right into his heart, into himself, so that it was his misery. It was more his than that of those who suffered it. He took it from them and laid it on himself...He humbled himself in their place."[11]

The phrase "to have compassion" is used by Jesus himself in three of the most significant parables. It describes the action of the Good Samaritan (Lk 10:33), of the father of the prodigal son (Lk 15:20), and of the king in the parable of the Unforgiving Servant (Mt 18:27). It was used three times in association with acts of healing, where Jesus is "moved by compassion" to perform the deed of healing in question. Both forgiveness and reconciliation underline the dimension of solidarity of God and us.

The Paschal Mystery and the Resurrection

Jesus' death on the cross cannot be isolated from the life and mystery of Jesus; nor can it be isolated from the resurrection. And in the same way that the cross cannot be isolated from the life and ministry of Jesus, the resurrection cannot be isolated from the entire life of Jesus, which is gathered up on the cross. Easter was the outcome of Jesus' life and death.[12] Cross and resurrection are bound together most closely, distinguishable but never separable. Between the event of Jesus' death and the event of his resurrection from the dead there prevails a unique relation which forbids that one event be viewed in isolation from the other. The themes of crucifixion and resurrection must be drawn together into the closest unity possible. This is evident in Paul's writings (see Rom 4:25; 8:34; 1 Cor 15:3-4; 2 Cor 5:15). As Hodgson writes: "Only the Crucified is risen, and the dominion of the Risen one extends only so far as the Crucified is served."[13]

The resurrection does not do away with the cross. On the contrary, it is the manifestation and confirmation of what happened on the cross, and therefore of what happened in the life of Jesus. It is not a question of choosing between two different interpretative contexts—Jesus' life or his resurrection. No dichotomy may be imposed between Jesus' life, ministry, and death, and his resurrection.[14] To understand the cross Christologically is to see it as the cross of the one Jesus who lived, suffered, and died, and was raised from the dead.[15] According to Moltmann, "The historical Jesus is not 'half Christ' nor is the risen Christ the other half of Jesus. It is a question of one and the same person and his unique history. The risen Christ *is* the historical and crucified Jesus, and *vice versa*."[16] There is real continuity between the life and death and the resurrection of Jesus, and therefore a real continuity in the faith of the disciples before and after Jesus' death.[17]

Jesus' death must be understood as the determinative free act that gathered up the entire human life of Jesus in its utter abandonment to the Father. The resurrection must be understood as the Father's simultaneous, irrevocable acceptance of Jesus' life and death. The resurrection is the significance of Jesus' life and death accepted by the Father and set free to work. It is the Father's *yes* to the person and the life of Jesus. It cannot, therefore, be isolated from the cross simply as another event in its own right. Rather, Good Friday and Easter should be seen as two separate aspects of a strictly unitary event of the existence of Christ that are essentially related to one another. The resurrection reveals Jesus precisely as the crucified Lord; the cross remains the signature of the risen One (see Rom 4:25; 8:34; 1 Cor 15:3-4; 2 Cor 5:15). The resurrection is simply the other side of Jesus' death, the definitive acceptance by God of Jesus, his activity and preaching, his self-awareness, in short, his life of filial obedience. The confession that Jesus is risen can and must be determined in light of his ministry and death. The resurrection does not give meaning to the life, ministry, and death of Jesus, but confirms their validity in the face of rejection.

Because the paschal mystery is the interpretative framework for the life, ministry, death, and resurrection of Jesus, it is also the interpretative framework for the soteriological dimension of these realities. While the full soteriological dimension of Jesus' death was worked out after the resurrection event, its foundation lies in Jesus' life, suffering, and death. If this were not so, the core of the gospel message would come close to being simply a subjective interpretation. The basic theological interpretation of Jesus' death is found in Paul's affirmation that "Christ died for our sins" (1 Cor 15:3).

Jesus and Salvation

There is an implicit soteriology in the life, ministry, and death of Jesus. A wholly accidental death would carry the interpretation that death is given meaning entirely from outside, from God. It would mean that Jesus' death was simply chosen by God as redemptive. Jesus was done violence to; he was killed on the cross. There is, however, a personal dimension to this death. Jesus' life, his twofold solidarity with the Father and with outcasts, led to his condemnation. Precisely because of his double solidarity, Jesus was executed. Jesus' self-identity offended both the religious and political leaders. Jesus' life was one of dedication to the neighbor.

The radical obedience of Jesus to his Father, which led to his death on the cross, expresses who he is and further, manifests the radical integrity of his life to the extent that he was killed for being who he was. Jesus' solidarity with the Father, expressed in his obedience, and his solidarity with outcasts and the rejected, manifested by his concern and care for them, constitute his self-identity. The redemptive and salvific interpretation of Jesus' death has its foundation in the unity of Jesus' life and message and death. The atoning effect rested upon his willingness to give his life in solidarity with God's salvific purpose and human suffering. Paul and the writer of Hebrews see Jesus' death and resurrection as being redemptive; the redemptive force of Jesus' death and resurrection lies in his solidarity of love. The redemptive dimension of Jesus' suffering does not lie with the negativity of death, as such, but with the positiveness with which he accepted it. In a sense, redemption occurs not because of Jesus' death but despite it.

The concept of solidarity is expressed clearly in the letter to the Hebrews: "Therefore he had to be made like his brethren in every respect, so that he might become merciful...For because he himself has suffered and been tempted, he is able to help those who are tempted" (Heb 2:17). "We have not a high priest who is unable to sympathize *(sympathein)* with our weakness, but one who in every respect has been tempted as we are" (Heb 4:15). Jesus is the one for others, the one who identifies with others.

This concept of solidarity is also enlarged to indicate representation. Representation, as a concept, is employed in the New Testament to explain salvation history (Mk 1:41; Lk 7:13; Mt 20:34). Phrases referring to it occur five times in Matthew and Mark as part of a formula that describes Jesus as he is moved with compassion for the crowds. The expressions "in our place" and "on our behalf," which designate the deepest sense of Jesus' compassion, also anticipate the oldest soteriological category for interpreting the death of Jesus, a category taken over and refashioned by Paul: "But God shows his love for us in that while we were yet sinners Christ died for us" (Rom 5:8). Jesus' compassion is possible because of his solidarity with us. According to Paul, a real exchange has happened in Christ: "Though he was rich, yet for your sake he became poor, so that by his poverty you might become rich" (Rom 5:8). "Who, though he was in the form of God, took the form of a servant" (2 Cor 8:9). For Paul, this exchange, this solidarity, is a reconciliation, a *katallage,* which means "a becoming other." Reconciliation implies a forgiveness. Both forgiveness and reconciliation underline the dimension of solidarity of God and us.

Salvation and Solidarity

In Jesus Christ the saving nearness of God was made present through a historical life of care for men and women. The death of Jesus on the cross was vicarious because it occurred in solidarity with us. Theology cannot neglect the circumstances of Jesus' death and consider that death in isolation and still ascribe to that death a universal, saving meaning. Without the specifics of Jesus' life, his death is deprived of its saving significance and has to be given a meaning elaborated in mythological terms. The salvific meaning of Jesus' death is rooted in the salvific meaning of his life, in the radical dimension of his love. Jesus' love is radical in the sense that he was not concerned with the consequences of this love for his own life. The vicarious death of Jesus is an instance of the law of love. Love is made manifest in personal relationship; it presupposes the distinctness of the persons concerned. But it is the very nature of love to transcend the boundaries of personal distinctness and to weld persons together in a unity in which it is the most natural thing for one to act vicariously for another. There is no need to refer Jesus' death to an arbitrary decision on the part of the Godhead; it has sufficient basis in the love with which and in which Jesus identified himself with us. Jesus' whole life is the interpretation of his death. The very substance of salvation is present to that life, and in that sense Jesus' death is tied in with his mission of salvation. In his life Jesus showed what love brings about—relief of physical suffering, the healing of illness, the abolition of hunger and discrimination. Through Jesus' love the depth of interdependence in reality is revealed to us: "No man has ever seen God; if we love one another, God abides in us and his love is perfected in us" (1 Jn 4:12). One cannot say that God required the death of Jesus as compensation for our sins. It is not possible to make God responsible for what human injustice has done to Jesus. We should not look for a divine reason for the suffering and death of Jesus.[18] As a matter of history, Jesus' death comes as a reaction to his life and ministry, as the consequence of his love.

Salvation and Resurrection

Seen by itself, isolated from Jesus' life and from the resurrection, the death on the cross appears as the ultimate absurdity. In the light of the resurrection what appeared to be absence and abandonment on the part of God becomes presence. In the light of the resurrection the utter futility of death as expressed in the Old Testament is shown to be deceptive. Death cannot destroy an authentic living communion with God. God's love is stronger than death.

The resurrection means the death of death. The resurrection does not mean that Jesus, who suffered death, now leaves death behind and returns to life. The resurrection of Jesus is not a resuscitation like that of Lazarus. Lazarus, who returned to life, has death still before him. The death of Jesus, in which God shares, is the transformation of death itself. As Paul wrote: "For we know that Christ being raised from the dead will never die again; death no longer has dominion over him. The death he dies he died to sin, once for all, but the life he lives he lives to God" (Rom 6:9-10).

In the light of the paschal mystery, suffering and death take on a different meaning. Yet suffering and death still remain impenetrable.

Jesus' resurrection is the object of our faith, of our hope. As Schillebeeckx writes:

> Our faith in the Resurrection is itself still a prophecy and a promise for this world—*qua* prophecy unsheltered and unprotected, defenseless and vulnerable. And so the life of the Christian is not visibly "justified" by the facts of history...The servant is not greater than his Lord. Just as Jesus did, the Christian takes the risk of entrusting himself and the vindication of his living to God; he is prepared to receive the vindication where Jesus did—beyond death.[19]

The absence of God is what we experience daily.

Jesus' resurrection is a promise that ultimately we will not be abandoned, not a promise that God will remove our suffering, pain, and death. Jesus in his cry from the cross offers no palliative for death. Even in the context of hope in the resurrection, death is recognized to be death. Death—Jesus' death as well—is a negative reality.

Then to what extent and in what manner is Jesus' death for us? Are we spared anything because of Jesus' death? We are not spared death and suffering. We are not spared from working out our salvation in fear and trembling. We cannot collapse the eschatological dimension of the cross into a salvation already realized and brought about. Pannenberg writes: "Whoever is bound up with Jesus no longer dies alone, excluded from community with God, above all no longer as one who is divorced from community with God and his future salvation...Whoever is bound up with Jesus dies, to be sure, but he dies in hope of the life of resurrection from the dead that has already appeared in Jesus."[20]

Solidarity with God in Jesus means salvation ultimately from death. It means salvation for all. It is in this sense that Jesus' death has vicarious significance for all humanity. In the crucified Jesus, God has revealed what authentic salvation is: God's unconditional grace, which brings justice to those who have been oppressed and makes righteous the unrighteous. Like the parable of the Prodigal Son, the cross shows that God's love does not depend on whether or not it is reciprocated: "If you love those who love you, what reward have you?" (Mt 5:46). In the parable of the Prodigal Son, the father forgives and condones without exacting suffering and pain. The father's forgiveness wipes away the guilt; there remains only the fact and memory of having sinned. The father did not need to be placated. Before the son "came to himself" the father was already awaiting and desiring his return. "This parable," according to J. Macquarrie, "stresses the unchanging character of God's attitude and work, which is always one of reconciliation...No historical event changes God's attitude or makes him from a wrathful God into a gracious God, or allows his reconciling work to get started."[21]

The basic experience that engendered Christianity was that of the paschal mystery. The Christology of the New Testament is at once a consequence of the paschal mystery and its expression. As such, it is best viewed as a kenotic Christology. The kenotic motif arises immediately out of the experience of the paschal mystery; the whole of the New Testament gives evidence of the kenotic motif.

The understanding of the kenosis of God in the person of Jesus is simply an inevitable outgrowth of the full Christian faith in Jesus Christ as the presence of God's salvation. The basic experience that led to an incarnational Christology was one of salvation, one of having been encountered by God in the person of Jesus Christ: in the presence of Jesus there is a new creation. In Jesus Christ God has been met in a startlingly new way, in a human life beset with the limitations, suffering, and death that all must endure. The early church was led to believe that God had gone where each one of us goes in death and yet remained God. The principal element of the kenotic motif is that divinity is supremely manifested in human self-giving, specifically in the human self-giving of Christ.

In the kenotic motif *astheneia* ("weakness") reveals God's divine power. "For Jews demand signs and Greeks seek wisdom, but we preach Christ crucified, a stumbling block to Jews and Greeks, Christ the power of God and the wisdom of God. For the foolishness of God is wiser than men, and the weakness of God is stronger than men" (1 Cor 1:22-5). God's action and presence are manifested at the point when Jesus is most clearly human. The weakness displayed on the cross is the power of God. Whatever we affirm about the divinity of Jesus cannot erase what was true of his authentic humanity. When we speak about incarnation, it must be recognized as an abasement and a mission. New Testament kenosis sees in Christ's full acceptance of the conditions of human existence the supreme manifestation of the limitless love of God for his unworthy creatures. When Paul wrote that "Christ died for us while we were yet sinners, and that is God's own proof of his love toward us" (Rom 5:8), he summed up a truth inherent to the gospels.

Jesus' message about God was a message of good news about forgiveness and compassion. God does not stand outside the range of human suffering and sorrow. Jesus proclaimed a new presence of God. "God was in Christ reconciling the world to himself" (2 Cor 5:19). The Christological hymn of Philippians 2:6-11 presents the self-emptying of Jesus as the revelation that to be God is to be unselfishness itself. In his life Jesus pursued a style of service even to the act of complete self-giving. He did so not simply as the exemplary man but as a revealer of divine reality. God's eternal happiness is not freedom from suffering; rather, it is the victory of God's suffering over evil. Divine suffering does not indicate any weakness or limitation in God, but rather a voluntary self-limitation and self-sacrifice and love for humankind. The kenosis hymn presents a revelation of what it means to be God. God knows no holding back, no selfishness, no fear of loss of power. As revealer of God's inner life, Jesus, in the words of Mark, came "not to be served but to serve" (Mk 10:45). The theology of Philippians 2:6-11 requires Calvary as the prelude to salvation.

CHAPTER THREE

The Christological Journey
in the New Testament

T he beginning of the good news of Jesus Christ, the Son of God"
(Mk 1:1). These are the first words of Mark's gospel, and they express the
major concern of Christology: What does it mean to confess that Jesus is
the "Son of God"? Jesus' life, ministry, message, death, and resurrection
confronted the disciples with fundamental questions about God and
humanity—about God who revealed himself in Jesus, and about their relationship to the God of Jesus. These questions were answered in light of the
resurrection. Yet in Philippians 2 and in the gospel of Mark what is most
revealing about God, Jesus, and themselves is found in Jesus' self-emptying. "Surely now that we have been justified by his blood, will we be saved
through him from the wrath of God" (Rom 5:9). In Philippians 2 Jesus'
saving action is expressed as self-negation, and the disciples are invited to
be of the same mind as Jesus. "For those who want to save their life will
lose it, and those who lose their life for my sake will find it" (Mt 16:25).

Jesus as the Christ

Mark speaks of Jesus' earthly mission in terms of Sonship culminat-
ing in the proclamation at Golgotha. For Mark, Jesus' Sonship comes to
expression in his faithful fulfillment of the mission God had given him.
His aim is to show that the gospel of God was effectively proclaimed by
Jesus. The gospel is about God; Jesus' mission was to reveal God. Jesus'
question "But who do you say that I am?" has no other aim than to pro-
voke an answer to a question about God. Jesus is asking, "Who then is
God if it is I who am the Christ, the Son of the living God?" That is the
existential question about the ultimate meaning of our own existence.

That Jesus is the Son of God or the Christ does say something about
Jesus, that what is revealed to us in him is the answer to our question
about God. So the professions that were originally intended to express
the event of Jesus as gospel, that is, in its meaning-for-us, cannot be
treated as though they were simply assertions about the person of Jesus
in his own being. In Mark, the proclamation of the gospel of God is

embodied in the entire mission of Jesus ending in his death and resurrection. He is the servant of God who inaugurates the Reign of God.

The earliest interpretations of the meaning of Jesus as the Christ were not "ontological" but functional. They were concerned not with who or what Jesus was but with what he was meant to do. None of the titles attributed to Jesus by his earliest followers explained Jesus' identity in and of himself, but only his identification with God's definitive presence and saving action.

As Christology developed it had to ask the ontological question of who Jesus himself was, as the one in whom salvation is achieved. To affirm that God has saved us in Jesus Christ is already to confess faith. To speak of Jesus in himself is a different kind of affirmation. Schillebeeckx sees the history of the Christological dogmas "to lie in the plane of 'second order' affirmation, albeit with the purpose of, and real concern for bearing out the first order of affirmation."[1] The relationship between first-order and second-order assertions raises the question of Jesus' divinity.

Christology and Salvation

The experience of salvation in the early church is the foundation of Christology. The tradition has attempted to define the actual person of Jesus in terms of the salvation that he brought about. In the new light of the resurrection the early church concluded that God acted decisively in the person of Jesus for the salvation of men and women. Paul wrote, "So if anyone is in Christ, there is a new creation: everything old has passed away; everything has become new" (2 Cor 5:17). And, "For as all die in Adam, so all will be made alive in Christ" (1 Cor 15:22). The Christological titles descend from this. Jesus must be interpreted from within God's plan of salvation. In the New Testament Jesus is from God, his activity is from God, and that defines him. If salvation has taken place in the person of Jesus, then certain questions must be asked: Who is Jesus in himself and what is his *ousia*, his "essential being"? How is it possible that in the presence of Jesus we are faced with God's salvific action? What does this mean for the person of Jesus? These questions attempt to interpret Jesus Christ as God's self-disclosure and self-giving, as God's communication with humanity. Christological titles express the conviction that Jesus encountered men and women from the side of God.

The Development of Christological Titles

The New Testament makes evident a trajectory in the scope of its witness to Jesus as the one who meets men and women from God's side, from doxological affirmations taken from the language expressing the hope of Israel to the universal affirmation of Colossians (1 Col 15:22).

The life and death of Jesus of Nazareth, together with those events that brought the disciples to believe in the resurrection, formed a complex historical event, the Christ-event, which was placed by the early church in the context of Israel's paradigmatic history. Inherent to Israel's history is the consciousness of being the chosen people. With Abraham, a new race (Gn 12:1, 2) is constituted, and with the Exodus a new people is created (Dt 4:35-40): "the people of the Lord." Israel is a people different from other people; "for you are a people holy to the Lord your God; the Lord your God chose you out of all nations on earth to be his special possession" (Dt 7:6). It is a people with a mission: "By my self I have sworn, from my mouth has gone forth in righteousness a word that shall not return, to me every knee shall bow, every tongue shall swear" (Is 45:23). In fact, at the time of Jesus' appearance we find an unparalleled period of missionary activity for Israel.[2] In Romans 2:17-23 Paul describes how the unshakable certainty of the Jewish people that they possessed the revelation of God found expression in a sense of duty incumbent upon them to make this revelation known to the nations.

Although the New Testament relates that Jesus forbade his disciples during his lifetime to preach to non-Jews—"Go nowhere among the Gentiles, enter no town of the Samaritans; but go rather to the lost sheep of the house of Israel" (Mt 10:5)—we find the disciples involved in intensive missionary work very soon after the resurrection. The early church saw the resurrected Jesus as the embodiment of all God's promises and the Christ-event as the fruition of God's salvific action in the world. The Christ-event took on a universal and ultimate import. The primitive community of faith understood itself as the new chosen people, the people of a new covenant, the "firstfruits" of what was to be in the consummation of all things. What had happened to them was symbolic of the purposes of God in and for all history.

The New Testament tells us that in Jesus Christ time is fulfilled (Mk 1:15), the fullness of time has arrived (Gal 4:4), and the scriptures have been fulfilled (Lk 4:21). The Fourth Gospel begins with the affirmation that Jesus Christ is the Word of God through whom all things have been made. Jesus is the "last Adam" (1 Cor 15). In him is accomplished and fulfilled the promise made to Abraham for all the people of the world (Lk 1:55, 73). Jesus Christ is presented as the one who sums up and fulfills in his own person the whole history of the people of Israel. That is to say, for the early Christians Jesus represented the right relationship to God. C. F. D. Moule writes: "It is in Jesus, as in no other figure in Jewish myth or history, that his followers found converging all the ideal qualities of a collective body of persons in a right relationship with God; and if Paul speaks of the Church as the Body of Christ (or as a body because incorporated in Christ), that is partly because he has found in Christ all that the People of God were designed to be."[3]

Paul affirms a universal Lordship to Christ. Christ dominates the centuries and sums up all creatures in himself because he is the pre-existent Son of God, risen from the dead and seated at the right hand of God. "He is the image of the invisible God; the first born of all creation" (Col 1:15). Jesus Christ is the one through whom God made everything there is (Heb 1:2), the Son "sustaining the universe by his powerful command." The covenant established by God with creation, the covenant established with Israel, becomes focused in the one person of Jesus Christ. "There is salvation in no one else, for there is no other name under heaven given among mortals, by which we must be saved" (Acts 4:12). Jesus' existence and words are understood to be disclosive of God. Jesus' significance for Paul is grounded in the fact that in him the final eschatological destiny of humanity to Sonship has already appeared (Rom 8:29). Everything is predestined toward Jesus, and he is predestined to be the summation of the whole cosmos.

The universalism of the New Testament has its source and foundation in one person: Jesus Christ. In every part of the New Testament, in every stage of the early tradition, we find that the coming of Jesus Christ has completely transformed the human situation. Our eternal destiny depends on the decision we make concerning our relation to this one Jesus of Nazareth. It is because of him that the prospect of the future has changed. So Schillebeeckx writes:

> Although Jesus' historical message about the kingdom of God is of abiding value, there is no single instance, either pre-canonical or in the New Testament, of an attempt to imple-ment the task of carrying forward this good news without linking it intrinsically with the person of Jesus. The heart of Christianity is not just the abiding message of Jesus and its definitive relevance, but the persisting eschatological rele-vance of his person itself.[4]

How seriously this definitive character of the person of Jesus is taken becomes clear in the fifth chapter of Romans. Here we find the synthesis of all the previous material. Just as there has been a first Adam, so there is a second Adam; this is deliberately reiterated. His com-mission means a complete change in the situation of humankind in that he brings new life and inaugurates a new and final era of history. Because Adam is the father of the old humanity, Adam is the prototype who foreshadows Jesus Christ. With the coming of Jesus Christ a new age has been inaugurated, an age of grace. Jesus Christ is seen as the fulfillment of all promises made in the past.[5]

As the fulfiller of the promises made in the Old Testament, Jesus is perceived by some of the authors of the New Testament as a supernatural agent; pre-existence is attributed to him. This leads to the understanding of the Christ-event in incarnational terms. As the fulfiller of God's promises, Jesus has a mission that no one else has ever had or will ever have. "Let it be known to all of you and to all the people of Israel: that this man is standing before you in good health by the name of Jesus Christ of Nazareth, whom you crucified, whom God raised from the dead" (Acts 4:10). Both understandings of Jesus, as fulfillment of God's promises and as involved in a unique way in bringing about such a fulfillment, are expressed by the Christological title Son of God. The title is prominent in Paul, in the epistle to the Hebrews, and in John.

Christ as the Son of God

The title Son of God, like most other Christological titles used in the New Testament, has different meanings. Rudolph Schnackenburg has considered the variety of opinions on the title Son of God and has discerned four possible approaches.[6] There is the conservative affirmation that Jesus himself used the title in a messianic sense and understood himself as the unique Son of God. There is the religio-historical explanation of the title in terms of the Hellenistic concept of the divine man, the *Theios Aner*. Some scholars have attempted to discern in the teaching of Jesus the seeds of later development in the church. J. Jeremias, for one, sees an original "servant" understanding behind the title Son of God in the baptismal narrative that was later reinterpreted in terms of Sonship.[7] And finally, O. Cullman and B. M. F. van Irsel, among others, see a link between the title and Jesus' own consciousness of a filial relation to God.[8]

According to Bultmann and Hahn, the traditio-historical approach accounts for all the uses of the title within the developing theology of the early church. The self-consciousness of Jesus is not a legitimate concern, since we have no sources for such knowledge. According to Hahn and Fuller, the title Son of God was first applied to Jesus in the early Palestinian church with reference to his future work as Messiah. Only at a later stage (Hellenistic Jewish Christianity) was it applied to him with reference to his exalted position after the resurrection.[9] Hahn's evidence for his view is to be found in Luke 1:32f., Mark 14:61f., and 1 Thessalonians 1:9f., which testify to the Palestinian view, and in Romans 1:3f., Acts 13:33, Hebrews 1:5 and 5:5, Colossians 1:13, and 1 Corinthians 15:15-28, which testify to the Hellenistic-Jewish view.

Fuller bases his case on Romans 1:3f. This text has long been recognized as a pre-Palestinian formula established by Paul. Fuller argues that the passage "who was made of the seed of David...who was designated Son of God by resurrection from the dead" means that Jesus was foreordained to be the Son of God at the parousia.[10] The Sonship referred to in this text expresses a dignity and a function rather than a natural Sonship. The function implied here is one of sanctifying *(pneuma agiosunes)*. The dignity of the Son of God with power designates a function that began at a certain moment in time and, while it might presuppose the eternal divine nature in the one who exercises it, does not designate it explicitly. The resurrection is perceived as effective and declarative of Jesus' divine Sonship.

According to Hahn, it is from royal messianism that the use of the title Son of God in the primitive Christian tradition can be explained.[11] As the concept of the Messiah went through a process of transformation, Son of God became a characteristic title of the exalted Jesus, who has been adopted by God and installed at his right hand.[12] Here the title Son of God pertains to a two-stage Christology already outlined in Romans 1:3ff., "according to the flesh" and "according to the spirit."

Descent from the line of David qualifies the time of the earthly Jesus, denoting the Messiah in the condition of his humanity and lowliness. In the realm of the Spirit, the second stage, Jesus is anointed Son of God. This Sonship of God cannot be taken in a physical sense but must be understood as the conferring of a dignity and office. The two stages indicate a contrast between the sphere of weakness and transience and the sphere of divine power, life, and salvation. The designation as Son of God has taken place not under earthly conditions but under the exclusive operation and within the unlimited rule of the Spirit of divine holiness.

In his heavenly mode of existence the One born of the seed of David and risen from the dead has assumed the authoritative function of the Son of God and is thus known truly as Messiah. It is the resurrection that proclaims Jesus to be the Son of God. The resurrection authenticates; it exercises a retroactive power. Some of the New Testament texts affirm a real effect of the resurrection on the person of Jesus. It is clear that the resurrection should not be reduced to a mere incident in the totality of the Christ-event. Jesus is not the same before as after the resurrection.

Jesus' transformation at the resurrection is related to the presence and work of the Spirit. There is a uniqueness, according to Paul, in Jesus' relation to the Holy Spirit. This uniqueness is underlined in texts such as 1 Corinthians 15:45 and in Paul's characterization of the Holy Spirit as the Spirit of Christ, the Spirit of the Son, the Spirit of Jesus Christ (Rom 8:9; Gal 4:6; Phil 1:19). From being a man under the direction of the Spirit, Son of God, according to the Spirit, Jesus becomes by virtue of his resurrection Son of God in full power of his Sonship, that is, in full power of the Spirit. After the resurrection and the exaltation, Jesus impressed his character on the less defined nature of the Spirit.[13]

Jesus' miracle-working had already caused him to be regarded as a charismatic man of God, a new Moses. Jesus provided with the Spirit by God has power over unclean spirits. Because of this power to work miracles, Jesus was considered as divine-man *(Theios Aner)*. In the Jewish context the *Theios Aner* is conceived as a man under divine inspiration, a man provided by God with the wherewithal for a special mission. The baptismal scene in Mark links the concept of *Theios Aner* as a man endowed with the divine Spirit and the concept of the Son of God. For Hellenistic Judaism, "the constitutive element of the *Theios Aner* conception, the divinity of man as the possibility of his participating in what is divine—indeed of his deification—is unthinkable."[14] Yet in the baptismal scene the Spirit of God descends and unites with the human person of Jesus. Jesus is thereby endowed with the messianic dignity of the Son of God, a dignity understood as a special supernatural power. It is not a process of transformation that is at work here but the bestowal of the Spirit of God. Temptation clarifies the real value of the title Son of God: "The Son of God may not misuse his power either in helping himself or in working a spectacular miracle; he must use it in what he is commissioned to do."[15] Divine Sonship implies obedience even unto death.

In the infancy narratives the dimension of divine Sonship is further determined by the theologumenon of the virgin birth. Here, through the begetting by the Holy Spirit, divine Sonship is predicated of Jesus not simply by indwelling "but by a special act which precedes the whole of his work on earth."[16] Divine Sonship rests upon the creative act of election and separation in Mary's womb.[17]

The gospel of Luke traces Jesus' Sonship ("He will be great; and will be called the 'Son of the Most High'" [Lk 1:32]) to a special creative act by God at his conception, although nothing is said of a physical Sonship. But when Matthew simply recounts that "the birth of Jesus the Messiah took place in this way. When his mother Mary had been engaged to Joseph; but before they lived together she was found to be with child from the Holy Spirit" (Mt 1:18), this formulation approaches the conception of physical Sonship.

Hellenistic Gentile Christianity construes the title Son of God on a twofold process: "The divine Sonship established through the bestowal of the Spirit is understood in the sense of a pervasion of being, and this then leads on to the idea of an original giftedness in nature."[18] Here the endowment by the Spirit is understood not as a provision but as an apotheosis.[19] "Therefore the step was taken from a concept of the divine Sonship that was messianically and therefore functionally determined to one that was understood in reference to being, even if to begin with an act of appointment was still adhered to."[20] Hellenistic Christianity interpreted the divine Sonship as intrinsic, a giftedness in nature. Here two approaches were available: "The one provided from the event of a virgin begetting; the other, from the idea of pre-existence."[21]

For Paul, the title Son of God implies the dignity of the Son and the Son's subordination to the Father. It is the Father to whom final honor belongs. His power and honor are the goals of all history. Paul finds the divine Sonship expressed clearly particularly in Jesus' suffering (Rom 5:10; 8:32; Gal 2:10). "Son" describes the close bond of love between God and Jesus and emphasizes the greatness of their sacrifice. Although Paul presupposes the pre-existence of the Son of God, he does not stress it. The title Son of God describes the greatness of the saving act of God, who offered up the One closest to him. Paul's understanding deepens the tradition of the divine Sonship; for him, it is no longer grounded in the heavenly glory of the exalted Jesus or the general institution of Jesus as Messiah but rather in suffering and rejection.

In the epistles that may confidently be attributed to Paul there are only a few places where he uses the word *Son* in a context which seems to refer to a pre-existent relationship with God (Rom 8:3, 32; Gal 2:20; 4:4). In these texts what seems to be meant is that God is giving God's self in the sending of the Son. The pre-existent Sonship of Jesus expresses the self-giving character of God.

Son of God in the Gospel of John

The gospel of John uses the title Son of God infrequently but emphatically. The title can only be understood within the basic theology of John. Edward Schweizer writes:

> When one considers what was already the formalized use of "Son of God," especially in demarcation from false faith, one can hardly deny that the title has already become a cipher which pre-supposes a unity of essence between Father and Son without defining it more precisely. But when one examines the basic passages, it is also evident that this unity of essence is grounded in the love between Father and Son and is thus an ever new unity of willing and giving on the part of the Father and of seeing, hearing, and responsive obeying on the part of the Son. It is not an ephemeral unity which has to be attained and which might be broken off at any time, but is grounded in the depth of God's being...The heart of Johannine theology is to be found in the emphasis on the unity of love which lives on in Jesus' dealing with his people.[22]

The event of salvation is anchored in the most intimate union between Father and Son. The Son lives only on the basis of the Father (Jn 6:57); he is one with him (Jn 10:30) and has unlimited participation in him (Jn 16:13; 17:10). The affirmation that "the Father loves the Son" (Jn 3:35) is not meant emotionally or mystically but is closely bound up with the commissioned work of the Son (Jn 8:16, 29). Love, then, is the deepest expression of the relation between the One who reveals himself and his agent (Jn 15:9; 17:23f.).

The title Son of God addresses both attributes of Jesus: being the fulfillment of God's promise, and the one chosen to do God's work. The various stages evident in the attribution of the title Son of God to Jesus indicate clearly that there was a real development in New Testament Christology. The designation of Jesus as God's Son took place within the church. The church associated this designation with various aspects of Jesus' life and ministry, always understanding it to be contingent upon the resurrection. This title is the declaration that Jesus in his life, ministry, death, and resurrection is the genuine revelation of the one God and Father.

Whether the filial relation of Jesus to the Father leads to the affirmation of a distinction within the Godhead is a question that is not dealt with in the New Testament. According to Bruce Vawter:

> It would be a mistake to regard the functional sonship...as a provisional level of Christology from which the Church graduated into a higher conception of Christ's relation to God. On the contrary the theology of adoptive or functional sonship continued throughout New Testament times to protect the truth it had first asserted, namely that the work of salvation was one of grace and not of value, that Jesus Christ was Savior not in virtue of the "flesh" but of the "Spirit."[23]

While one of the Christological climaxes in the Fourth Gospel is to be found in the affirmation "I and the Father are one," it is impossible to elude the distinction between Jesus and the Father. What is essential for John is that Jesus is the true revelation of God: "Anyone whose teaching is merely his own, aims at honor for himself. But if a man aims at the honor of him who sent him he is sincere, and there is nothing false in him" (Jn 7:18). As God's agent and fulfillment of his promises, Jesus is from God and stands for God.

In the writings of Paul and John, Jesus is presented as the definitive Word of God to men and women, as the unique and absolute revealer. The office of revealer is so closely bound up with the person of Jesus that he himself becomes the embodiment of revelation.

The Logos of God

The climax in the New Testament development of Christological thought is reached in the Fourth Gospel in the affirmation that the "Word became flesh" *(o logos sarx egeneto)*, the most influential New Testament text in the history of dogma. "The Word dwelt with God, and what God was, the Word was" (Jn 1:1). John identifies Jesus with this Logos—and in so doing makes the Logos personal. In a Hellenistic context no greater opposition could be conceived than that of *Logos* and *Sarx*. *Sarx* points to what is most ordinary in human beings, to their human frailty. John's affirmation underlines the sharpness of the antitheses and the depth of the synthesis of *Logos* and *Sarx*. When predicated of the *Logos*, *Sarx* underlines the fact that God's Word has entered completely into our human existence. No triumphalistic incarnational theology can be deduced from John's *Logos Egeneto Sarx*.[24]

The subject of becoming is the Logos. It is first said of the Logos that from eternity the Logos is with God, and that the Logos becomes flesh. The Logos is the subject of the event. Divine and human attributes are asserted of one and the same subject. It would be historically mistaken to seek the fully developed two-natures doctrine of Chalcedon in the Johannine writing. The emphasis to be recognized here is not two natures in one subject but a succession of events in history.

It is clear that in understanding Jesus as the fulfillment of God's promise to Israel and as God's special agent in bringing about salvation, the early church attempted to define more fully the person of Jesus. It was inevitable that questions would be asked that would lead directly into the Christological dogmas. What must the origin and nature of Jesus have been in order for Jesus to have been what he was and continues to be in the structuring and restoration of human existence? The basic question about the person of Jesus is the question of his relationship to God. This question ultimately led to the Christian dogma of consubstantiality of Jesus with the Father, to the "very God of very God." We find in the New Testament a variety of formulations relative to the question of the human and the divine in Jesus: the Son of God becomes man (Gal 4:4; Rom 1:3; Phil 2:7); he gives up in some fashion his divinity to take on our humanity (Phil 2:7); the fullness of the divinity dwells in him corporally (Col 1:19; 2:9); God appears or is manifested in the flesh (1 Tim 3:16); he is the Logos become *Sarx* (Jn 1:1). In the New Testament we find a variety of foundations for doctrines concerning the relationship of Jesus to God: there are passages of adoption, identity, distinction, and derivation. In the end, the passages of derivation control the development of Christology. These passages refer to Jesus as being of the Father, not only in time but also eternally. The two titles expressing that dimension of derivation are Son of God and Logos. These titles came simply into being to reinforce the conviction that Jesus—his person, life, message, death, and resurrection—is from the side of God. They underline the theocentric dimension of salvation history.

The passages of derivation eventually became the key to the orthodox understanding of both the passages of identity and the passages of distinction. The title Son of God is more prominent than that of Logos in the New Testament, yet it is the Logos title that is most prominent in the development of Christology in the Patristic period. In the Old Testament the term *Logos* gradually underwent a transformation as it developed from its basic meaning of an eternal word spoken by Yahweh, through the notion of an inner word or thought of Yahweh, to the indication of God's personal appearance to human beings. There is a tendency to hypostatize the Logos, which is clearly present in those biblical passages where the Word is understood as active subject. In Proverbs 8:22 we read about the pre-existence of *hachma* (Wisdom), the identity of Wisdom with God's plan for creation, and also the understanding of Wisdom as the instrument of creation. It is this tradition that lies behind the prologue to the gospel of John.

The dimension of pre-existence attributed to Law in the Psalms and to Wisdom in Proverbs is transferred to the Logos of the prologue to the Fourth Gospel. The only really explicit references to pre-existence occur when Paul identifies Jesus with pre-existent Wisdom (1 Cor 8:6; Col 1:15ff.; 1 Cor 1:24). What is radically new in John's and Paul's use of Wisdom language is the application of such titles as Logos and Wisdom to a historical person, to Jesus of Nazareth.

Christ: The Revealer of God

In the Logos become *Sarx,* in Jesus Christ, God is revealed as a personal God in the concreteness of divine, free activity. The answer to the question Who is God? must arise from the answer to another question, How has humanity experienced God in its history? God's omnipotence is primarily revealed through God's free operation in salvation history. God's attributes are not to be deduced in an a priori way from a metaphysical understanding of God, but from the nature, the reality, of God's Word made flesh. They are to be understood in relation to the free revelation of God in Jesus Christ. Karl Rahner writes, "A person does not, strictly speaking, have attributes with respect to another person: he has freely and personally adopted attributes."[25] To consider God's attributes is to question how God behaves in relation to God's creatures, not simply to ask what can be deduced from the essential structure of God's nature.[26]

In the New Testament, God's attributes of love and forgiveness, God's mercy and compassion, are not deduced through a philosophical process. They have been revealed in Jesus Christ. "It was there from the beginning; we have heard it; we have seen it with our own eyes; we looked upon it, and felt it with our own hands; and it is of this we tell. Our theme is the word of life" (1 Jn 1:1). The letter continues: "We have come to know and to believe in the love God has for us." St. Paul has a profound conviction of being loved by God: nothing "will be able to separate us from the love of God that comes to us in Christ Jesus our Lord." It is in the Christ that God's love is concretely objectified and finally realized once and for all, because nothing in the future can ever make this presence void (Rom 8:38). In the person of Jesus, God is revealed as absolutely free. God's love is not a calculable principle but an unfathomable mystery of freedom.

The parabolic nature of Jesus' life, ministry, death, and resurrection is our revelation of God's compassionate love.[27] This parabolic life is marked by Jesus' referring to God as Abba. Hammerton-Kelly remarks that "Abba means that God is love: it is a representation of the primordial experience of reality as good, expressed three thousand years before Christ in the hymn to the Moon god, Sin from Ur—'Compassionate and merciful Father in whose hand the life of the whole land lies.'"[28] Jesus places the understanding of fatherhood and the reality of the Kingdom of God at the center of his doctrine of God. Throughout the gospel narratives and in the words and gestures of Jesus, his trust in and loyalty to the universal love of God are made evident. In Luke 12:30-31 Jesus assures his disciples that there is no need for anxiety because God's rule is benevolent. One can trust God because God is really Father, Abba. The Kingdom of God is the rule of God, Creator-Father. The coming of the Kingdom is the realization of salvation.[29] The Kingdom's completion means the fulfillment of all human yearnings and the end to human suffering.

The Kingdom of God is embodied in the person of Jesus. In his understanding of his relationship to God as Father we are given a parable about creation and Creator. In the person of Jesus, in his life, ministry, death, and resurrection, we accept the revelation of Creator and creation, of the right relationship between Creator and creation. The early church perceived Jesus as the fulfillment of scripture because he was the fulfillment of humankind-in-relation-to-God. Jesus embodied the true Adam, a renewed humankind. At Jesus all the lines of God's relations with men and women are found to be meeting. What Israel was meant to be in relation to God, Israel had fallen short of, but Jesus succeeded. According to C. F. D. Moule, "Israel represented the position intended in the Genesis creation stories and in Psalm 8, for Adam: mankind, obedient to God."[30] Jesus is perceived as the second Adam and is understood as gathering into himself the destiny of Israel and so of all humankind. In Paul's letter to the Romans salvation is understood as the reversal of Adam's fall; it is the reshaping of each person into the image of God. Salvation is the restoration of the human race to that image in which Adam had been created. Jesus is the indispensable model or pattern for this process:

> For it is not Adam, unfallen Adam, who is the image into which believers must be transformed, but Christ: it is God's purpose to conform believers "to the image of his Son" (Rom 8:29); "as we have borne the image of the man of dust, we shall also bear *(phoresomen)* the image of the man of heaven" (1 Cor 15:49); it is Christ who is the "image of God" (2 Cor 4:4; Col 1:15; cf. 3:10).[31]

Jesus' entire life and death are marked by these characteristics. "Christ's earthly life was an embodiment of grace from beginning to end, of giving away in contrast to the selfish grasping of Adam's sin, that every choice of any consequence made by Christ was the antithesis of Adam's."[32] The transition from salvation in Jesus to Christ, Son of God and Eternal Word, makes a kenotic Christology manifest.

CHAPTER FOUR

In the Form of a Servant:
The Kenotic Hymn

While the "Christological hymn" in Philippians 2:6-11 has not had the same influence as the prologue of John in the development of Christology, its Christological value has always been recognized. It was to be expected that with the advent of contemporary biblical criticism this text would become the subject of much exegesis.[1] In terms of Christological material, probably the most important single development has been that which concerns the nature of the text as a poem. The poetic form and narrative nature of the text have much to say about the various Christological issues. This text is a piece of poetry, a hymn which may have had its early existence in the liturgy of the community. Poetry, as has often been stated, has its own laws; its manner of expressing reality is more open than, for example, metaphysical language. Affirmed as poetry, this text is a hymnic sketch, an inspired hymn of praise. It is a document of the prophetic spirit of the end-time, a product of the earliest post-Easter enthusiasm.

As a poetic structure Philippians 2 has its own value. No amount of theological or philosophical reflection, valid as they may be, can replace the poetic and narrative texture of the hymn. Consider the distribution of this hymn into three parts, each part containing two balanced tercets. This division tends generally to support a three-stage, descent-ascent pattern in Christology: pre-existence, incarnation, and exaltation. Yet what is crucial to the theological element of the text is to be gleaned from a narrative perspective where not three, but two parallel parts are contracted and pivot on the affirmation "Therefore God has highly exalted him" (2:9a). The heart of this hymn is the experience of the cross. The text considers the cross from a post-temporal perspective, and from that perspective what is crucial is "taking the form of a slave," "humbled." The subject of the verses is God (2:6), God the father (2:11), to whose glory the whole action and movement of the verses are directed. This is the reason the hymn does not employ a linear time structure with three equal "ways" or "stages."

Pre-existence

The study of the kenotic hymn has brought to prominence one of the most penetrating questions of Christology: the issue of the pre-existence of Christ and the nature of that existence. Pre-existence has always been understood to be essential to both an incarnational model of Christology and a kenotic Christology. It is an understatement to say that exegetes are widely divided in their interpretations.[2] In R. P. Martin's survey of the exegesis, the affirmation of pre-existence seems to be taken for granted.[3] Since Lightfoot and Lohmeyer, there has been a general consensus that the hymn refers to the pre-existent Christ.[4] This position has been challenged.[5] J. Murphy O'Connor, among others, argues that it is the human Jesus who is the subject of kenosis and exaltation.[6] To support his position, O'Connor suggests that the hymn's frame of reference is not Paul but the book of Wisdom and its anthropology.[7] To James Dunn the Christological hymn does not imply any kind of belief in a pre-existent Christ.[8] This text, he points out, differs from the prologue to the gospel of John in that in Philippians there is no stress on what is before time. The saving significance of Christ is not grounded in his pre-existence but in his humble existence in time.

The Adam Typology

Exegetes may and do differ on the issue of pre-existence in the Philippians hymn, but they tend to be in agreement on its Adam-Christ typology. Monica Hooker states:

> An unnecessary antithesis has been set up by interpreters between a rather superficial interpretation of Pauline ethics on the one hand—an interpretation implying that Christian behavior is simply a case of following Jesus—and on the other hand the conviction that the passage is to be understood only as the recital of saving acts, to which the Church responds in adoration.[9]

Following Kasemann,[10] many exegetes interpret the passage as expressing the event of salvation as a drama. R. P. Martin sums up this position:

> The hymn is loosely dependent upon the ethical dimension, yet...supplies the objective facts of redemption on which ethical appeal may be made. The Apostle's summons is not: Follow Jesus by doing as he did—an impossible feat—rather: Become in your conduct and church relationships the type of

persons who, by that kenosis, death, and exaltation of the
Lord of glory, have a place in his body, the Church.[11]

The hymn does enumerate the events of salvation. But it also invites the
disciples to conformity, "for," according to Monica Hooker, "what Paul
urges the Philippians to do is to be conformed to what they ought to be—
and what they did become in Christ—results from what Christ is and did;
one cannot separate the Christian character from Christ himself."[12]
Whatever the original intention and context of the hymn may have been,
Paul uses it as a basis for his ethical appeal to the Philippians and links
the self-emptying of Christ to the life of the Christian community.

The everyday conduct of the authentic disciple should be characterized as the type of life Jesus Christ himself led. "The appeal to act in a
certain way is directly linked with the action of the Lord Jesus Christ."[13]
And what is the life of Jesus Christ? It is explained in terms of a contrast
between Christ and Adam: "An Adam created in the form and likeness of
God misunderstood his position, and thought that the divine likeness
was something which he needed to grasp; his tragedy was that in seizing
it, he lost it. Christ, the true Adam, understood that Christlikeness was
already his, by virtue of his relationship with God. Nevertheless, he empties himself."[14]

The parallel with Adam is important to our understanding of what
the *morphe theou* means. The position of Adam in Judaism distracts us
from the recognition that the hymn presents an incarnate God. Jewish
anamology forms the literary context of Philippians 2:6-11, although, as
we know, Paul was familiar with the parallelism of the two Adams.[15]
Paul's Adam-Christology is essentially an Israel-Christology; Jesus as
Messiah is man as originally conceived.

An important element of Paul's Adam-Christology is the fact that
Christ was obedient even to death on the cross. Thus he becomes the last
Adam, the Adam that gives life. The apocalyptic belief that Israel is the
last Adam is the correct background for the Adam-Christ typology. As
the last Adam, Jesus reveals God's compassionate love, reenacting it by
becoming obedient even unto death. Christ is the great contrasting figure
to Adam, and the contrast lies in the interpretation of what it means to
be *morphe theou*. "You know the grace of our Lord Jesus Christ, that
being rich he became poor for your sake, that you through his poverty
might become rich" (2 Cor 8:9). Here we have the essence of salvation.

In the Form of God

Adam typology provides the proper context for the interpretation
of the *morphe theou*. For classical exegesis this term is the key to the
entire hymn. But first-century liturgy is far removed from the subtle

distinction of thought found in Plato and Aristotle. There are several clusters of interpretations. There is a philosophical exegesis, in which *morphe theou* is understood formally. Accordingly, Christ is understood to have existed before his incarnation as essentially one with God. Another interpretation finds the roots of *morphe theou* in the Septuagint. Here the word *morphe* would have the meaning of the outward form or appearance of the thing so described. There is yet another conviction that a doctrine of the primal man, the *Urmensch,* lies at the heart of the hymn.[16] This third exegesis recognizes that the hymn uses the framework of a myth in order to structure its Christological message. Within this framework *morphe* indicates not merely the outward form and shape in contrast to the being, but the whole realm of existence. The *morphe theou* is the field of reference in which the encounter between God and Christ took place.[17] The most convincing way of understanding the *en morphe* is Kasemann's: it denotes the sphere in which one stands, the force-field. *En morphe* is less a statement about personal nature than a statement about origin. Its fundamental meaning here is that the divine realm is not in opposition to the human; being in the *morphe doulou* is not in opposition to the *morphe theou,* though there is no greater contrast than that between *Kyrios* and *Doulos.*

The Self-Emptying

The verb *kenoo,* which characterizes the transition in verse seven from the divine to the earthly realm of existence, has no particular philosophical use in Greek. It means "to empty" or "to make void, of no effect." "He emptied himself" is a graphic expression of the completeness of Christ's self-renunciation. Elsewhere in Paul the verb is used in a figurative meaning, "to make void" (1 Cor 9:15; Rom 4:14). It could be translated "he made himself powerless." Making himself powerless meant that he took the form of a slave, one who has no rights or privileges, one who does not even own his or her own body.

The reflexive form "he emptied himself" has no object to define that of which he emptied himself. He empties himself as one pouring himself out. "For you know how generous our Lord Jesus Christ has been; he was rich, yet for your sake he became poor, so that through his poverty you might become rich" (2 Cor 8:9). It has been remarked that "the one who is truly what man is meant to be—in the form and likeness of God—became what other men are, because they are in Adam."[18]

C. F. D. Moule has translated the text thusly:

Jesus did not reckon that equality with God meant snatching: on the contrary, he emptied himself. This would mean that whereas ordinary human valuation reckons that God-likeness essentially means having your own way, getting what you can, Jesus saw God-likeness essentially as giving and spending oneself out.[19]

Precisely because Christ was in the form of God he recognized equality with God as a matter not of getting but of giving. Height is equated with depth; humiliation is identified with exaltation. What is called emptying is really fulfilling. "*Kenosis* is actually *plerosis* which means that the human limitations of Jesus are seen as a positive expression of his divinity rather than as a curtailment of it."[20]

For Monica Hooker, the real paradox in the text is that

> precisely because he (Christ) is truly in the form of God (or God's image)...he is prepared to take on the form of a slave...In becoming what we are, Christ becomes subject to human frustrations and enslavement to hostile powers; but his very action in becoming what we are is a demonstration of what he eternally is—ungrasping, un-selfcentered, giving glory by all of his actions to God.[21]

God's glory is demonstrated in shame and weakness. Divinity issued not in self-aggrandizement but in generous self-giving.

The Exaltation

The last section of the hymn opens with the conjunction *dia*, meaning "in consequence of." *Dia* indicates a causal relation with that which went on before. The exaltation resulted in a real change of status; something was given and accepted that was not previously possessed. Christ became the one who is worshiped. The exalted Jesus is more closely related to God than he was in his pre-existence. Traditional exegetes have been inclined to deny the real dynamic of God in Christ as strongly stated in this hymn. They transformed the "exaltation" to a new and higher status into a "return to the full glory of the Godhead." It seemed to them that no new status could be given to Christ, who held equality with God from the beginning. Exaltation was thus traditionally understood as the revelation of the true divine status, which, having been obscured during the earthly ministry because it was veiled in flesh, was now made manifest.

This traditional view overlooks evidence of the exaltation to new status. The new status given to Christ on account of his obedience unto death is not his alone to possess. In Philippians 3:20-21 Paul affirms that the power given to Christ to transform will enable him to bring us into conformity with him; we shall become like him. "He will transfigure the body belonging to our humble state, and give it a form like that of his own resplendent body, by the very power which enables him to make all things subject to himself" (Phil 3:21; 4:1).[22]

In Philippians 2 God reveals divinity in Jesus Christ not primarily in *doxa* ("glory") but in the human kenosis, in the form of a servant. The meaning of this kenosis is that "God so loved the world that he gave his only begotten Son" (Jn 3:16). The Lordship of God cannot be more fully demonstrated than in servitude. In humiliation God's majesty—God's superabundant divinity—is revealed.

Classical kenotic Christology requires an affirmation of pre-existence. This appears in the New Testament as a direct consequence of the community's confession of Jesus as Lord and as a reflection on the mystery of Jesus, his relation with God, and his work. Pre-existence should not be seen as the existence of personal essence capable of choice. Nor can the affirmation of pre-existence in these texts be interpreted according to later developments of trinitarian doctrine not found in the New Testament itself. Historical study has demonstrated that it was later trinitarian doctrine that made the pre-existent Christ and the exalted Christ of equal status.[23]

What is affirmed in Philippians 2:1-11 is the life of Jesus as a life of voluntary self-surrender to humiliation and obedience. What Jesus became is due to his life of service, his true greatness, his authentic divinity. Divinity manifests itself in humility and in service. Christology in Philippians 2 pictures the life of Jesus as fully human; it connects this humanity to God's work of salvation.

It is as servant of God, the *ebed Adonai,* that Jesus' human existence, his suffering and death, are perceived as salvific. There is a close relationship between the servitude of Jesus and the servant portrayed in Deutero-Isaiah.[24] The word meaning "self-emptying" is not found in Greek literature; the word is found in the Old Testament most characteristically in the fourth suffering servant song (Is 53). The servant "poured out his soul to death" (Is 53:12). Christology in Philippians 2 is servant Christology.

The kenotic hymn is concerned with the connection between suffering and salvation. Allusions have been traced in the text to Wisdom 3 and 4 and to the Book of Isaiah (Is 49:4; 53:8; 53:12; 44:7). The hymn emphasizes the self-emptying and unjust suffering of the historical person of Jesus, but his humiliation is not the last word. Humility and obedience are characteristic traits of the servant of the book of Isaiah and the righteous One. The life of humiliation and suffering is recognized as possessing innate value.

The Kenotic Motif in the New Testament

Kenotic Christology as a fully articulated incarnation Christology cannot appeal to Philippians 2 as its primary or unique source. The validity of kenotic Christology does not depend upon any specific exegesis of the passage in Philippians. What is of unique value is the focus on the humanity of Jesus and on what characterizes this humanity, which is given a name that is above all names. Whatever may be said about Jesus the Christ cannot ever take away the picture of Jesus as it emerges from the modern critical approach to the New Testament. In this picture Jesus is not immune from limitation and weakness; he remains a Jew of the first century.

The kenotic motif is the ground of the New Testament. While the word itself is rare in the New Testament, the kenosis motif shapes and informs the various approaches to the meaning of Jesus Christ. Martin Hengel finds the notion of kenosis in the scandalous death of Jesus on the cross and perceives the epistle to the Hebrews to be a commentary on the hymn in Philippians. I myself affirm that the gospel of Mark also is a long commentary on that hymn. Kenosis is not a Pauline innovation; it is a recurring recognition of the meaning of Christ's life and death. It is inevitable in any Christology that claims to be rooted in the New Testament.

The Kenosis and the Gospel of Mark

Various methodologies have been applied in the recent past to the exegesis of the gospel of Mark.[25] Mark has been perceived as bringing together a variety of traditions about Jesus (form criticism) or as a redactor (redaction criticism) in the production of the first "gospel." Mark is also perceived as the creator of a new literary work on Jesus.[26] Recent studies on Mark have not only followed different methodologies, but they have also concentrated on themes such as Christology, eschatology, discipleship, and suffering. While none of these themes can be interpreted in isolation from the others, it is the Christology, especially a suffering Christology, which seems to me to be of unique importance in Mark.[27]

In recent years Mark has been interpreted as the opponent within the early church of a triumphalist movement that emphasized a theology of glory and a "divine man Christology."[28] While the category of "divine man" has been imprudently used, this does not invalidate the perception of Mark as a Christological controversialist. Perrin maintains that "a major aspect of the Markan purpose is Christological: he is concerned with correcting a false Christology."[29] The gospel of Mark is a theological document concerning the relation of Jesus to God and ourselves; the theology is a Christology. Mark's Christology is limited and defined by earlier traditions, which were not monolithic but diversified and often mutually opposed.

Mark's is a narrative Christology.[30] Narrative Christology is fundamentally open-ended Christology capable of further additions and interpretations. As narrative it is open to paradox; it can live within ambiguity. For this reason the parabolic nature of Jesus is more finely realized and has more power in the gospels than in the Chalcedonian formula. Above all else, Christology is paradoxical. It affirms that in Jesus we have one who is truly divine, truly human, and truly one. An authentic Christology must affirm that Jesus' life is simultaneously characterized by power—divine power that comes to expression in miracles—and by powerlessness, as is made apparent in the passion narratives. Mark affirms both aspects of Jesus' life: power and powerlessness. Yet the gospel narrative does not present a simple juxtaposition of two conflicting Christologies. At the center of Mark's story there stands a theology of Jesus' suffering and death that recalls the kenotic theme of Philippians 2. The parable form serves Mark well as an expression of the kenotic vision. Parable, as is well known, offers a view of reality in which expectations are reversed.

Mark and the Gospel Genre

Mark's gospel was the earliest written. He created a new literary form that was also a major theological achievement. It is a work of real symbolic dimension. This gospel shocked the complacency of the Markan community as much as it supported certain elements of the communal vision. In this sense Mark's gospel follows and closely resembles the function and purpose of Jesus' own parables. As we have already observed, the parables have as their objective the disruption of the hearer's world view in order to effect a radical change of heart. The gospel of Mark is a parable about God's kenotic love for us, shown in and through the person of Jesus Christ.

Mark's work commences: "Here begins the gospel of Jesus Christ, the Son of God" (Mk 1:1). The gospel is the salvation of those who believe (Mk 16:15). It is the story of God's eschatological intervention in this world, of God's unprecedented, incomprehensible love that, in the person of Jesus, seeks us out and finds us and overcomes all obstacles to do so.

Mark immediately declares that Jesus is God's agent, chosen to establish God's sovereignty upon earth. This inauguration (1:1) is announced as the fulfillment of the time of deliverance, as the drawing near of God's rule (1:15). John, the herald of his coming, whose role is itself foretold in scripture, points to Jesus as the mightier one whose authority will be made evident through the divine Spirit.

It is through the Spirit that Jesus is declared to be God's beloved Son, and it is the same Spirit that accompanies him on his mission. This mission begins with power: miracles of healing and exorcism. In keeping with the miracle tradition the gospel of Mark affirms God's omnipotence and Jesus' share in this omnipotence, "Who is this, that even the wind and the sea obey him?" (4:41). There is here no rejection of power.[31] Yet

Mark's Christology is expressed not in the miracle, but in the suffering tradition.

Christology and the Passion Predictions

Mark's Christology is most clearly stated in two key sections of his gospel: the incident at Caesarea Philippi (8:27-10:45) and the passion narrative (14-15). It has been shown that in 8:27-10:45 there is a three-fold repeated pattern: a passion prediction; the disciples' misunderstanding; and corrective teaching discipleship intended to correct the disciples' misunderstanding of the authentic nature of Jesus' mission. The Christological climax of this section is at 10:45: "For even the Son of Man did not come to be served, but to serve, and to give up his life as a ransom for many." These verses have a parallel in Luke:

> "For which is greater
> one who sits at table, or one who serves?
> Is it not the one who sits at table?
> But I am among you as one who serves" (Lk 22:27).

In both Mark and Luke, Jesus is presented as a servant *(diakonos)*. But the disciples must be servants also. In this section, the theological heart of Mark's gospel, the disciples are presented as called to follow Jesus.[32] Jesus and the disciples are shown as being "on the way" (8:27; 9:33, 34; 10:17); the end of the journey is Jerusalem, where Jesus will be crucified. The journey is a journey toward suffering. The teaching about Christology is deeply intertwined with teaching about discipleship.

Disciples are invited to follow Jesus' "way," which, for Mark, is the way of the cross. They are invited to shed their "Christological blindness" to follow Jesus' way and to discover the authentic nature of his mission.[33] For Mark, as we have said, discipleship is intimately bound up with Christology.

The Passion Predictions and Discipleship

Each of three passion predictions is followed by a scene in which the disciples argue heatedly about what Jesus has revealed concerning the journey of *discipleship*. This discord serves a variety of purposes. Most important, Mark's account of the disciples' response enables Jesus to elaborate on the reality of service and its correlative powerlessness. *Powerlessness* here refers to those who have little or no power of their own and to God's special relationship with them. Because their human situation is so vulnerable, they are especially open to receive God's Kingdom. Discipleship in Mark demands relinquishing human power and resources; paradoxically, it is the losing of one's life in order to save it (8:34). Power is to be measured within the community of disciples in terms of servanthood and willingness to suffer for the Kingdom of God. While Mark speaks in various ways of the powerlessness of the disciples, the dominant image is that of cross-bearing (8:34). No symbol of relinquishing power is greater than that of cross-bearing, because to bear the cross is to suffer shame and rejection.

In Mark's Christology power is comprehended in terms of a servanthood exemplified by Jesus' own servanthood; it demands self-denial (8:34). Jesus' invitation underscores the danger of possessions. In chapter 10 Mark tells us of the rich young man called to dispossess himself of material goods. This challenge closely resembles Paul's affirmation, "For you know the grace of our Lord Jesus Christ, that though he was rich, yet for your sake he became poor, so that by his poverty you might become rich" (2 Cor 8:9). Possessions in this world are always an indication of power, as L. T. Johnson writes:

> Possessions do not merely express the inner condition of a man's heart; they are also capable of expressing relations between persons and the play of power between persons. Indeed, when all the aspects are brought together, power appears as reality which underpins them all. Possessions are a sign of power.[34]

Renunciation of property and possessions is, for Mark, the clearest indication of authentic discipleship.

Caesarea Philippi is the geographic point at which Jesus makes a deliberate change of direction. Turning, he begins to journey south toward Jerusalem, anticipating the possible consequences of such a journey. Theologically Jesus abandons the way of power for the way of powerlessness. The real question of 8:27-33 is not so much that of Jesus' identity, which has already been raised at 4:41 ("Who is this, that even the wind and the sea obey him?"). It is, rather, a question of what kind of Messiah Jesus is. For Mark, this is the fundamental issue.

No one is prepared for Jesus' abrupt self-disclosure at this point in the gospel, particularly in light of the power so far made evident in his proclamation of the Kingdom. Peter's reaction is not at all surprising. He may speak for himself (and thus for Satan) in his attempt to dissuade Jesus from the path of rejection and death, but he is thinking in terms of common experience (v. 33). His beliefs about power are based on human experience, yet it is precisely because of this that the Kingdom is a *mystery,* radically overturning the expectations of this world. The Kingdom overthrows humanly constructed theology as well as human values with regard to the nature of power.

The Garden of Gethsemane

In the passion narrative the theological and Christological issues of power and powerlessness are dramatically displayed. It is here that Jesus' own experience of powerlessness is made evident; the focus of concentration is no longer the disciples but Jesus himself. On the journey to Jerusalem Mark's Jesus foretells the passion with what appears to be detachment: "The Son of Man must suffer many things" (8:33; 9:31-10:32). In the garden of Gethsemane, however, he expresses deep anguish. He cries out in his agony, "My grief is enough to kill me" (14:34a). In the garden of Gethsemane there is no escape from choice: between the exercise of power and the giving up of power, between his divinity and his humanity. While "everything is possible for God," for Jesus there is no escape from this agony of mind and spirit. The language of suffering is made explicit in 14:33: Jesus "shudders in distress" *(ektham beisthai)* and "anguishes" *(ademonein)*. Each phrase evokes horror and distress.[35]

Jesus pleads for what he knows cannot be granted. "Father if it were possible the hour might pass from me. All is possible to you: turn aside this cup from me" (14:36). Yet Jesus dies on the cross. The theme of the death of Jesus dominates the gospel of Mark. He dies not as the hero but as the victim. He is "delivered into the hands of men" (9:31; 10:33); he will "be rejected." On the cross Jesus experiences abandonment by God.

The Dying on the Cross

It is clear from Mark's description that Jesus' suffering exceeds that of physical pain. The cross marks his defeat by the forces of evil and his abandonment by God. Jesus suffers the absence of God. Jesus is "delivered up" (14:10, 11, 18, 21, 41, 44; 15:1, 10, 15) not merely into the hands of the Jewish-Roman power structure but beyond that into demonic darkness and God-forsakenness. God's noninterference at the cross, his abandoning Jesus in the hour of his greatest need, constitutes the ultimate depth of Jesus' suffering.

In the accounts of Mark and Matthew, Jesus dies with the words "My God, my God, why hast thou forsaken me?" (Mk 15:34; Mt 27:46). This saying posed difficulties from the beginning.[36] Luke already found it intolerable; he makes Jesus die with the words "Father, into thy hands I commit my spirit" (23:46). In John, Jesus dies with the cry of victory, "It is accomplished" (19:30). Even before the biblical traditions had become fixed, therefore, it was considered scandalous that Jesus should die abandoned by God.

It must be acknowledged that the cry "My God, my God, why has thou forsaken me" is a quotation from Psalm 22, which has clearly influenced the whole passion narrative. According to the practice at the time, to recite the opening verse of a psalm implied the whole psalm. And Psalm 22 turns into a song of thanksgiving. The religious man's suffering is experienced as abandonment by God, but in his suffering and in the agony of death he finds that God, who has been and is forever Lord, saves him and brings him into new life. Consequently, Jesus' words are in themselves not a cry of despair but a prayer confident of an answer, one that hopes for the coming of God's Kingdom.

As the text makes manifest, Jesus' faith did not give way. Even so, he experienced the darkness and distress of death more deeply than any other human being. When he cried out to God in death, he called not only on the God of the Old Testament but also to the God he called Father in an exclusive sense, the God with whom he felt uniquely linked. In other words, he experienced God as One who in his very closeness withdraws, who is totally other. Jesus experienced the unfathomable mystery of God and God's will, but he endured this darkness in faith. This extremity of emptiness enabled him to become the vessel of God's fullness. His death became the source of Life. It became the other side of the coming of the Kingdom of God—its becoming in love.

The Markan crucifixion drama contains various themes and motives. Among these the motif of Christological identification (15:32) is not only central but also crucial Christology that has a primal significance for this evangelist, a centrality manifested both by the fact that the centurion's Christological confession serves as the climactic point of the crucifixion scene and by the major role Christology plays in the crucifixion story and in the gospels as a whole.[37]

Jesus and the Son of God

It is in the context of the passion that Mark shows Jesus to be the Son of God. Mark makes it clear that we can truly see Jesus as the Son of God only if we understand that Jesus shows himself to be such in his passion and death. To be truly God's son is to be dedicated unconditionally to God's purpose even to death. The Son of God title receives its definitive and correct meaning in the centurion's confession (15:39). The centurion, in contrast to others in the drama, proclaims Jesus the Son of God—not because he witnessed one of Jesus' miraculous feats, as Jesus' adversaries mockingly demanded for their proof, but because he saw how Jesus died. The only person on the scene with real power in the eyes of the world reinforces Jesus' Christological status—not because Jesus awed him with his power but because Jesus died a suffering and powerless death. The confession of faith is not made by a pious disciple of Jesus, nor by a Jew, but by a Gentile Roman centurion. For Jews, the centurion's confession means the end of the significance of the Temple; for Gentiles, the opening of the way to God through Jesus' death.

The Resurrection of the Crucified Christ

In the gospel of Mark the resurrection is subordinated to the cruci-fixion. Mark, like Paul, stresses the crucified character of the risen Jesus. Mark's account of the resurrection is astonishingly stark. Female disci-ples find an angelic being in the empty tomb and are overcome with trembling, "and they said nothing to anyone, for they were afraid" (16:8). The evangelist ends his gospel not with an account of Jesus' appearance at his resurrection but with the starkness of the passion. Unless rooted in the cross, the resurrection does not carry in itself a sote-riological significance. While Easter commemorates the cross, the cross is the condition *sine qua non* of Easter. The resurrection marks the beginning of Jesus' absence from the community.

> Mark's is the gospel of "Jesus' absence," and above all the gospel of the earthly Jesus recollected and the expectation, in hope, of the coming heavenly son of man, an expectant awaiting of his exaltation, which is to usher in the eschato-logical kingdom, the rule of God. He has an anti-triumphalist Christology and puts at the center the rejected Jesus of Nazareth. Since Jesus' departure we find ourselves living in a rather drab but necessary interim period (13:9-13) in which Christian faith will be severely tested. But anyone who accepts this Christology will be saved (13:10-13). This is Mark's theologia negativa.[38]

If the absence of Jesus from the community is a Markan experience, then the absence of God suffered by Jesus on the cross appears in a new light. In his God-forsakenness Jesus suffers the plight of the Markan Christian. He anticipates in exemplary fashion the traumatic experiences of the gospel audience. The disciples' life is now conformed to the cross. The actual way of the Christian community in this world has been marked out by the earthly, crucified Christ, and not by the risen Christ in his glory. But as Jesus' death on the cross was taken up into resurrection, so the way of Christians in this world shall receive ultimate vindication.

Mark's Kenotic Christology

In attempting to reveal in Jesus, who is one and the same, two rad-ically different characteristics—the human and the divine—Mark's gospel offers an authentic Christology. While Mark does not use the language of the two natures, he uses two kinds of language with regard to Jesus: the language of suffering and powerlessness, and the language of omnipo-tence, of power. Jesus is simultaneously the Son of God possessing divine power and a victimized human being abandoned on the cross. In

Mark, Jesus is both on the side of God and on our side. The Christological question has always been this: Since he is on the side of God, how and in what way can he possibly be thought or said to be on our side? In Philippians 2 and in Mark the answer is given in terms of kenosis. The gospel of Mark is an account of the unprecedented and incomprehensible incarnate and kenotic love of God.

In the first part of the gospel Mark presents Jesus as someone marked by the power of God; the disciples appear as men encouraged to value their discipleship in triumphalistic terms. For them, the emphasis is on power not powerlessness. With Mark's Jesus this is manifestly not so; he is utterly human, wholly identified with the weakness of humanity. While absolutely from and on the side of God, Jesus is completely on our side also. In our reading of the gospel of Mark the Christological title Son of God must be understood in the context of these words from the author of Hebrews:

> In the days of his earthly life he offered up prayers and petitions, with loud cries and tears, to God who was able to deliver him from the grave. Because of his humble submission his prayer was heard: son though he was, he learned obedience in the school of suffering (Heb 5:7ff.).

Christology and Discipleship

The essence of Mark's Christology is to be found in his unique emphasis on the relationship of Jesus to his disciples. The truth about Jesus Christ is to be found in the communal life of the disciples. Jesus chose his disciples "to be with him" (3:14). Mark intends to present Christ at work with his disciples.[39] Christ's truth may at times appear compromised by the mortal weakness and failings of the disciples, as Mark narrates them; it is in no way compromised by Mark's Christology. For Mark, there cannot be an abstract Christology; every Christology must be a particular commitment. Mark's Christology is an applied Christology. Christology is not possible without discipleship, and authentic discipleship is the key to understanding. Markan Christology is not only bound to the cross and binding to the cross—the basic essential for a kenotic Christology—but it is also bound to discipleship. This is the fundamental reason why Mark's Christology is fully kenotic. Christology and discipleship in Mark are one topic in the same way humanity and divinity are one. With Mark it is never a question of one or the other. Jesus' identity is revealed through and in true discipleship; true discipleship is revealed through and in the identity of Christ.

Jesus, as Mark presents him, is the suffering servant; he thus fulfills some of the characteristics of the figure of the righteous sufferer of the psalms, and of the Deutero-Isaian servant of the Lord (Is 50:4-9, 52:13–53:12).[40] Much of the suffering typology of the Markan passion narrative is inherited from pre-Markan tradition. Such types, as originally employed, had an eschatological dimension both in themselves and in their application. It is the mission of the servant to establish justice in the whole earth (Is 42:4) and to extend Yahweh's salvation to the ends of the earth (Is 49). Mark presents the death of Jesus as an eschatological event. Jesus' suffering embraces the suffering of the disciples who are to take up their cross and follow him (Mk 8:34).

Since the Christology of Mark is one of servanthood, it is also one of discipleship; the way of discipleship is the way of the suffering servant. "If anyone wishes to follow after me, let such a one deny oneself and take up one's cross and follow me" (8:34–9:1). At the same time, Jesus' death is not to be undergone merely as a form of imitation; there is no value in violent death itself. But such a death may be suffered at the hands of the powers of this world in order to witness to the truth of Jesus and the gospels (8:35).

Mark's gospel is at once radical and intensely personal. His message is, "Follow me on the journey to the cross" (Mk 10:32); "Follow me for my sake and the gospel," "for the sake of my name" (Mk 10:29). The necessary trial is action. The gospel of Mark is salvation history. Our response must be at the existential level of confrontation, of choice, of enactment. The decision to follow Jesus is in the act of following him. Jesus' way is paradoxical. Its power is the way of the cross, the way of powerlessness. "For you know how generous our Lord Jesus Christ has been: he was rich, yet for your sake he became poor, so that through his poverty you might become rich" (2 Cor 8:9). "For the divine nature was his from the first yet he did not think to snatch at equality with God, but made himself nothing, assuming the nature of a slave" (Phil 2:6ff.). "For even the Son of Man did not come to be served but to serve, and to give up his life as a ransom for many" (Mk 10:45). Jesus' primary service is his self-sacrifice; in the ultimate renunciation of power the way of salvation is opened to all.

Christological titles in Markan tradition, however they may have arisen, stress the continuity between Jesus' inaugural role in the redemptive purpose of God and the work the community has been commissioned to carry forward in his name. Hence the use of corporate metaphors; the designations Son of Man and servant alternate, as in the Old Testament tradition, between representing an individual and a community. Hence also the emphasis upon the reality of the Kingdom. In the first fifteen verses Mark affirms the triumph of God's Kingdom, points to the one through whose agony the triumph is to be achieved, and indicates the suffering that all true disciples must undergo as God's Kingdom comes to fulfillment.

The motif of the Kingdom is announced (1:15), declared to be a mystery reserved for the elect (4:4), promised as a revelation to be made within the lifetime of Jesus' contemporaries (9:1), said to be accessible only to those willing to undergo self-denial (10:14ff.; 10:23ff.), described as being anticipated in the eucharistic meal (14:15), and named as the object of expectation (15:43).[41]

The Kingdom of God is understood as an eschatological reality. The followers of Jesus are told that some of them will live to see the Kingdom come with power (9:1). The futurity of the Kingdom is referred to explicitly (14:25; 15:43). Christ's work continues in the world and is deeply involved with the fidelity of the disciples, to whom the Kingdom of God has been given.

Conclusion

That a theology of the cross lies at the center of Mark's gospel is, I believe, not a matter of dispute. As a theology of Jesus' suffering and death it has marked affinities with the Pauline kerygma in Philippians 2. Thus the topic of power is central to the image of the Kingdom as it is generally understood. The coexistence, in paradoxical relationship, of power and powerlessness is most intensely realized not as one might expect in the resurrection, but in the crucifixion. In Mark the theology of the cross appears to be the power to renounce power. It is only through God's power that Jesus is able to accept powerlessness and face the necessity of the cross.

The presence of God is to be found not in the human institution of power but in those places where human beings experience powerlessness as an oppressive and life-denying force. The powerlessness experienced by Jesus is not to be equated with defeat, for it is through such means that the Kingdom is established. Though the cross appears to be defeat and absence, it is in reality ultimate victory and presence. In Mark we see a paradoxical "presence in absence," for the powerlessness that usually indicates the absence of God is now revealed as the very presence of God.

Philippians 2 and the gospel of Mark establish a paradox that must permeate all Christian life. Salvation and well-being are attained not by conquest, not by domination of the other, but by self-effacement and self-giving love. This is the paradoxical process that ultimately leads to self-realization. The coming of the Kingdom is realized through self-actualization of the other. Real authority and real power lie in compassionate, persuasive love, in choosing weakness instead of strength.

Mark's passion narrative effects a transvaluation of existing images of authority and power. The prophetic destruction of the Temple was accompanied by a cry of triumph, but the cry on the cross is one of dereliction. And yet this very dereliction is the means whereby the Roman centurion, the representative of coercive power, is brought to affirm the power of the powerless Christ. The crucifixion story in Mark dramatizes the mysterious paradox of authentic Christian existence: "Power comes to its full strength in weakness" (2 Cor 12:9).

In 1 Corinthians 1:23 Paul says that the crucified Christ is "a stumbling block" for the Jews and "folly" for the Gentiles. A crucified Messiah, Son of God, must have seemed a contradiction in terms to anyone—Jew, Greek, Roman, or barbarian. In proclaiming this paradox the gospel of Mark, like the hymn to the Philippians, shatters all analogies. In the person of Jesus the solidarity of the love of God with us is given historical and physical form. God in Christ took up the "existence of a slave and died a slave's death for us." John's "Logos become *Sarx*" shatters all analogies. In this radical kenosis, which is at the heart of the gospels, God communicates and reveals Godself.

CHAPTER FIVE

Patristic Christology and Kenosis: God's Immutability

A survey of the New Testament clearly demonstrates that a kenotic Christology lies at its center. A pervasive theme in the New Testament, it found little reception in the formative period of the church's Christology. Classical Christology proposed an ontological understanding of the incarnation and Logos by which divine Sonship was to be understood in terms of metaphysical categories. This type of Christology was first advanced against Arius and given expression at the Ecumenical Council of Nicea in 325. At Nicea Jesus was defined as simultaneously truly human and truly divine (*homousios* with the Father). The Son of the New Testament, according to the council and the opponents of Arius, is not simply the most perfect of all creatures but is equal to the Creator. The fundamental tension of such a formula lies in the great temptation to emphasize one role over the other.

Chalcedon witnessed the last phase of the Christological debate. Here the unity of the true divinity and the true humanity of Jesus was upheld. Unlike the Council of Nicea, Chalcedon did not begin with the concrete unity of Jesus as a historical human being, but with the two different natures or substances. While the starting point of the Nicene Creed corresponds to the twofold way of understanding Jesus "according to the flesh" and "according to the Spirit," as found in Romans 1:3-4, at Chalcedon the starting point was no longer a concrete event but a metaphysical reality. Patristic exegesis consistently connected the kenosis of Philippians 2 to the incarnation and consequently attributed such a kenosis to the pre-existent Logos or to the God-man. Yet, according to the Fathers, such a kenosis cannot be understood strictly as affecting or touching the pre-existent Logos-Son.

Exegesis of Philippians 2 was dominated at this time by dogmatic concerns issuing in the anti-Arian controversy, so the text was never really read on its own terms. At the center of the Arian crisis was the question of the full divinity of the Logos. The Arians had interpreted the term *morphe theou* in Philippians 2 according to their own Christological pattern; that is, the Logos is not fully God but "in the form of God," meaning in the image or reflection of God.

Anti-Arians interpreted *morphe theou* metaphysically. The eternal Logos is the form, the reality of God. To use the term *morphe theou* is to move into the trinitarian context: the Logos is the eternal Son, the Second Person of the Trinity. Eternally equal to the Father and equally unchangeable as the Father, the Son incurs no change in the mystery of the incarnation. The kenosis is to be interpreted primarily as a veiling of the divinity. The *morphe* of Philippians 2:6-7 was replaced by *ousia,* and with that translation it was given a metaphysical bent from which it would never recover.

Most of the Latin Fathers and many of the Greeks concentrated so intently on the need to combat Arianism that they could not read in Philippians 2 any dimension of condescension, only the affirmation of rightful divinity. This is Hilary's reading of the kenotic text in his commentary on Psalm 2: He who was "in the form of God" took "the form of a slave." It is because of his having taken this "form of a servant" that he demands the glory of God, within which he had always remained, by saying "now, Father, it is time for you to glorify me with that glory I had with you before the world was" (Jn 17:5). He is not asking for something new; he does not desire something that was foreign to him. He simply prays to the Father in order to be what he has previously been, that is, engendered in view of what was truly his. Novatian, in his tract on the Trinity, affirms basically the same understanding.[1]

Cyril of Alexandria found Philippians 2 useful in his struggle against the Antiochian Christology of Nestorius, who, according to Cyril, understood the incarnation as an exaltation of the human subject. For Cyril, the incarnation is the abasement of the Logos, a self-limitation. Incarnation is a self-abnegation on the part of God.

> We say that the Only begotten Word of God Himself, who is begotten from the Father's very Substance, who is Very God from Very God, Light from Light, through whom all things were made both in heaven and in earth, came down for the sake of our salvation and abased Himself unto emptying and was incarnate and lived as Man...not indeed casting off what He was, but even though He became Man by the assumption of flesh and blood He still remained God in nature *(physis)* and in truth.[2]

Yet for Cyril this self-emptying changes nothing in the form of the eternal Son; the kenosis is simply the acceptance of a human disguise.

His divinity remains impassible even through the most intense suffering of his humanity. Incarnation is a divine renunciation made out of love, an emptying that leads to no increase in God.

Stressing the reality of this self-emptying, the Fathers nevertheless insist that nothing changes in the eternal Logos. And here we find a singular problem, which has been carried into contemporary theology: How may divine immutability be reconciled with divine self-emptying? The theology of the Fathers on the immutability of God does not do justice to the kenotic dimension of New Testament Christology. It is in the interpretation of the kenotic dimension of the New Testament that the latent tension between the New Testament and the Greek-Hellenist metaphysics reached a breaking point.

It is true that the starting point of the Fathers' Christological deliberations is the historical figure of Jesus Christ, not a figure of mythology. Nor did Nicea and Chalcedon invent the fundamental affirmations of the scriptures, affirmations that in Jesus Christ we have someone who is truly divine, truly human, truly one. The Bible and Chalcedon are not opposed to one another. The formula of the "one person in two natures," who is Christ, has a clearly recognizable basis in scripture. The whole history of the development of the Christological formula is nothing but the history of essentially biblical patterns, among which John 1:14 occupies a predominant place. Tensions, which could be perceived already in the New Testament, continue throughout the whole history of the Christological kerygma up to our own time.

The Fathers did not invent the Christological paradox of holding simultaneously divinity, humanity, and unity. As Peter Brown has put it, for a late-fourth-century Roman "to accept the Incarnation would have been like a modern European denying the evolution of the species: he would have had to abandon not only the most advanced, rationally based knowledge available to him, but, by implication, the whole culture permeated by such achievements."[3] What the Fathers accomplished was an apprehension of the biblical paradox in their own cultural context.

The Greek Fathers, however, brought into their interpretation of the incarnational paradox a concept of God that was clearly not of biblical origin. For the Greek mind God was immutable. While the monotheism of the Bible is dynamic and personalistic, covenantal and dialogical, that of Greek thought is static and abstract. Greek thought posited a fundamental distinction between the eternal and unchanging world of becoming and the world of being. If God changes at all God only changes for the worse, since we cannot suppose God to be deficient either in virtue or beauty. It is impossible that God should ever be willing to change, being, as is supposed, the fairest and best that is conceivable.[4]

Because God is pure act, God exists forever beyond change or passion. God is the unmoved mover.

Patristic development of New Testament Christology was strongly influenced by the term *Logos,* as used by the Apologists, who gave it a key position in their own Christology and who found in it a fruitful means of treating the relationship of Jesus and his Father within the Godhead. *Logos* is probably the most characteristic word in the Greek language, relating as it does to philosophy, science, and religion, and thereby offering a comprehensive term for our overall understanding of reality. So understood, the Logos is regarded as the rational principle of the cosmos, as our key to the knowledge of truth and morality. The Logos is understood as the interpretation, revelation, and expression of the Father, as the necessary interpreter of God's *fiat* on the creation of the world and in the word of incarnation.

The Apologists, in turn, had been influenced by the Jewish philosopher Philo. Philo's formulation of the Logos involved the blending of Old Testament, Middle-Platonic, and Stoic ideas. He believed that the Logos had three stages of existence: two before the creation of the world and one after creation. The Logos existed from eternity as the thought of God. Before the creation of the world the Logos was created by God as an instrument and as a plan in the creation of the world. After the creation of the world the Logos was inserted in the world to be an instrument of God's providence. The Apologists adopted and changed Philo's concept, but they did not change the basic understanding behind Philo's development and use of the Logos: the absolute transcendence of God. God the Father is to be understood as having such an absolute transcendence that he could not possibly deal actively with his creation.

And thus the idea of the impassible God was imported into theology. This idea is so foreign to Hebraic-Christian thought that it seems to make nonsense of the revelation of God in the Old Testament. It makes the incarnation no real incarnation, the kenosis an impossible contradiction, and reduces the suffering and death of Christ to a purely human work. The idea seems simply to be assumed rather than argued for and is placed in paradoxical juxtaposition with the New Testament affirmation that God was in Christ's suffering and death reconciling the world to himself.

This paradoxical juxtaposition characterizes the thought of one of the earliest of the Fathers, St. Ignatius. In his "Letter to the Romans" he writes: "Let me imitate the Passion of my God," but in the letter to Polycarp (3.2) he writes: "Be on the alert for him who is above time, the Timeless, the Unseen, the One who became visible for our sakes, who was beyond touch and passion, yet who for our sakes became subject to suffering, and endured everything for us." Again, in the "Letter to the

Ephesians" (7.2), Ignatius writes: "There is only one physician—of flesh yet spiritual, born yet unbegotten, God incarnate, genuine life in the midst of death and suffering, from Mary as well as God, first subject to suffering, then beyond it—Jesus Christ, Our Lord." The paradox is explicit; God is impassible—yet in Christ God suffers.

A good example of the influence of such thought on the development of the concept of God, and therefore on Christology, is to be found in the writings of Irenaeus. Irenaeus held that God is impassible (*Adv. Haer.* 2.17, 6) and that the Logos, who is also from God, is impassible (*Adv. Haer.* 2.17, 17); he stressed the eternal coexistence of the Logos with the Father. Because the Logos is divine, the Logos is thereby immutable. The Logos could descend to take up his dwelling in a human life, but the work of the Logos was limited to those activities that were compatible with divinity.

> For just as he was man in order that he might be tempted, so, too, he was Logos in order that he might be glorified. When he was being tempted and crucified and dying, the Logos remained quiescent: when he was overcoming and enduring and performing deeds of kindness and rising again and being taken up, the Logos aided the human nature (*Against the Heresies,* III, 19.3).

The same crux is found in the writings of Clement of Alexandria: If God is immutable how can God experience genuine incarnation?

> God is impassible, free of anger, destitute of desire. And He is not free of fear, in the sense of avoiding what is terrible; or temperate, in the sense of having command or desires. For neither can the nature of God fall in with anything terrible, nor does God flee fear; just as He will not feel desire, so as to rule over desires (*Stromata,* IV, XXIII). Man, on the other hand, possesses "flesh with its capacity for suffering...by nature subject to passion" (*Stromata,* VII, II, 6.77).

Clement's Christology is conditioned by his idea of impassibility, and yet Clement does not deny the reality of the incarnation. In *Protrepticos* (106.4) he writes about "the God who suffered." For Clement, however, the incarnational suffering of Jesus is not essential to his role; Jesus' suffering is accidental to the divine condescension and salvation. What Jesus brings about is a noetic redemption. Clement understands Jesus to function as humankind's teacher and to exist as the "impassible man" (*Stromata,* V, XIV, 94.57). While the Logos has taken to himself our flesh, so that the incarnation is real *sarko phoros,* he

trains this flesh toward impassibility. The incarnate Logos leads humanity to an imitation of the immutable God. According to Clement, "the way
to the Immutable is by immutability" (*Stromata,* II, XI, 51.6).

Origen knows better than Clement that Jesus' passion and death
are at the heart of divine love and salvation. However, since he also
knows that the divinity of the Logos means absolute impassibility, God's
entry into humanity does not allow him genuine participation in the suffering of the human soul and body he assumes. Origen feels compelled to
grant that God experiences suffering, yet he cannot fit this affirmation
into his philosophical-theological framework.[5]

The implications for Christology of this doctrine became evident in
the Arian controversies. The fundamental premise of Arius's system is
the affirmation of the absolute uniqueness and transcendence of the
unoriginate Source of all reality. If the Logos is truly flesh, then, according to Arius, the Logos cannot be equal to God, since the transcendent
God cannot become flesh.

Athanasius, in his *Discourse against the Arians* (III.4), affirmed
the consubstantiality of the Logos with the eternal Father. He insisted at
the same time on the unchanging nature of the Logos.

> For the Father is unalterable and unchangeable, and is always
> in the same state and the same; but if, as they (the Arians)
> hold, the Son is alterable, and since not always the same but
> an ever-changing nature, how can such a one be the Father's
> Image, not having the likeness of his unalterableness?

The Son, since he is of the same substance as the Father, is also
unchangeable. This same Logos is the sole principle and unique subject
of all statements about Christ. The human element in Christ is determined by the Logos. Although the relation between the Logos and flesh
is not accidental, yet no change is possible in the Logos who becomes
flesh. The suffering and weakness of Jesus cannot be attributed to the
Logos. That would be attributing them to God and, as Athanasius wrote,
"the faith of Christians acknowledges the blessed Triad as unalterable
and perfect and even what It was, neither adding to It what is more, nor
imputing It any loss" (ibid., I.18).

The unchanging character of the Logos has direct consequences for
redemption. Redemption is the restoration of human nature into the
incorruptible image of God. "For he was made man that we might be
made God; and he manifested himself by a body that we might receive
the idea of the unseen Father; and he endured the insolence of men that
we might inherit immortality."[6]

Athanasius is so concerned to affirm the unity of the Logos with the flesh that he is sometimes moved to affirm that the Logos suffered, but he never fully follows that inclination. He writes in the *Discourse against the Arians* (III.32): "It becomes the Lord, in putting on human flesh, to put it on whole with the affection proper to it; that, as we say the body was his own, so also we may say that the affections of the body were proper to Him alone, though they did not touch Him according to his God-head." All weakness and suffering are attributable to the flesh. Yet Athanasius writes that the Logos is the sole physical subject of Christ's life and actions.

At Nicea, Jesus Christ was confessed to be the Second Person of the Trinity, coequal, consubstantial with the Father; thus his being is eternal and unchangeable. At Nicea the unchangeableness of the divine nature in Jesus Christ was emphasized. At the same time any suggestion of Christ's subordination was eliminated. Reacting against Arianism, the true divinity of Jesus Christ was so emphasized that the true humanity was lost sight of. This becomes clear upon reading Apollinarius. God, who is immutable, can create a finite human life only if the humanity of Jesus is not complete, if the Logos takes the place of the human soul. The Logos uses the human *sarx* simply as an instrument.

Later Christologies, Cyril of Alexandria's is an example, affirm the full humanity of Jesus while maintaining the impassibility and immutability of the divine Logos. The human Jesus is the subject of suffering. Such a Christology risks loosening the intimate link between the divine Logos and human nature of Jesus. In expressing the nature of the incarnation Cyril uses the phrase "hypostatic union." He writes: "We believe therefore, not in one like us honoured with Godhead by grace...but rather in the Lord who appeared in servant's form and Who was truly like us in human nature, yet remained God, for God the Word, when he took flesh, laid not down what he was, but is conceived of the Same God alike and man."[7] The two natures, divine and human, are so united in Jesus that we may speak of one Person; we may say, "God suffered" and "God died." Yet the Logos remains in his own nature impassible; he remains "external to suffering as far as pertains to His own Nature, for God is Impassible."[8] Cyril finds he must simultaneously affirm the impassibility of the Logos and the suffering of the Logos, because the suffering and death of a mere man could not have effected redemption. The Logos suffered in the human flesh and since this flesh is the Logos's very own, the Logos suffered, but impassibly. Cyril sets out his difficulties with the question of Jesus' suffering and divinity in the following terms:

And though Jesus be said also to suffer, the suffering will belong to the economy; but is said to be His, and with all reason, because His too is that which suffered, and he was in the suffering Body, He unknowing to suffer (for He is impassible as God); yet as far as pertained to the daring of those who raged against Him, He would have suffered, if he could have suffered.[9]

Cyril's doctrine of the incarnation clearly expresses the difficulties inherent in accepting an understanding of God as changeless, eternal, and impassible, of identifying the Logos with such a God, and of attempting to attribute real suffering to the incarnate Logos. The Logos is sympathetic to the suffering of the flesh but does not itself suffer. The divine in Christ is untouched by the suffering of his human nature. Rather than be affected by becoming flesh, the divine Logos imparts its attributes to human nature. There is a deification of the human, but no humanization of the divine.

Hilary presses the idea of impassibility to a point where the exemplary nature of Christ's experience in his humanity almost completely disappears. In *On the Trinity* (X, 23) Hilary affirms: "When, in this humanity, He was struck with blows, or smitten with wounds, or bound with ropes, or lifted on high, He felt the force of suffering, but without its pain...He had a body to suffer and he suffered: but He had not a nature which could feel pain. For His body possessed a unique nature of its own." In fact, Hilary believed that Jesus Christ never needed to satisfy bodily longings: "It is never said that the Lord ate or drank or wept when he was hungry or sorrowful. He conformed to the habits of the body to prove the reality of his own body, to satisfy the custom of human bodies, by doing as our nature does. When he ate and drank, it was a concession, not to his own necessity but to our habits" (X, 24). This approach evacuates the passion narratives of their force; suffering undertaken for the sake of men and women yet without pain certainly is not suffering. According to the later opinion of the Monophysitos, an act of pure grace on the part of the Logos allows the body of Jesus to experience suffering since, apart from such grace, suffering could not touch it.

At Chalcedon the Orthodox faith was expressed in terms of the doctrine of two natures and one person. This solution to the Christological controversies followed from the logic of the earlier trinitarian doctrine. It resulted from the affirmation at Nicea that the Son is consubstantial with the Father. It resulted from the rejection by Nicea of those who claimed there was a time when the Son did not exist or that he did not exist before he was begotten. The framework of this doctrine is still that of an impassible God and Logos. Being of one substance with the Father, the Second Person of the Trinity shares the immutability of the Father. This immutability must necessarily affect the nature of the Logos's consubstantiality with us. Consubstantiality cannot mean any real sharing in the experiences of suffering, want, or change.

This immutability also involves a soteriological motif: human nature finding salvation and immortality by participating in the divine nature. God becomes man that men and women might become Godlike, that is, immutable. It is evident that the Patristic idea of God colored the whole development of classical Christology and has posed a problem for theology ever since. The Patristic idea operated with an understanding of God that was inadequate to bear the full meaning of the New Testament texts. The Fathers insisted at all costs on the impassibility of God and the Word. One of the predominant ideals of Greek intellectual life is stability—permanence—and the idea of perfection is inseparable from the idea of changelessness. Becoming is the opposite of being, and being is reality. The very idea of change is to be excluded from the essence of the divine, and the life of God is eternally changeless contemplation of the eternally changeless. The Stoic ideal of *apatheia* was transferred in idealized form to the inner life of God. Thus it was difficult for the Fathers to find a proper place for the humanity of the Logos and for the reality of suffering. God was understood as eternal, without change, and impassible.

The Fathers' struggles with the issue of Jesus' suffering clearly illustrates the way in which their theology influenced their understanding of the incarnation. If the Son is consubstantial with the Father and therefore inherently perfect and incapable of change, progress, or suffering, how is he truly one with us, consubstantial with us, an authentic mediator? The Christological controversies that took place in the early church were concerned with the seemingly insoluble problem of how the eternal Logos, incapable of change or suffering, could be incarnate at all. The two major opponents in the controversy that finally led to the formula of Chalcedon were unable to solve the problem. The Antiochenes insisted on the difference between the two natures and had real difficulties in accounting for the unity between them. The Alexandrians stressed the oneness of the nature of the Logos enfleshed; nevertheless, they were in agreement that the Logos could not suffer on the cross.

P. Van Buren states the problem clearly:

> On the one hand, the Fathers said that God was in Christ in an indissoluble union with Christ's human "nature." On the

other hand, they said that Jesus Christ had actually suffered and died on the cross. If they had been more consistent in saying that God is unknown apart from his self-revelation and that we must begin with Jesus Christ in order to know anything about God at all, they might have been able to begin with the cross as the event of self-revelation of a God who is quite able to take suffering to himself and whose glory is so great that he can also humble himself. Had this been done, the course of the development of classical Christology would have been quite different.[10]

Emphasis on the immutability of God had radical implications for all Christologies, but especially for a kenotic Christology. Classical Christology affirmed that in the act of redemption the Logos is involved not only as man but also as God: the Son of God himself lived, suffered, and died. The Fathers spoke of the "sufferings of my God," of "the suffering God," of the "crucified God," yet such statements lost their full implication when accompanied by the affirmation of the immutability of God.

Patristic theology recognized the need for a *communicatio idiomatum* ("the exchange of attributes") between the divine and human elements in Jesus Christ. In the context of the affirmation of the immutability and impassibility of God the *communicatio idiomatum* cannot get beyond a paradoxical affirmation. The Logos remains untouched, absolutely impassible. Within this framework no true kenotic Christology can emerge, nor can a full interpretation of Philippians 2 be given.

Kenosis, while touching the humanity of Jesus, does not reach the divinity. Patristic exegesis of Philippians 2 tends to deny any movement from God to Jesus. The exaltation never means a transformation for Jesus but rather a simple return to an original glory. As Dawe has put it: "No new status could be given, since there is full equality with God from the beginning. Hence exaltation was traditionally taken to mean the revelation of true divine status which has been obscured during the earthly ministry because it was veiled in flesh."[11] The text, however, does speak of a new status arrived at because of the suffering and "obedience even unto death." The transition from the status of slave and crucified to that of exaltation is marked by the word *dia,* which is a causal word, "on account of" or "because of."

Since the patristic doctrine of impassibility penetrated the tradition, later authors have the same problem construing Philippians 2:9. Their exegesis excludes a dynamic and transformative understanding of kenosis. The Philippian hymn was understood in most of the tradition as "proof text" for the two–nature Christology; the "form of God" *(morphe theou)* was taken to be a metaphysical term. The kenosis was perceived figuratively as a veiling of the divinity. Thus, while kenosis marks the Christology of the New Testament, it failed to develop into a fully articulated Christology until much later.

CHAPTER SIX

The Incarnation as a Mystery
of Divine Self-Emptying

The development of Christology from Chalcedon down to our time has been dominated by the "God-man formula": Jesus Christ is "truly God" and "truly man." All the formulas that have emerged in the course of history were intended as logical explanations of this union. The crux of the whole Christological tradition is the simultaneous living unity of God and man in Jesus Christ, and the continuing differentiation of the two: the personal unity of God and man in Jesus Christ. This has been classically expressed in the doctrine of the hypostatic union, which claims that God is present so radically in Jesus' own subjectivity that Jesus' own identity is God-given and yet his own. The hypostatic union is the affirmation that while God and man are radically different they are one in Christ.

Kenotic Christology emerged as an attempt to deal with the nature of God's immanence revealed in Jesus.[1] Early kenoticists set the question of Christ's kenosis within the limits of God's immutability, whereas the real question to be asked should be: Who is God in light of the kenosis? What is needed is a reevaluation in our understanding of God so that kenosis will appear not as a process of de-divination but rather as an attribute of God's love disclosed in the compassionate existence of Jesus.

The earlier kenotic Christologies arose out of a desire to deal seriously with the newly emerging concepts of personality and a critical restudying of the New Testament that emphasized the reality of Jesus' humanity. The Chalcedonian doctrine of person had been expressed in ontological terms. The psychological dimension of the person, with its insistence on consciousness and growth, was entirely foreign to it. Exponents of kenotic Christology in the nineteenth and twentieth centuries saw in kenosis the means of integrating the new understanding of personality into the traditional understanding that the center of Jesus' personhood was the eternal Logos. For these theologians God in some way had to limit Godself so that the presence of the divine in Jesus did not destroy the human dimension of his personhood.[2]

84

The great weakness of the kenoticists was that they did not go far enough. "The new humanistic thrust in theology demanded nothing less than that Christology be stood on its head, so to speak, and that it should find its starting point in the humanity of Christ."[3] In their fear of the extreme positions of men like Strauss and Feuerbach, the early kenoticists clung to the traditional framework as alone making possible a real incarnational theology. For more recent kenoticists the humanity of Jesus Christ has become the pivot of reconstruction and a new question is asked: Given the integrity of the human in Jesus Christ, how is it possible to speak of the presence of the divine?

Contemporary kenotic Christology fully accepts J. Moltmann's affirmation that the cross is the basis and standard of Christology: The crucified Christ "becomes the general criterion of theology."[4] "What does the cross of Jesus mean for God himself?" "There can be no theology of the incarnation which does not become a theology of the cross." The suffering of Christ must be thought of "as the power of God and the death of Christ as God's potentiality."[5]

Jesus as God-Man

In a kenotic Christology, as in any Christology, the basic question is the hypostatic union; this doctrine, laborious and involved as it is, is simply an attempt at a conceptual and ontological expression of the New Testament affirmation that God is manifest with eschatological finality in Jesus Christ. The development of this conceptual model, as we have said, has been dominated by the "God-man formula," the "two natures-one person approach."[6] The major objection to the traditional understanding of the hypostatic unity is that its initial approach is ontic and tends to regard the hypostatic unity primarily as a synthesis; that is, the ontic approach does not take as its starting point the unity of the concrete person Jesus of Nazareth but rather the difference between the human and divine natures. W. Pannenberg puts it well: "The pattern of thought thus moves in the opposite direction from the formula, *vere deus, vere homo*. Jesus now appears as a being bearing and uniting two opposed substances in himself. From this conception, all the insoluble problems of the doctrine of the two natures result."[7] Jesus cannot be understood as the synthesis of the human and the divine, of which only the human side can be seen.

The Concept of Person

In the midst of the Christological controversies, Christian understanding of God shifted from the radical monotheism of the Bible to a trinitarian monotheism. This transformation evolved from the development of the concept of person and its application to the Godhead. This development did not occur in the same way among the Latin Fathers as it did among the Greek Fathers. According to T. DeRegnon, the Greek Fathers began with the three divine persons and concluded with the one divine nature. The Latin Fathers started from the one divine nature and proceeded to the three persons.[8] R. Cantalamessa remarks that while there is truth in DeRegnon's observation, it is more precise to say that while the Latins and Greeks both start from God's unity "this unity is conceived by the Latins as impersonal or pre-personal—it is God's essence which then becomes specified as Father, Son and Holy Spirit (although of course this essence is not thought of as pre-existing the persons). The Greeks on the other hand conceive of an already personalized unity."[9] The divine reality is personalized because it is of the Father, from whom proceeds the other two persons. "For the Latins, God is the divine essence, for the Greeks, the person of the Father."[10] The Latin view has been criticized because it gives too much importance to the impersonal God of the philosophers; the Greek for leading to subordinationism.

While in the Christological controversies both *persona* and *hypostasis* were used to refer to an objective individuality, *persona* stressed the individuality, and *hypostasis* the objectivity. The use of the word *persona,* however, did not involve the idea of a subject implying self-consciousness. The word *persona* referred to substance, not to self-reflecting consciousness. Augustine writes: "When we speak of the person of the Father, we mean simply the substance of the Father."[11] According to the formula of Chalcedon, the person of Christ does not first come into being from the concurrence of the Godhead and manhood but is pre-existent. The Logos was a person in the fullest sense. At the incarnation he did not become an individual; he became human without ceasing to be divine. The incarnation is the mystery of the Logos uniting himself hypostatically with Jesus' human substance, thus the formula of two natures and one person.

The classical affirmation of trinitarian theology states that there are three persons in God. The Logos is one of these persons and exists as such from all eternity and independently of the incarnation of the Son. This divine person assumes a complete human reality through a union that is affirmed to be hypostatic because it is not a mingling of natures but a matter of the hypostasis of the Son. Jesus' human nature is joined in such a fashion to the Logos's hypostasis that this hypostasis becomes that nature's subject and is united to it substantially. So the human nature may be said to be truly predicated of the Eternal Logos. The divine and human natures coexist inseparably. The union is not a merging into a third nature; the subject does not emerge from the union but exists prior to the union. The uniqueness of the subject is the ground for the doctrine of the *communicatio idiomatum*—the interchange of predicates.

Theories about the Hypostatic Unity

This formula led to a theological explanation of the unity of the two natures in the one person known as *enhypostasis*. According to this doctrine, the man Jesus in his concrete reality has the ground of his existence, his hypostasis, not in himself as man but "in" the eternal Logos, the Second Person. That is, the human nature of Christ exists in the divine hypostasis of the Logos. Pannenberg explains the matter thus:

> The unity of the man Jesus with the Son of God is expressed in post-Chalcedonian Christology with the formula of the enhypostasis of Jesus in the Logos. According to the Chalcedonian decision, an independent reality (hypostasis) of its own form of manifestation (person) could no longer be attributed to Jesus' human nature. By itself Jesus' humanity would not only be personal in the modern sense of lacking self-conscious personality, but taken by itself Jesus' human being would be non-existent. Hence it can be conceived by itself only by abstracting from the actual reality of Jesus' existence. In his concrete reality the man Jesus has the ground of his existence (his hypostasis) not in himself as man but "in" the Logos.[12]

Enhypostasis provided the grounding for various medieval formulations of the action of the eternal Logos relative to the human nature of Jesus. Pannenberg identifies three categories: the *assumptus* theory, the *habitus* theory, and the subsistence theory.[13] According to the *assumptus* theory, the Logos assumed a complete man at the incarnation, yet that man is not a person. The *habitus* theory sees the incarnation as a form of vesting, the putting on of a garment. And in the subsistence theory the eternal Logos simply dons a human nature, which finds the substance in him and so is united with him. According to this theory the human nature of Jesus loses nothing by receiving its subsistence from the eternal Logos; it receives a higher dignity than if it had possessed a human personality and its own existence.

All of these theories demanded the establishment of a distinction between nature and person or hypostasis.[14] Their arguments and assumptions regarding what the person is in itself were essentially metaphysical. In a contemporary context where it is assumed that a person is a psychological subject of interpersonal relations, the traditional enhypostasis theory has been challenged. What is being affirmed today is that one cannot be truly a human being without being a human person. If we are to think of Jesus as truly a man, we must think of him as a historical person. Contemporary Catholic theology attempts to take into consideration this new development in the concept of the person by attributing to Jesus a human subjectivity, a human "I."[15] In so doing, it has pointed out quite clearly the difficulties of the enhypostatic way of understanding the hypostatic unity. According to this doctrine, the man Jesus has the ground of his existence, his hypostasis, not in himself as man but "in" the Logos. The absence of individual concreteness in Jesus' human nature as such, apart from its unification with the Logos, makes the completeness of Jesus' humanity problematic. In Christ the divine person is understood to substitute for the human person. The subject of Jesus' thoughts, feelings, and actions is the divine Logos. Our foremost difficulty with this is the fact that personal subsistence is an important element in a human being. Can one be truly a man without being a human person? G. H. W. Lampe reflects the thought of many contemporary theologians: "The great defect of this idea is that in the last resort it almost invariably suggests that Christ's manhood is no more than an outward form, like a suit of clothes in which God the Son was dressed up as a man—the king disguised as a beggar."[16] The theory of the enhypostasis makes the personal agency of Jesus' humanity problematic. As Hodgson puts it: "The Logos is conceived as an active, personal suprahuman agent who incarnates himself in generic human flesh or nature and who constitutes the personal individual subjectivity of that flesh in lieu of a human subjectivity, while the flesh itself is merely instrumental to the action of the Logos."[17]

The Unity of Jesus with the Father

Yet while the whole theological tradition sees the unity of Jesus as hypostatic in and with the eternal Logos, the Second Person of the Trinity, the New Testament sees the unity of Jesus primarily as that of Jesus with the Father. According to the New Testament, Jesus' human consciousness is turned not to the Logos but to the Father. Jesus knows himself to be one with the Father. Jesus' unity with the Father is expressed in his behavior toward the Father—obedience and total dedication to the point of self-sacrifice. Jesus relates to the Father as a free subject to a free subject. Karl Rahner writes:

> The human nature of Christ as the person of the Logos must be understood in such a way that Christ in reality and in all truth is a man with all that involves: a human consciousness which is aware in adoration of its own infinite distance in relation to God: a spontaneous human interior life and freedom

with a history which because it is that of God himself, possesses not less but more independence, for the latter is not diminished but increased by union with God.[18]

Jesus stands before God in free human obedience. He is mediator, says Rahner, "not only in virtue of the ontological union of two natures, but also through his (Jesus') activity, which is directed to God (as obedience to the will of the Father) and cannot be conceived of simply as God's activity in and through a human nature thought of as purely instrumental, a nature which in relation to the Logos would be ontologically and morally, purely passive."[19] The unity of Jesus with God can be found only in the historical existence of Jesus in his message and actions. The foundation for the question of hypostatic unity is in the history and destiny of Jesus of Nazareth, his relation to the Father in dedication and obedience.

From what can be discerned of Jesus' own message, it is apparent that he was a pointer to the Father and to the Kingdom of the Father. As Jesus is confessed to be the Christ by the early church and becomes the focus of its preaching, the centrality of the Father is not forgotten. God the Father still remains the focus of the New Testament.[20] The basic issue in Christology is the question about God and humanity, about the transcendence and immanence of God: God being fully God and fully human.

The Incarnational Model

God's relationship to Jesus' humanity has been expressed in the symbol of the incarnation. This symbol can already be discerned at work in the New Testament, albeit in a language not specifically its own.[21] At Chalcedon the symbol of incarnation attained its classical expression. While there has been a marked tendency in recent Christologies to abandon the notion of hypostatic union,[22] the question about Jesus the Christ still remains a question about the God and man. As a theological symbol incarnation speaks in a very specific way of God's presence and initiative, of God's graciousness and self-communication in Jesus Christ. The specificity of the symbol has been described as an approach "from above" to the mystery of the self-communication of God in Jesus Christ.[23] While this approach proves to be problematic, the primary question in any Christology remains that of the relationship of God to the human, the unity of God and the human, the transcendence and immanence of God. In its theological meaning the symbol of incarnation says that God belongs to the world of God's creatures; the incarnation is a characteristic of God's being with us. God's transcendence is not from another world; it is a transcendence for men and women. The incarnation as a symbol expresses something decisive about the relationship of the human to God, and this specifically in Jesus Christ.[24]

Theologizing about Jesus becomes a real discussion about God's union at a particular point in time with the earthly corporality of the man Jesus.[25] Christology's primary function is to illuminate our experience and our understanding of God. God remains the one, absolute mystery defining all other mysteries, including that of Jesus Christ. While the person of Jesus Christ leads us into the mystery of God, he himself is defined by God. The fundamental question of Christology is the question of God, of God's agency and causal relation to the human reality of Jesus. Is a human history capable of mediating the action and presence of God? Can the history of the man Jesus be at the same time the history of God? Kasper sees the primacy of God in Christology in terms of the fundamental problem of freedom. Human freedom that is not grounded in the freedom of God is destined to self-destruction. The question of a unity of God and man in Christ has to be rethought in such a way as to show that this unity is not the antithesis of human emancipation but the condition of its possibility.[26]

The question of the unity of the divine and the human in Jesus must therefore be conceived as having a deeper intensity than could be expressed by any form of synthesis. At the same time, one cannot speak of two persons in Christ; no dialogue can be assumed between the divine and the human person within the one Christ as between Christ and the Father.

Nor can a Christology that begins with the historical Sonship of Jesus appeal to the eternal Sonship to establish the transcendence of Jesus' human existence. A Christology from below must establish Jesus' transcendence from Jesus' human existence.[27] It must establish Jesus' transcendence precisely in his manhood. The incarnational model risks removing the transcendence of Jesus from his humanity for reasons Schoonenberg notes: "One need not worry then about Jesus' humanity, seeing that the second person of God's Trinity stands 'behind' it with his divine nature."[28]

The Personal Unity of Jesus with the Father

The unity of Jesus Christ with God is primarily a personal community with the Father expressed in total dedication and obedience. Although our categories begin historically and existentially, ultimately they must open up into the realm of ontology.[29] The ontological issues arise when the question about the ground of Jesus' historical dedication to the Father is posed. Is the personal community of Jesus with the Father also a community of essence? This same question can also be asked differently: Is Jesus the eternal Son of God?

The resurrection reveals that Jesus' life was grounded in Godself. The personal community of Jesus with the Father is not simply accomplished through Jesus' dedication to the Father; it is given, it is from the Father. The basis of Jesus' unity with the Father does not reside simply in Jesus' humanity; it is to be sought from the side of humanity but found on the side of God. Here the incarnational model is correct in affirming that the unity of Jesus with the Father was from the beginning. The incarnation underlines the fact that in the life of Jesus there is no independence from God. What is true from the perspective of the resurrection is true for the totality of Jesus' person from the beginning. Jesus' unity with God is one of complete dependence expressed historically in dedication and obedience. The Easter event revealed the truth about Jesus' unity with the Father, about Jesus' nature; it did not constitute that truth.[30]

God's acceptance of Jesus from the very beginning is the expression of God's fatherhood toward Jesus. This is what is revealed in the resurrection. Jesus' dedication and obedience to God can be characterized in terms of Sonship. As the one fully obedient and responsive to the will of God, Jesus is the one in whom the fullness of divinity dwells, the one to whom God is fully present. To Pannenberg, "Such personal community is at the same time essential community. It is so first of all in the sense that it is the essence of the person itself to exist in dedication...To be submerged in the 'Thou' means at the same time, however, participating in his being. Thus the divinity of Jesus as Son is mediated, established through his dedication to the Father." Also, "Through personal community one achieves a share in the essence of the other in spite of the continuing personal distinctiveness. An 'essence' common to both emerges in the course of their interaction."[31] Jesus' unity with the Father and his identity with the eternal Son of God is dialogical. This unity and identity emerge fully only in the history of Jesus' existence.

A Christology "from above" begins with the unity of the man Jesus with the eternal Son of God. It is a given. In a Christology that begins with the historical particularity of Jesus' Sonship to the Father, there is no such given. Nor can Jesus' Sonship be related to the eternal Sonship as one person to another person. Pannenberg sees the unity of Jesus to the eternal Son in Jesus' dedication to the Father. "Only the personal community of Jesus with the Father shows that he is himself identical with the Son of this Father."[32] Again, "In the execution of this dedication, Jesus is the Son. Thus he shows himself identical with the correlate Son already implied in the understanding of God as the Father, the son whose characteristic it is not to exist on the basis of his own resources but wholly from the Father."[33] "Nonetheless, with the special relation to the Father in the human historical aspect of Jesus' existence, his identity in the other aspect, that of the eternal son of the eternal Father, is given."[34] It must be emphasized that the possibility of moving from Jesus' historical dedication to God his Father to affirming that through this dedication he is identical to the eternal Son implies the requirement of the possibility of historical transcendence. Jesus' dedication must have a depth, a God-given depth that makes the transition possible.

To say that the unity of Jesus with the Father can be found only in the historical participation of the man Jesus is to say that transcendence is fully situated in the human. The experience of the historical Jesus must, in some way, be so profound that it becomes the experience of the transcendent in our midst. Jesus' personal community with the Father can be said to be a community of essence only if Jesus' dedication to the Father is rooted in a transcendence characterized by self-emptying love. This community is as the coming together of God's self-emptying and Jesus' acceptance. Without the divine self-communication and Jesus' receptivity there would be no incarnation. Two activities, each requiring and complementing the other, are indispensable to the full and irrevocable coming together of God and man. It is impossible for God to become incarnate apart from human response and human responsibility, and therefore human transcendence expressed in self-emptying.

Incarnation and Anthropology

A dialogical unity between God and man requires a line from below: the open transcendence of the human subject as spiritual being oriented to the absolute being of God. The essence of human beings as openness for and toward the other constitutes in its own way the presupposition for an incarnation. God's self-communication constitutive of Jesus' humanity establishes the necessary condition for the acceptance of such a gift. For Rahner, "God's self-communication or offer is also the necessary condition which makes its acceptance possible."[35] The offer of the gift is already an orientation, an openness to the gift, a God-given openness. This orientation is also the source of the radical poverty of the human race; fulfillment can only be from God. So Rahner writes: "In our poverty we are oriented toward the mystery of fullness."[36] "All beings and above all the created spirit in its transcendence towards absolute being, partake of the mysterious character of God insofar as all beings are referred to God and cannot be adequately understood without this relationship and hence without the term of this relationship."[37] Human nature needs to be understood as "emerging." As we read in John, "It does not yet appear what we shall be" (1 Jn 3:2). The finite is capable of the infinite because the infinite is present to the finite as gracious offer. According to Rahner, "The finite itself has been given an infinite depth and is no longer a contrast to the infinite, but that which the infinite himself has become, to open a passage into the infinite for all the finite, within which he himself has become a part."[38]

The essence of human nature as openness for and toward the other constitutes in its own way the transcendental presupposition for an incarnation. Human nature, as it is created through God's self-bestowal, must be conceived as an active transcendence, as an opening ultimately toward God.[39] Humanity, therefore, and Godhood cannot be taken to be fixed natures infinitely far apart. Rather, the essential characteristic of the human is an open, emerging reality transcending toward God, because it has been created as such by God. The human reality from the very depths of its God-given being is an openness to God perpetually opened by God. That openness is the receptivity for God's self-communication as the possible, free, and radically deepest answer of God to what the human reality itself is. In the incarnation God does not enter a realm foreign to Godself, for human finitude does not exclude God. Men and women exclude God from their lives through sin. Human limitations do not of themselves alienate the human from God. This is God's world. The uniquely full relation between God and man seen in Christ is grounded in God's initial relation to all humankind.

In the incarnation God's self-communication is the communication of a personal agent to a personal agent. What is communicated is not a thing but a self, God's own personal being. In this self-communication God posits Jesus fully in his own intrinsic humanity as a human person, as a personal agent free and able to respond yes and no. Jesus stands before God in free human obedience. He is mediator, according to Rahner,

> not only in virtue of the ontological union of the two natures, but also through his (Jesus') activity, which is directed to God (as obedience to the will of the Father) and cannot be conceived of simply as God's activity in and through a human nature thought of as purely instrumental, a nature which in relation to the Logos would be ontologically and morally purely passive.[40]

In the mystery of the incarnation the decisive question is not that of the otherness of creation; it is the question of the unity of God with the other. To see creation as a kenotic act through which God posits what is differentiated from God through a gift of self is not yet to see God's unity with what is differentiated from God. That act is, nonetheless, the foundation of any such unity from God's side. The possibility of creation is grounded in the fact that God has the capability to give Godself to what is not God; thus the possibility of the incarnation.

In a kenotic approach creation and incarnation are understood as two phases of "the one process of God's self-giving and self-expression."[41] God is already in a self-limiting relation with the whole of the created order. The kenosis in Jesus the Christ is the precise articulation of God's kenotic love for creation. The uniquely full relation between God and man in Jesus is grounded in God's initial relation to all humankind. Kenosis means that there is a movement in the divine life that is directed toward human life; it is expressed in creation and consummated in the incarnation.

The Kenosis of God

In a kenotic Christology, God is considered as absolute letting-be, as self-giving, as self-spending. Kenosis is understood as the way God relates to the world; creation is a work of love, of self-giving. A kenotic Christology is built on that fundamental conception of God's nature as eternal *agape*. God's love expressed in self-giving, while manifested in creation, is supremely manifested in Jesus Christ. In a kenotic Christology God poses the humanity of Jesus as "other," through self-emptying. God in absolute freedom has the possibility of becoming "the other" without endangering God's own identity. "The other" is brought about, constituted, as God's own reality by an act of kenosis, by a dispossession on the part of God, by a giving away of Godself. The incarnation is not an assumption of a human nature on the part of the eternal Logos but rather a self-emptying on the part of God. The personal humanity of Jesus is not prior (and so we do not have adoptionism) but comes to be and is constituted in essence and existence when and insofar as God empties Godself.

For Karl Rahner, this is the fundamental way to understand the incarnation.

> God, in and by the fact that he empties himself, gives away himself, poses the other as his own reality. The basic element to begin with is not the concept of an assumption, which presupposes what is to be assumed as something obvious, and has nothing more to do than to assign it to the taker—a term, however, which it never really reaches, since it is rejected by his immutability and may never affect him, since he is unchangeable, when his immutability is considered un-dialectically and in isolation—in static concepts. On the contrary, the basic element, according to our faith, is the self-emptying, the coming to be, the kenosis and genesis of God himself, who can

come to be by becoming another thing, derivative, in the act of constituting it, without having to change in his own proper reality which is the unoriginated origin. By the fact that he remains in his infinite fullness while he empties himself—because, being love, that is, the will to fill the void, he has that wherewith to fill all—the ensuing other is his own proper reality. He brings about that which is distinct from himself in the act of retaining it as his own, and vice versa, because he truly wills to retain the other as his own, he constitutes it in its genuine reality. God himself goes out of himself, God in his quality of the fullness which gives away itself.[42]

When the Logos becomes man, his humanity is not prior but comes to be, insofar and inasmuch as the Logos empties himself. Jesus as such is the self-utterance of God, "because God expresses himself when he empties himself."[43]

We have here not an impersonal humanity but the full humanity of Jesus as the proper vehicle for divinity in the space-time context, and this without eliminating the distinction between God and man. Through God's self-communication as constitutive of Jesus' humanity, Jesus belongs to the divine mystery rather than to himself, but he does so through his own human acceptance. While Jesus exists as the kind of person he is in and because of his relationship to that mystery which God is, yet his unity with God is understood primarily in terms of his human dedication to the Father and to the neighbor, a dedication that comes to fulfillment in the crucifixion. The person of Jesus is constituted by a reciprocal movement: of God to Jesus, of Jesus to God. It does not emerge from the synthesis of two static natures. We have here a unity of agency rather than of substance, of activity rather than natures, a *homo-praxis* rather than a *homo-ousia,* a personal, because dialogical, unity. The locus of unity is the self-emptying of God, which is essentially a letting-be of Jesus as Jesus and the corresponding self-emptying of Jesus, which is also a letting-be of the Father as Father. When the capacity for self-emptying and letting-be is raised to an absolute level, a particular personal being can be of one essence with the Father, the primordial being. Here personal community is also essential community. The unity is dialogical.[44]

The mystery of the incarnation as understood kenotically implies that when God gives of Godself, even in the fullest extent, God does not do violence to "the other," but gives it full authenticity. Jesus is the one who sees himself and the whole of his life in the context of receiving and giving. Receiving is the fundamental expression of his being. In self-surrender, in self-emptying, in accepting to be fulfilled by God, Jesus posits his own existence. This is actualization by letting-go. In Jesus we have the affirmation that the more deeply we are accepted by God and taken into God's own existence, the more we discover ourselves, the more radically we are made free for our own possibilities. Being accepted and being independent are not opposed; they correspond to one another. Jesus of Nazareth is the one who, from the very depths of his being, has surrendered himself to God and has been accepted by God. Jesus lived his life in complete dependence on his Father. Such dependence does not destroy human personality. Indeed, we are never so truly and fully personal as when we are living in complete dependence on God. Here we come into our own. This is not impersonal humanity, but humanity at its most personal, since what appears to be radical dependence upon God is in fact interdependence.

Jesus of Nazareth is the one who, from the very depth of his being, a being grounded in God, has surrendered himself to God and has been accepted by God. According to Rahner, in the case of the incarnation we have the verification of the axiom that governs all relationship between God and creature:

> Namely, that the closeness and the distance, the submissiveness and the independence of the creature do not grow in inverse but in like proportion. Thus Christ is most radically man, and his humanity is the freest and most independent, not in spite of, but because of its being taken up, by being constituted as the self-utterance of God.[45]

The degree to which true selfhood is realized is the coefficient of the constitutive transcendental relation to God. Dependence and freedom are not in inverse proportion but in direct proportion. Human freedom perfects itself through dedication to God. Jesus is the man whose life is one of absolutely unique self-surrender to God.

The Self-Emptying of Jesus

Since receiving is Jesus' fundamental nature, his life is lived out in giving, in a pouring out of self, and ultimately in a consummate gift, his dying on the cross. Jesus' answer to God's self-emptying is in his own self-emptying. By emptying himself Jesus participated fully in the life of God, the plenitude of being. Self-emptying, the principle of the kenotic Being of God, became the law of Jesus' own life. Jesus universalized this law: "Whoever would save his life shall lose it, and whoever loses his life for my sake and the gospel will save it" (Mk 8:35; Jn 12:24). All personal reality must go out of itself in order to preserve itself. The "I" must empty itself for a "Thou" in order to gain itself in "the other." Whatever exists finds its identity not through an absolute, aloof being-in-itself, but concretely, and only through a relationship. Jesus does not find his nature in being a hypostasis, a self-subsistence, though that has been regarded in the tradition as the highest perfection; instead, he is the one who stands up for others and identifies with others. Jesus' personhood possesses both passive and active qualities. On the one hand, and this is primary, it contains the element of surrender or self-negation in relation to the Father; on the other hand, it invites a dedication to the neighbor. The "Thou" of the Father and the "thou" of the neighbor are constitutive of Jesus' own personhood. The depth of Jesus' personhood is measured in terms of his relation to God and to the neighbor. These relations determine the concrete essence of his person. Jesus' "I" comes not from himself but from beyond himself, from the Father and from the neighbor. To be constituted by these singular relationships is to be unconditionally responsive. In being fully responsive to the Father and to the oppressed, Jesus is the Son of God. Jesus' divine Sonship is his radical humanness. Jesus is the Son of God.

Kenosis and the Pre-existent Son

Is this doctrine consonant with what tradition affirms about the eternal pre-existent Son of God? In Jesus we do not have two persons: the divine Son and the man Jesus. What is being affirmed in our kenotic Christology is that the unity of the personal cannot be thought of in the form of an individual self but only in the mutuality of personal relations. The eternal Son does not stand alongside Jesus as another person. Anything said about the eternal Son can only be said fully when reference is made to the man Jesus; anything said about Jesus can be said fully only by recourse to the eternal Son. In the economy of salvation, in the event of the incarnation, the abstract personality of the eternal Son became concrete through a free self-limitation. There is no Son of God apart from the son of flesh. This is not made explicit prior to the incarnation, but the inner logic is there in God's self-communication in creation and to Israel. Through an identification with a creature, God introduces within Godself a real opposition and the possibility of inter-personality. The incarnation as a kenosis allows God to become existent in the world in this radical sense.

The *egeneto,* the becoming, of John's gospel carries the implication of a historical existence. *Egeneto* is the predicate that by essence belongs to creaturehood; it now exists as the predicate of the Creator. It is not simply that the eternal Son has become conditioned in some manner by flesh, as though the flesh were an external and temporary condition of the eternal Son. The eternal Son has become truly flesh, has entered into the experience and existence of creaturehood. The transcendence of God has become historical.[46]

God's transcendence is the act by which God moves outside and beyond immanent freedom. The transcendence of God is God's placing of self into concrete, historical relation to the creature. Transcendence means that God can become for another because the power of becoming belongs to God's own being in God's own inner, kenotic act. Christhood may be understood as that point at which humanity and divinity come together and divinity is manifested and mediated in God-humanhood. Macquarrie writes, "So we can understand how it is that Christ has a complete human nature and what was meant by saying that at the limit of existence, that is to say, at the furtherest point along the road toward fulfilling or unfolding the 'nature' (existence) he manifests divine Being."[47] Christ is the chief exemplification of God's gracious giving of self; in Jesus we have the unique culmination of creation's own response. In his personal unity with God, Jesus is the fulfillment of the human destiny.[48]

Human destiny is to have its origin permanently in God, to be permanently grounded in absolute mystery, to be radically different and yet one with God. Being from God and being totally dependent upon God in no way cancel out human personhood, individuality, or independence. The deepest self is constituted by its relationship to God, which is directly related to the human's capacity for the infinite. The actualization of that capacity through God's graciousness constitutes the deepest dimension of a person's self-being. The more a creature participates in God's being, the more the creature *is* itself. To think of God or the creature as threatening "the other" by its existence is to fail to think of "in itselfness" and "for the otherness" as mutually fostering, mutually inclusive. In other words, it is a failure to think dialogically.

In a kenotic framework the divinization of Jesus, the *gratia unionis* is a humanizing action; the greater the proximity to God, the greater the intrinsic reality of the human being. The greater the unity, the more a distinct reality is posited. Genuine independence and self-coherence increase, not in the inverse but in direct proportion to radical dependence upon God. Jesus is autonomous because of, and real in spite of, total dependence on the Creator.[49]

What we have in the person of Jesus as the Christ is intensified creation. In Jesus Christ the dimension of creatureliness is sharpened, not eliminated. So, says J. B. Metz, "The human nature of Christ is not 'lessened' by being taken up into the divine Logos, made simply into a dead tool, a mere accessory, a gesture of God within the world, but given its hitherto unsuspected full, human authenticity: Jesus Christ was fully man, indeed, more human than any of us."[50] Being accepted by God is freeing, because it is fundamentally a kenotic act: "God's divinity consists in the fact that he does not remove the difference between himself and what is other, but rather accepts the other *precisely as different from himself*."[51] To be accepted by God is to be set free to be oneself.

Incarnation and the Character of God

Incarnation becomes, then, a characteristic of God's being with us. The incarnation of Jesus is a specific case of what is true about God's presence. Incarnation expresses something decisive about God's self-communication to the total creation. Here the problem of Jesus' difference causes no embarrassment. The hypostatic unity is not so much intended as a quality that makes Jesus different from the rest of us, as it is a decisive point in the history of God's gift of self to creation. The once-and-for-all dimension of the incarnation is to be understood eschatologically. Jesus is the eschatological fulfillment of God's involvement with God's creation. As eschatological, the drama of the incarnation is not yet over: "having come about historically" is a characteristic of God's presence. God's presence is in the form of a servant; it is not absolutely transparent. While Jesus Christ is in glory, the world is not yet "resurrected"; it is still on the cross, the Kingdom of God is still to come. As historical and eschatological, God's presence in Jesus Christ is essentially revelational.

Since Jesus is the self-utterance of God, and since God expresses Godself when God empties Godself, then Jesus as the Christ is the revelation of God. The presence of God in Jesus is dialogical and therefore revelational. And it is not in spite of being a human person but because of being a human person that God is revealed in Jesus Christ. Incarnation in a man is a mode of communication peculiar to the Logos. Human nature is specifically designed to reveal the eternal Logos. The flesh is not a veil but a revelation of the Logos.[52]

Since kenosis is necessarily a personal act, the most personal of all acts, then God's revelation occurs in Jesus as a person. In the person of Jesus, of Jesus crucified, God's Word comes to speech, and not only comes to speech but is dependent upon this person to be spoken fully. God's Logos depends upon an embodiment for its coming to speech in the world. Jesus' humanity is God's self-interpretation. In Jesus' life of perfect obedience the Logos expressed himself. By definition the Logos is that which in God is able to express God in that which is not God. The Logos is God's ability to express Godself in history.

Christ as the Revelation of God

God's presence in Jesus is revelatory. Revelational identity, while combining presence as appearance and substantial presence, emphasizes

presence as appearance.[53] The human form of Jesus is the personal revelation of God and is therefore God for us. Here the "is" does not express a
real identification in the content of subject and predicate as would be the
case if one affirmed that John is a man. Relative to his humanity, Jesus *is*
not God, nor *is* God, relative to his divinity, man in the sense of real identification. As revelational and concrete expression of the divinity, Jesus
in his human personhood is a symbol. For any concrete assertion about
God must be symbolic. Jesus the Christ, insofar as the unconditioned
transcendent is envisaged in him, is a symbol. In his human personhood
Jesus Christ is a historical symbol, and only as such may a kenotic God be
manifested and revealed.

For Macquarrie, Jesus Christ "is for Christian faith the decisive or
paradigmatic revelation of God...we can call him the 'symbol of
being.'...In using the word 'symbol' no diminution or unreality in
Christ's relation to Being is intended."[54] Macquarrie affirms that God is
present and manifest in Christ. This expression "present and manifest"
is peculiarly appropriate when we think of Christ as the revelation or the
revelatory symbol of God; "presence" in Greek is *parousia,* and "manifestation" is *epiphaneia,* and these are the words that traditionally have
been used for the revelation of God in Christ—*advent* and *epiphany*. In
Christ, the advent of God takes place, God's coming to be present or
dwelling among us. In Christ likewise the epiphany of God takes place,
the manifestation or showing forth of God's grace and truth.[55]

Christ as the Symbol of God

The understanding of Jesus as the symbol of the Godhead or the
revelation of God is not incompatible with the affirmation that in Jesus
Christ, God has acted decisively and once and for all. To speak about the
presence of God in Jesus Christ as revelational and of Jesus Christ as symbol of God is simply to unfold the kenotic nature of God and Jesus Christ.
In "The Theology of the Symbol" Rahner elaborated an understanding of
symbol that sheds light on what we have just now affirmed. To Rahner,
"All beings are by their nature symbolic, because they necessarily
express themselves in order to attain their own nature."[56] The primary
function of the symbol is to make another present primarily for itself and
also for others. Because of the unity and multiplicity of being, one thing
can be the expression of another. This is true even for God, since God is
revealed as a distinction of persons in God's own simplicity. Plurality in
unity is not a deficiency. While unity precedes plurality, and plurality is
the consequence of an original unity, yet for a being the condition for the
possibility of its self-possession in knowledge and love is the act of constituting itself as a plural. Self-presence or self-realization is the "coming

to itself" of a being in its expression, its emergent and intrinsic plurality. Every being is primordially symbolic to the degree of self-possession.[57]

For Rahner, a being "comes to itself in the measure in which it realizes itself by constituting a plurality."[58] This means that each being is itself primarily symbolic. "It expresses itself and possesses itself by doing so. It gives itself away from itself into the other and there finds itself in knowledge and love, because it is by constituting the inward 'other' that it comes to its self-fulfillment, which is the presupposition or the act of being present to itself in knowledge and love."[59] Strictly speaking, then, the symbol is the self-realization of a being in "the other." "Where there is such a self-realization in the other—as the necessary mode of the fulfillment of its own essence—we have a symbol of the being in question."[60] For Rahner, the notion of symbol highlights the characteristic of entities that requires that they express themselves in order to be themselves. Reality is symbolic because by essence it is kenotic: "self-possession" is attained through self-expression. It is the very essence of personal reality to express itself in "the other." In order to be oneself, personal identity is always realized in and with "the other."

The Logos, as we have said, is the expression, image, and word of the Father. The Logos is the symbol of the Father, both in the inner life of God and in the world. "It is because God 'must express' himself inwardly that he can also utter himself outwardly; the finite created utterance *ad extra* is a continuation of the immanent constitution of 'image and likeness.'"[61] So the Logos is the expressive presence of the Father in the world. In the incarnation the humanity of Jesus is the appearance, the symbolic reality, the genuine self-disclosure of the Logos. The Logos's humanity is not alien to the Logos; it does not function simply as a sign. If this humanity were simply a sign, "The Logos would make himself audible and perceptible through a reality which was of itself alien to him, had intrinsically and essentially nothing to do with him and could have been chosen at random from a whole series of such realities."[62] The humanity of Jesus as expressive of the Logos is constituted by the Logos as he exteriorizes himself.[63]

Humanity as the Symbol of the Logos

Humanity can be understood as the symbol that emerges when God expresses Godself exteriorly. In its quality as symbol, such a humanity possesses an unfathomable depth, which faith alone can sound.[64] Christ is the expression of God's self-presence in that which has been constituted as "the other." Because humanity constituted by God is also symbolic, Christ as symbol is the outward expression that calls to life and feeds what is already part of our own inner dispositions. It shows us what we are and thus enables us to actualize our potentialities as children of God.

The truth of human existence is expressed in Jesus Christ. In the affirmation of Jesus as Christ we find the symbolic expression of the transcendent possibility of what it means to be fully human.

> If human nature is conceived as an active transcendence towards the absolute being of God, a transcendence that is open and must be personally realized, then the Incarnation can be regarded as the (free, gratuitous, unique) supreme fulfillment of what is meant by "human being." Christ's "humanity" can be seen as that which results when God in his Word literally becomes other to himself in a creature. In this way Jesus Christ is the summit of creation, the Lord and Head of the human race because he is one of its members, the "Mediator between God and creatures."[65]

Christ is the eschatological symbol of the presence of the universal and eternal God in human history. Just as God's initiative in Jesus is part of a larger history of God's self-communication, Jesus' acceptance is also part of a larger history of human response, which prepared the way for Jesus' acceptance and is in part contradicted by Jesus' obedience. Jesus' human freedom is rooted in and yet transcends the history of human freedom, which precedes him. Incarnation is not simply an act of God; it is rather a cooperative act of God and man, a kenosis on the part of God and a kenosis on the part of man.

The entire Christ-event must be understood in terms of kenosis. In the incarnation God's self-limitation already evident in creation is embodied with ultimate radicalness. Incarnation is the utmost that is possible to God's self-surrendering love and therefore the unsurpassable self-definition of God. In the particularity of Jesus' life, in a particular time and at a particular place, meaningfulness is given for the world. To confess that God is incarnate in Christ is not simply to affirm that God is incarnate in Jesus, but that God is incarnate in the large and complex human reality, in the order of interpersonal relationships. The incarnation is not exhausted in the one unique historical person of Jesus of Nazareth, but as Teilhard de Chardin could affirm, it is a process that strives toward the Christification of the cosmos.

Conclusion

The proper framework for kenotic Christology is simultaneously an anthropology that emphasizes openness and a trinitarian theology, particularly in its willingness to introduce kenosis within the Godhead and to accept the possibility of change within God. The divine self-emptying is directly related to the understanding of God as the Person who loves in freedom. The self-emptying of God in creation and in the incarnation originates in the primal possibility of God's love. God is love that moves to fill the void and so create "the other." The very concept of Person is understood, in kenotic terms, as the one who exists in self-dedication. The ultimate meaning of Jesus' personhood is existing for others.

As we have observed, the original impetus for a kenotic Christology was an attempt to understand anew the concept of incarnation within the humanistic trend initiated by Schleiermacher. For Macquarrie, the major cause of the failure of nineteenth-century kenotic Christology was its determination to retain the traditional incarnational framework of Christology. Macquarrie claims that the kenoticists, while right in holding on to the incarnational framework, failed to realize that that is possible only if the framework emerges at the end of Christology.

Macquarrie suggests—and this would seem to be an important step for any contemporary focus of kenotic Christology—that the incarnational framework "must emerge only at the end and must not be presupposed."[66] Pannenberg had anticipated this point. "Methodological reasons," he affirmed, "do not permit us to work with the incarnation as a theological presupposition. To do so would be to make the humanity of Jesus' life problematic from the very beginning."[67]

What is being affirmed here is the necessity for a methodological shift. One cannot commence Christology with a fully developed concept of God and the trinitarian life and then by some process, kenotic or whatever, decide "how much of the divine being can be brought within the limits of human existence."[68] But we cannot avoid affirming the full divinity of the one whom we confess to be Lord. Such an affirmation should follow the full acceptance of Christ's humanity.

Within the context of this basic methodological shift, the priority of questions concerning kenosis must change. "The question of kenosis is no longer: How is kenosis possible in the light of God's nature? The more fruitful question is: What does the reality of Christ's God-manhood tell us about the nature of God and Man?"[69] Macquarrie suggests that within this methodological shift, the eternal self-emptying of the Logos should only be spoken of in the light of human self-emptying. "The theological value of this idea lies in the fact that it points to what is deepest both in man and in God and so in the God-man, Jesus Christ."[70] We first experience and understand self-emptying in our own experience; we then encounter it at a unique depth in Christ and confess it as the manifestation and presence of God:

> This is the paradox of personal existence, that emptying and fulfilling, kenosis and plerosis, are the same; and he who

utterly emptied himself, Jesus Christ, is precisely the one who
permits us to glimpse that utter fullness that we call divine.[71]

The Christ's kenosis is not a dimming down, a curtailment of the divine
nature, but a positive expression of it, "the very expression of that
nature at its deepest and most significant level."[72]

From its beginning Christian theology has held to the axiom that
God is immutable, unchanging and unchangeable. Since God is impassible, God cannot suffer. Despite some questioning of this position, and
despite the fact that the mystery of the incarnation was perceived as
problematic in the context of a doctrine of the absolute immutability of
God, the theological tradition has remained consistent in its affirmation
of God's immutability.

The theologians of the nineteenth century admitted that God had
really limited himself in his kenosis and redefined the absoluteness of
God. The Hegelians, realizing that kenosis implied a whole new doctrine
of God, developed a doctrine of God where change was a possibility. They
were criticized for having made God dependent. What is really needed is
a way of understanding God's independent existence that also compre-
hends his relatedness.

In the Middle Ages scholastic philosophy and theology had developed the doctrine of the nonreciprocity of relation between God and creation. Applied to the doctrine of the incarnation this meant that real
change was not to be located in God but in humanity. But Christology
taken seriously is not compatible with a God devoid of real relationships.
At the heart of the incarnation is the God who stands related to someone
other than Godself. To say that God has suffered is to say that God is
actively engaged in dealing with a history that is real to God. In our time
theological reflection is inclined to maintain the reality of the relationship of God, the God of grace to all creation. Such a reflection leads to the
conclusion that the most central Christian model for God is the person of
Christ and that the cross is central to our understanding of God. On the
cross the incarnation of God reaches its true meaning, so that ultimately
the Christ-event must be understood in terms of the cross; it is the cross
that reveals the nature of God's love, the nature of self-surrender. On the
cross God's kenotic love becomes historically present and visible. As
Kasper writes, "The cross is the utmost that is possible to God in His self-
surrendering love; it is 'That than which a greater cannot be thought'; it
is the unsurpassable self-definition of God."[73] The nature of God's divinity is revealed on the cross; the powerlessness of the cross reveals the
power of love.

CHAPTER SEVEN

Kenosis and the Holy Trinity

Christianity unceasingly affirms that God is revealed in the life, death, and resurrection of Jesus Christ. Jesus Christ is God's revelatory word, God's clearest self-expression. In Christ is revealed what God is like; Christ defines who God is for humankind and for creation. It has been said that "incarnation means initially that God's love and power had been experienced in fullest measure in, through and as this man Jesus, that Christ had been experienced as God's self-expression, the Christ-event as the effective, recreative power of God."[1] The humanity of Jesus is the appearance, the sacrament and symbolic reality, the genuine self-disclosure of God; this is the mystery of the incarnation. The advent of God takes place in Jesus Christ, his coming to be present or his dwelling among us, and there likewise the epiphany of God takes place, the manifestation or showing forth of God's grace and truth.

Scripture and tradition have ventured to interpret the advent of God in Jesus Christ as a divine self-emptying. The self-emptying of Jesus Christ makes manifest the kenosis of God. Yet Christianity has hesitated to attribute to God that authenticity of kenotic love that it has recognized in Jesus.[2] The purpose of this chapter is to reflect upon the nature of divine love in the light of Jesus' kenotic love.

Creation reveals the character of God. As we saw, in the Christian vision we cannot separate the mystery of the incarnation from the mystery of creation. Both are sacraments of God. In both mysteries God has revealed Godself as a loving God. In creating and in the mystery of the incarnation God has freely accepted limitations in the fulfillment of a loving will for fellowship with that which is "other" than God. The love of God in creating and in the incarnation is a kenotic love. God does not reveal Godself in the wisdom and power of the world but in the foolishness and weakness of the cross (1 Cor 1:18-25), in communicating to the weak and foolish of the world (1 Cor 1:26-9:2; 1 Cor 12:9; 13:4; Mt 11:25). That which is equal to God, the *morphe theou,* issues in poverty, lowliness, and death on the cross. He who is Wisdom, Logos become *Sarx,* is temporal, frail, delivered up to the power of sin and death (Jn 1:14).

Jesus and the Compassionate Love of God

In the kenosis of Jesus, God is revealed as a loving and compassionate God. The Christ-event, as kenotic, is fully and thoroughly a free act on the part of God, an act in which God's love and innermost life is communicated. When we think of the passion, we are meditating on the mystery of God. This revelation of God in the passion is profoundly challenging because it contradicts everything that we have commonly believed about God. The divinity revealed in Jesus is the divinity whose complete and sole activity is the activity of self-emptying. Jesus' self-emptying, his kenotic love in the poverty and humility of his historical existence, points to the eternal kenosis of God; instead of impairing the fullness of God's revelation it contains the heart and substance of that disclosure. In the vulnerability and precariousness of Jesus' love we have a disclosure of the nature and activity of God.

The self-limiting nature of God as revealed in the paschal mystery and in the act of creating extends to the inner life of God. Self-limitation in creating and in the incarnation is founded on the very nature of God. Creation and incarnation are the results of a movement of radically divine compassion. God's kenosis in creating and in the incarnation did not begin there but within the eternal Godhead. Divine possibility—the ability to remain other while being present totally to the other—does not begin with the act of creation or with the sending of the Son; they are the results of an eternal passibility. Creation and incarnation are not the beginning of divine passibility but the continuation of it with an intensification in time and space. Creation and cross are projections on the plane of history of that which is eternally true about God's nature.

A kenotic understanding of creation and incarnation can lead to a problem that directly threatens the Christian concept of God. Is the kenosis of God so radical that God has been deprived of what is most authentically God, so that God ceases to be God? If God died on the cross, must we not speak of the God who *was* love rather than of the God who *is* love? In Christianity, the mystery of the Trinity in all of its dimensions is the fundamental answer to that question. And the cross is the way into the Trinity.[3]

The Cross and the Trinity

For much modern theology the history of Jesus, who dared call God Abba and who ended his life on the cross, is the key to the mystery of the Trinity. The acceptance of this position does not necessarily imply that one has accepted Jurgen Moltmann's position on the God-forsakenness and abandonment of the Son by the Father.[4] Yet if the cross is to be understood as the revelation of God in Godself, then the cross must be accepted in Christianity as the way into God, especially into the triune

God. The cross affirms the otherness of the Father and Son in the economy of salvation. This reflects a distinction and otherness in God, a giving and receiving in Godself. So, to Eberhard Jungel,

> the grounding of trinitarian dogma on the act of Jesus on the Cross has hardly been sought in the theological speculation on the Trinity. The principle of immutability in the metaphysical conception of God, and the rule devised for avoiding tritheism ("the actions of the Trinity outside God are undivided") led to the distinction between "theology" and "economy" and the corresponding separation of the "immanent" from "economic" Trinity.[5]

Yet, as Moltmann affirms, "to recognize God in the cross of Christ, conversely, means to recognize the cross's inextricable suffering, death and hopeless rejection of God."[6] In some mysterious sense God is not Father, Son, and Holy Spirit without the world, so that the triune God is in process to the extent that one may refer to the trinitarian history of God. The humility on the cross reflects the eternal humility of God; the passibility of God on the cross points to the passibility at the heart of God. Karl Barth writes:

> If we would know what it was that God elected for himself when he elected fellowship with man, then we can answer only that he elected our rejection. He made it his own. He bore it and suffered it with all its most bitter consequences. For the sake of this choice and for the sake of man he hazarded himself wholly and utterly. He elected our suffering (what we as sinners must suffer towards him and before him and from him). He elected it as his own suffering. This is the extent to which his election is an election of grace, an election to give himself, an election to abase himself for the sake of the elect.[7]

The definition of God's being therefore relates to the death of Christ; the death of Jesus belongs to the concept of God. This implies that the cross is an actualization in human history of what is true of God's eternal being. God is most Godlike on the cross. Karl Barth has reversed the classical affirmation that the humanity of Jesus is revealed in the suffering of the cross and the power of the divinity in the resurrection. For Barth, the divinity is most manifested in the suffering on the cross.[8]

On the cross the incarnation of God reaches its true meaning and purpose. On the cross God's self-renouncing love is embodied with ultimate radicalness. The cross is the utmost that is possible to God in God's self-sur-rendering love. This kenosis of God on the cross is not a self-abandonment, not a self-dedivinization of God, but a true becoming of God.

In creating and in the "becoming flesh" God has revealed Godself as dynamic, as the "One who has freedom absolutely," as "the One who constitutes self and the world through an organic dialectic of relation-ships *ad intra* and *ad extra*."[9] The Johannine statement that "God loved the world so much that he gave his only Son" (Jn 3:16) seems to imply that there is within the Godhead a kenosis, an act of self-emptying that results in a letting-be, in the enabling of another to be. Kenosis in the Godhead means that there is "otherness" within God. God is triune because God is love. As Jungel writes, "Love is an ever greater selfless-ness in the midst of ever greater self-possession, freely going out from self and bestowing self."[10] God as personal agent exists in self-dedication to "the other," and God does this from within. God's "relativity" is in the first instance vis-à-vis God.[11] The begetting of the Son and the Spirit is a kenosis, a process of self-giving to "the other."[12]

John O'Donnell, commenting on Urs von Balthasar, affirms that

> the mission of Jesus which is fulfilled in the Cross has its ori-gins in the eternal Trinity. If we conceive of the event of the Cross as a divine drama involving the Father and the Son, then as Balthasar argues, this drama must be grounded in the eter-nal background of the divine life. The cross is the working out in history of the drama, that is, namely the eternal action within God himself. In other words, the only way to avoid see-ing the cross as the imposition of an alien obedience is to situ-ate the dramatic action within the eternal trinitarian drama. This is the merit of Balthasar's trinitarian theology. Balthasar wants to stress that the cross is a separation of Father and Son, but the dramatic caesura that rends the heart of God on Calvary has already been embraced from all eternity by the divine Trinity. From all eternity the Father has given himself away to the Son, has risked his being on the Son, and from eternity the Son has been a yes to the Father, a surrender to obedience. Thus the Father's risk of himself creates a space for the Son. The Father separates himself from himself, so that the Son can be. But this separation is also bridged eternally by the Holy Spirit, the communion of love of the Father and the Son.[13]

The Dogma of the Trinity

Historically the dogma of the Trinity arose out of the original neces-sity of Christian thought: to distinguish Jesus Christ from God, with whom he is simultaneously identified. This necessity in its turn arose out of the impression that Jesus Christ, in his life, death, and resurrection, made upon the minds of his disciples. Theologically speaking, we might almost say that it was in order to make intelligible the experience of the incarnation and the atonement that the doctrine of the Trinity was formulated.

What seems clear to contemporary theologians is that the divine Trinity should not be conceived of as a closed circle of perfect Being in heaven. This was, in fact, the way in which the immanent Trinity was conceived in the early church. In contrast to this, one should think of the Trinity as a dialectical event, indeed as the event of the cross and then as "eschatologically open history."[14] Karl Rahner has proposed that "the 'economic' Trinity is the 'immanent' Trinity and the 'immanent' Trinity is the 'economic' Trinity."[15]

The term *economic Trinity* is a way of speaking about the life and work of God; it refers to the three manifestations of God's activity in the world, which are correlated with the names Father, Son, and Spirit. In particular, *economic Trinity* denotes the missions, that is, the Father's sending of Son and Spirit in the work of redemption and divinization. These missions bring about communion between God and humankind.

The phrase *immanent Trinity* refers to the inner life of God: the reciprocal relationships of Father, Son, and Spirit considered apart from God's activity in the world. In Rahner's theology, which presupposes that God is essentially love and that love is ecstatic and therefore constantly self-communicating, the economic Trinity is the historical manifestation of that eternal ecstasy and self-communication in the mission of Jesus Christ and the Spirit. The identity of the economic and immanent Trinity means that what God has revealed and given in Christ and the Spirit is the reality of God as God is from all eternity. But the distinction between economic and immanent Trinity is strictly conceptual, not ontological. There are not two Trinities, the Trinity of experience and one beyond experience: God-in-Godself and God-for-us.

To relate the immanent Trinity to the economic Trinity is to affirm that the mystery of God's generosity expressed in creation and incarnation has infinite roots. This incomprehensible and ineffable mystery is not exhausted by God's self-giving in the history of salvation. Kenotic love is already present in the dynamic relationship within the being of the Triune God, already active, already completed and already triumphant. No dimension, no intensity of self-giving can ever exhaust the kenotic love of God. The kenotic love within God, which is the source of creation and incarnation, is not a love marked by neediness but by overflowing fullness.

God's Ecstatic Love: The Spirit

In a trinitarian understanding of God, the very substance of God is ecstatic love. Love is not an attribute of God but both the mode of God's existence and constitutive of God's being. Therefore the person of the Holy Spirit has a primary function with the Trinity. Within the inner life of God the Holy Spirit proceeds from the Father and the Son both as the interpersonal unity of their mutual self-surrender and their incomprehensible fruitfulness. As the third Person the Spirit is the expression that the divine love is inexhaustible and eternally new, that God's capacity as absolute lover is ever greater, ever newer, and ever more fruitful. The Spirit exists as the total boundlessness of God. Within the perspective of a kenotic Christology, emphasis must be given in the mystery of the Trinity to the Person of the Holy Spirit. This involves a reversal of the traditional order of trinitarian theology, yet belief in God the Holy Spirit is belief in the essence of God as ecstatic love: God is God precisely insofar as God is self-gift, as God is Spirit.

God is spirit both in divine essence and in person. God is, in essence, absolute self-possession poured out in love, and therefore God is also Spirit, in essence and as person. Thus the Holy Spirit has a wholly unique personhood. The Spirit is the expression of God's innermost being. The Spirit is the third Person precisely as the eternal "mode," the surprising "newness" and unending fruitfulness of this outpouring love. This Holy Spirit is also the expression in person of God's outermost being, the possibility and the reality of God's going outside Godself in love. The absolute mystery that God is and remains comes to its fullest expression in the Spirit.

The essence of God is self-giving love. The persons of the Trinity are understood as forms of surrender of the one divine love that flows from the Father as fountainhead of the divine. That divine self-possession, which knows itself as it is known in self-surrender, is the heart of a kenotic doctrine of God. The inner trinitarian kenosis is the eternal procession of the Son and the Spirit from the Father. The incomparable, immediate characteristic of the Spirit's personality is to be person "from" and "in" the other persons of the Trinity. Here it is possible to speak about the anonymity of the Spirit. It is possible to say that the Spirit is faceless. The face of the Spirit can reveal nothing else but the loving Father and Son.

Emphasis on the person of the Holy Spirit requires emphasis on pure relationality. In such pure relating there is a pure "being toward," a pure "being with," that issues in communion *(koinonia)*. In a sense, the Spirit's utterly unique personal identity is constituted in anonymity as the *We* of Father and Son. The third Person of the Trinity has no proper name. That which serves as a proper name—Spirit—could be applied to the entire Godhead. The Spirit as the personal unity of Father and Son personifies the ever-greater fruitfulness and freedom of God's kenotic love. The fullness of God's being precisely as trinitarian is characterized by that which is mysteriously ever greater. The Holy Spirit is the capacity of God to give in love eternally.

Spirit and Kenosis in God

A trinitarian understanding of God begins with a kenotic understanding of the incarnation: "...who, though he was in the form of God..." (Phil 2:6), "and the word became flesh" (Jn 1:14). Yet the kenosis of the Son in the incarnation points to a deeper kenosis within God: the procession of the Holy Spirit. The kenosis of the Holy Spirit is found in the same scriptures that express the kenosis of the Son. The meaning of the Holy Spirit within the immanent and economic Trinity can be traced back to the Hebrew word *Ruach,* which is translated in Greek by *pneuma.* The Greek noun *pneuma* derives from the verb *pneumo* and refers to air in motion experienced as wind, breeze, or breath. But even "breath" and "wind" express only a part of the more comprehensive sense of movement implicit in *pneuma.* The basic sense is that of energy, motion that is imperceptible except in its effects. In the Jewish scriptures *Ruach* is the creative energy of God and the vital energy of everything that lives. *Ruach* is God's saving power leading Israel out of slavery; it is the divine energy present in the prophets as the source of their compassionate ministry to the people. *Ruach* emphasizes activity; when it is affirmed of God it implies that God can be described as a tempest, a storm, a force; it is divine energy present and effective, immanently efficacious. When we affirm that God is *Ruach,* we are affirming that God is creative energy in all things created. The *Ruach* of God is understood as God in the midst of the people and the nations, God present and active in the world, God in closeness to us: Emmanuel. As Paul wrote:

> What no eye has seen, nor ear heard, nor the human heart conceived, God has prepared for those who love him. These things God has revealed to us through the Spirit; for the Spirit searches everything, even the depths of God. For what human being knows what is truly human except the human spirit that is within? So also no one comprehends what is truly God's except the Spirit of God. Now we have received not the spirit of the world but the Spirit that is from God, so that we may understand the gifts bestowed on us by God (1 Cor 2:9ff.).

Jesus and the Spirit: The Power of the Resurrection

Christianity traditionally speaks of the Holy Spirit as an eternal aspect of God, the third "Person" of the Holy Trinity alongside God the Father and God the Son. Yet the meaning of Holy Spirit in the canonical scriptures is less specific and more complex. This complexity is evident in Paul. Paul refers to the Spirit both as "the Spirit of God" (Rom 8:9, 11, 14; 1 Cor 2:11f., 14; 3:16; 6:11; 2 Cor 3:3; Phil 3:3) and as "the Spirit of Christ" (Rom 8:9; 2 Cor 3:18; Gal 4:6; Phil 1:19). Through his death and resurrection, Jesus, who has been given the Spirit during his life, becomes the giver of that Spirit. The resurrection has, in a sense, transformed Christ himself into the Spirit (1 Cor 15:45; 2 Cor 3:17). As such, he communicates his own dynamic qualities to others: "Where the Spirit of the Lord is, there is freedom" (2 Cor 3:17). This Spirit dwells in us as temples, making us belong to Christ (1 Cor 3:16; 6:19) and even making us "one Spirit with him" (1 Cor 6:17), just as we are "in the Spirit" and have "Christ dwelling in us" (Rom 8:9ff.). Paul seems to be thinking of an interpenetration of the Spirit and the human heart—their being "in" one another—that involves the re-creation in us of Christ himself, in his very passage from death to life. Having become the "life-giving Spirit" (1 Cor 15:45) Christ is completely filled with and penetrated by the Holy Spirit. Christ is the source and giver of the Spirit. The risen Son is the first work of the Spirit in the new creation; as Paul wrote to the Corinthians, "Even though we once knew Christ from a human point of view, we know him no longer in that way" (2 Cor 5:16). We know Christ no longer according to the flesh but according to the Spirit.

The Holy Spirit is the power of the resurrection, and the community of the risen Jesus is that place where the Spirit is manifested (Eph 1:19). The gifts of the Spirit are the energies of new eternal life. In these gifts the grace of God takes on specific forms. The Holy Spirit is not only a gift given through the resurrection but the gift of person. The risen Lord identifies himself with the realms of the Spirit. The fact that the risen Lord is identified with the Spirit does not end or deny the reality of the incarnation. The resurrection is the abolition of the limits freely chosen by God in the kenosis of the incarnation. This abolition occurs through the kenosis of the Holy Spirit; the Spirit is available to all and everywhere. In H. Wheeler Robinson's words:

> The kenosis involved when Holy Spirit dwells in sinful men raises new issues as compared with the kenosis involved in Creation or in the Incarnation of the Holy Son of God in a sinless human personality...In the light of the principle of kenosis, therefore, we shall neither look for a revelation of Spirit

divorced from any medium and consequently impressible, nor reject such revelation because it is conditioned by the medium it necessarily employs.[16]

The Holy Spirit is the medium into which the resurrection of Jesus takes place and also the mediator of this reality for all men and women; the Spirit is the person-gift. The gift of the Spirit, which manifests its power in the charismatic manifestations that give life and structure to the Christian community (1 Cor 12:4-11; 14:2, 12-15; Gal 3:5; 1 Thes 5:19f.), means for community and individual the beginning of a wholly new kind of life, a transformation, even an interior revolution parallel to Paul's on the road to Damascus. Its work is not yet fully done, our hearts not yet fully transformed, so "what the flesh desires is opposed to the spirit, and what the spirit desires is opposed to the flesh" (Gal 5:17; see also 3:3; 4:29; Rom 8:12f.). And on the level of religious practice the Spirit struggles against self-justifying formalism, slavery to the "letter" (Gal 3:2; 5:18; 2 Cor 3:6). In principle, however, victory is already won; believers are already "discharged from the Law...so that we are slaves not under the old written code but in the new life of the Spirit" (Rom 7:6). The Spirit, already given to us and bearing fruit in our daily lives, is the bridge to eternal, definitive salvation and freedom, the Christians' hope for the "firstfruit" of a greater harvest (Rom 8:23), the "seed" of eternal life (Gal 6:8; see also 1 Cor 15:44), the "down-payment" on the fullness of God's grace (2 Cor 1:22; 5:5). At the beginning of Genesis we are told that the "wind from God," "the Spirit of God," brooded over the chaos. In the second creation story it is through the "breath of life" that Adam is brought into existence. In creation it is God as Spirit who is operative and immanent.

Clearly the Christian experience of the Holy Spirit in and through the risen Jesus reflects the experience of the same Spirit in the Hebrew scriptures. The Spirit is the life-giver who at the beginning of creation hovered over the waters, who at the incarnation overshadowed the Virgin, and who in the resurrection raises Jesus to a new life. In the work of the Holy Spirit we see the unity of creation and incarnation as the eternal, self-communicating plan of God.

The Kenosis of the Holy Spirit

In the kenosis of the Holy Spirit we are given the continuous self-emptying of God in creation and in history. The incarnation is the symbol of the depth of the immanence of God. The immanence of God in the incarnate life cannot be discontinuous with creation and history, which are the grounds of the incarnation. It is God's personal presence as Spirit that culminates in the incarnation. In a world understood as an ecosystem in evolution, the *entelechia* ("inner energy") is the Spirit. In such a world view there cannot be a total discontinuity between human and world. God as Spirit is the energy immanent to creation that leads creation to fulfillment, from matter to personhood. Through the kenosis of the Spirit, God enters into dialogue with creation, submitting to a relationship in which creation is free to refute or respond. The presence of the Spirit to creation is the reason for the radical plasticity of the universe. As C. E. Raven writes, "From atom and molecule to mammal and man, each by its appropriate order and function expressed the design inherent in it, and contributes, so far as it can by failure or success, to the fulfillment of the common purpose."[17]

Through the presence of the Holy Spirit creativity and movement are ever present in the cosmos. The Spirit is the energy that pervades everything; the cosmos is the temple of the Spirit inhabited from the beginning by the Spirit. The Holy Spirit is the divine activity in the cosmos, the kenotic divine activity. To talk about divine action is to talk about personal action, about an action that does not take over, that does not dominate. As Spirit, God does not act coercively; rather, God lures, solicits, works pervasively from the inside of reality. The activity of the Spirit respects the boundaries of creation. The Spirit operates within the limits of memory, sight, and expectation.[18]

Through the Spirit God is in this world and this world is in God. Everything that is, is in God; God is in all things and yet God is other than all things. This panentheist understanding of God's activity is determined by the fact that Spirit characterizes the kenotic nature of God. Through the activity of the Holy Spirit, through the kenotic presence of the Holy Spirit, the world and its history mediate God; they are God's appearance, the possibility of God's self-manifestation. Through the Spirit the finite is the appearing of the infinite; the finite has its being in the infinite. In a kenotic understanding the Holy Spirit cannot simply be viewed as the Spirit of redemption, cut off from personal historical life and from the life of nature. The Holy Spirit is not simply the Spirit of the church; God's work is one, for God's Spirit is one. Creation, incarnation, redemption are the single continuous activity of the kenotic God.

The relatedness at the heart of the Trinity is the ground of the relatedness between ourselves and all other parts of creation. That ground is God—God as Spirit, God as hidden. This relatedness, which is the very core of God's nature and therefore the core of all life that God created, finds its especial force in the work the Holy Spirit does for us. That dimension of God is directly communicable to creation. Creation is the consequence of a divine self-limitation, of a kenosis. Creation as evolving, as incomplete and free to respond to the Creator, demands a special causal presence of God that is personal and nonintrusive. Such presence is through the Holy Spirit, by means of the kenosis of the Spirit.

The presence of the Spirit creates the space in which the "otherness" of creation can emerge. This kenosis of the Spirit is in effect the sacramentalization of the created order. The created is not inimical to the expression of, even the realization of, the divine. Spirit is God's unique manner in which God inspiring men and women and becoming involved with them does not cease to be God. The mystery of the incarnation as a kenosis of God the eternal Son is also a mystery of the kenosis of the Holy Spirit. During his earthly life Jesus was characterized by the Spirit. He was filled with the Spirit and led by the Spirit. In the incarnation the eternal Son acquired an irrenounceable pneumatological character. This is true of the entire life of Jesus, but it is more clearly true of the risen Jesus.

The presence of the Spirit of Jesus is the authentic beginning of the Kingdom of God and of the new creation in history. This presence of the Spirit is the authority in Jesus' preaching. It is through the presence of the Spirit that Jesus affirms that God is Abba. The Spirit is present even on the cross. It was in the Holy Spirit that Jesus suffered and died. The cross is not only the story of the suffering of the Son but also the story of the suffering of the Spirit. The Spirit leads Jesus to the acceptance of the cross, and it is the Spirit who brings Jesus to life. The Spirit participates in the dying of Jesus in order to give him new life.[19]

The prologue of the gospel of Mark describes the gift of the Spirit to Jesus as the descent of the Spirit. When we realize the effect of that presence in Jesus' life, ministry, death, and resurrection, we acknowledge a kenosis of the Holy Spirit, which emptied itself and descended from the eternity of God into the vulnerability of time and space. While the Spirit is the energy of Jesus' ministry, the Spirit does not turn Jesus into a superman; the Spirit participates in the weakness, suffering, and death of Jesus. Although the Spirit is present on the cross, Jesus cannot come down from the cross. The indwelling Spirit binds itself to Jesus' life and death. The Spirit surrenders itself wholly to the person of Jesus. The presence of the Spirit in Jesus is a kenotic presence; this presence reflects the nature of the Spirit within the trinitarian life—the person-gift, the Spirit of God existing in the mode of gift.[20]

As uncreated gift the Holy Spirit is the source "of all giving of gifts vis-à-vis creatures (created gift); the gift of existence to all things through creation; the gift of grace to human beings through the whole economy of salvation."[21] God in the mode of gift means God as immanent, God as compassionate, God whose "love has been poured into our hearts through the Holy Spirit" (Rom 5:5). William Hill recognizes that within the life of the Trinity, "the personal relating of Father and Son is above all a disposition of love. An 'achieving' of personhood in a pure giving to the other in the mysterious creativity of love..."[22] This personal relating is the very nature of the Holy Spirit, the third "hypostasis." Again, in Hill's terms: "This third in God answers now not to 'I' or 'Thou' but to what is expressed with the pronoun 'We.' God's being is a dynamism which brings forth the personally other in order that such being might consummate itself in love."[23] While the church has maintained from early in its history that the Holy Spirit is truly one of the three, a Person, this in no way implies that the nature of the Holy Spirit cannot be understood in dynamic categories as the efficacy of the Father and the Son. This efficacy has both an inner-trinitarian and an economic mode. Spirit is a mode of the Trinity's presence in creation, incarnation, and redemption. It is characteristic of this mode of presence to be hidden, secret, and silent. One can speak truly of the anonymity of the Spirit, of the faceless Spirit. When we use these categories to speak about the Holy Spirit, we are talking about the kenotic forms of the Spirit, forms of the Spirit's self-emptying.

The mission of the Spirit is one of self-emptying, a kenosis. The mission of the Son is likewise a self-emptying. Within the incarnation this self-emptying has a concrete, visible, and unique appearance in the historical humanity of Jesus. The self-emptying of the Spirit necessarily lacks this concrete and historical dimension. In an authentic sense the kenosis of the Spirit is a more radical kenosis than that of the Son. In the economy of God it is the nature of the Spirit to be self-effacing; the Spirit is "vehicle," "medium of transmission," the eternal "that-by-which." The Spirit perfectly expresses what the divine economy means: administration, provision for need.

The Spirit is faceless and anonymous inasmuch as the Spirit has no proper personal name, as do the Father and Son. The "face" of the Spirit could reveal nothing but the loving of the Father for the Son. In this perspective the Spirit can be spoken of both as the expression in Person of God's innermost being as love and the expression in Person of God's outermost being, the *ekstasis* of the divine love, the possibility and the reality of God's going outside God's self in love.[24]

In a real and mystical way, through the kenosis of the Holy Spirit, the Garden of Gethsemane has an ongoing existence. The cross reveals the rejection of God's self-giving, the tragic possibility that when all is given in love, all may be given in vain. Yet the resurrection comes as a proleptic manifestation of the ultimate victory of God's love. In the resurrection the Spirit brings to sacramental expression the truth that God's love is boundlessly fruitful. The resurrection manifests the ground of human hope: the presence of the Spirit. For in the Spirit are present both origin and consummation.

The purpose of the Spirit is the purpose of God: salvation for all through self-communication. The bestowal of the Spirit brings salvation. Here again the kenotic nature of the Spirit determines the mode of the presence of salvation. Salvation is present in a sacramental way; it is incomplete and in process. The presence of the Holy Spirit as sanctifier is a presence that accepts sanctification as processive and respectful of human freedom and of the possibility of rejection. The salvific presence of the Spirit is in no way triumphalistic. The presence of the divine on the cross of Jesus continues on the cross of the world. The Spirit makes present the powerful powerlessness of God, the hiddenness of God, Luther's God revealed hidden under his opposite *(Absconditus Dei Sub Contrario)*. Hans Küng writes that the Spirit reveals God's "spirituality confined in the flesh, his vastness in his limitation, his eternity in temporality, his omnipresence in being here, his immutability in growth, his infinity in privation and his omniscience in silence."[25] In a kenotic theology the Spirit is not revealing the nondivinity of God but rather the deepest divinity of the Godhead.

The suffering of God in Christ on the cross did not end at Easter but continues in the presence of the Holy Spirit. The ongoing, guaranteed presence of the Holy Spirit in the history of men and women in spite of their rejection expresses the long patience of God. As long as men and women refuse God's salvific gift of self, God continues to suffer. The presence of the Holy Spirit at the center of a world that is far from its goal manifests the ongoing dimension of God's passibility. The Holy Spirit fully suffers with the suffering, grieves with those who grieve. The Holy Spirit is truly the fellow-sufferer.

Through the Spirit, God participates in the ongoing struggle of creation. The Holy Spirit is involved in drawing nothingness into God's history. As we have already seen, God is passible because God is Spirit not as an attribute but in God's very self. God's capacity to suffer is the capacity of the Spirit, who is the active presence of the personal God in history. The Holy Spirit is the gift of God's own self to humanity. Such a gift means that God has made Godself dependent upon "the other." In kenotic love there is always present the possibility of loss, of tragedy, because love offered can mean love rejected. Creation and redemptive incarnation reveal a self-giving of God for a work that is ever precarious and ever poised between the possibilities of triumph and tragedy. The tragic and the triumphant are symbolized by the cross and the resurrection.

God's self-emptying in the Spirit involves a suffering that is not the expression of a lack, not a fated necessity, but an expression of God's kenotic freedom and love. God suffers out of love, which is the overflow of God's being, the Spirit. The experience of the Holy Spirit issues out of the depths of our redeemed and yet unredeemed world. There is a cry from the depths that is the Spirit's own cry. The cry for salvation is itself God's cry inherent in the human yearning for deliverance. Our experience of the world is too often the experience of the absence of freedom. The Holy Spirit empowers people to resist the actuality of the present exigency. The two key words to describe the function of the Holy Spirit are *anticipation* and *resistance,* which represent the dialectic of cross and resurrection.[26] In the resistance and the anticipation of Christian existence come together the mysteries of God's self-emptying in creation and incarnation, the kenosis of the Holy Spirit.

CHAPTER EIGHT

Kenosis and Creation

Christianity affirms that the character of God is revealed most fully in the life, death, and resurrection of Jesus Christ. It claims that there is nothing un-Christlike in God. What it means to be Christlike is expressed in Paul's letter to the Philippians and in the gospel of Mark: to be the servant of all, to let go, and to love without conditions, to accept suffering and powerlessness. For Christianity it is in the mystery of the incarnation that God's character is claimed to have been most fully revealed. But it would be intolerable to affirm that the character of God was solely revealed in Jesus Christ. God must always have been characterized by kenosis. So we must trace the story of divine self-giving love, of divine suffering, from Jesus to the inner triune life of God and to creation, the topic of this chapter.[1]

The Unity of Creation and Incarnation

The incarnational and redemptive presence of God in this world presupposes God's initial and ongoing creativity. Yet in the Judeo-Christian tradition there has been a tendency to separate the two. For Israel, the emphasis on historical salvation never permitted the doctrine of creation to attain an independent status. In Christianity, the primacy given to the mystery of the incarnation had the same results. Creation in both traditions has only an ancillary function: it provides support for faith in God's saving activity. According to many exegetes, belief in creation is founded upon faith in the historical events of salvation.[2]

Our theological tradition has witnessed the separation of nature from grace. This is the inevitable result of a theology in which creation has been separated from incarnation and redemption. The disadvantage of this polarization is evident in the obvious degradation that results from the dualism of opposing nature and grace, reason and faith, works and faith, evangelization and development, religion and politics. All these dichotomies suggest that certain elements of creation are autonomous—outside the realm of grace and the personal will of God—and must be without value unless brought by force to subjection to God. There is a tendency either to banish grace into the inner life, and therefore simply to accept the politico-economic status quo, or to force one's own Christian understanding upon the political and economic structure.

In the Christian tradition Augustine's declaration that grace pertains primarily not to the constitution of nature but to its cure introduced an opposition between nature and grace. Such an opposition can be construed from the New Testament. Paul writes in Philippians 3:30, "Our citizenship is in heaven," and in Colossians 3:1f.: "So if then you have been raised with Christ, seek the things that are above, where Christ is, seated at the right hand of God. Set your mind on things that are above, not on things that are on earth." The same can be heard elsewhere. "Here we have no lasting city, but we seek the city which is to come" (Heb 13:14). We find in the New Testament two different understandings of the meaning of the word *world*. The first meaning is the world as God's creation (Acts 17:24), the totality of all that is created (Jn 1:10; 1 Cor 3:22). To affirm that the world is created is a profession of faith that God is the Ruler and Lord of all. Yet the New Testament does not affirm unambiguously the lordship of God over all creation. The final rule of God over the world is always perceived eschatologically. Since God's sovereignty is not without ambiguity, the New Testament presents us with another meaning of the word *world*— the world as cosmos, as fallen creation. This fallen world is in longing for a future and different world.

Creation as Original Blessing

In Christianity there has always existed a tradition that sees creation as God's first grace and grace as the origin of nature. The doctrine of creation is not a theory about the beginning but an affirmation of the fundamental lordship of God and the essential goodness and orderliness of the world. Creation reveals itself as eminently complex and immensely variegated. As Charles Darwin observed:

> It is interesting to contemplate a tangled bank, clothed with many plants of many kinds, with birds singing on the bushes, with various insects flitting about, and with worms crawling through the damp earth, and to reflect that these elaborately constructed forms, so different from each other, and dependent upon each other in so complex a manner, have all been produced by laws acting around us...There is grandeur in this view of life, with its several powers, having been originally breathed by the Creator into a few forms or into one; and that, whilst this planet has gone cycling on according to the fixed law of gravity, from so simple a beginning endless

forms most beautiful and most wonderful have been, and are being evolved.[3]

In the first chapter of Genesis, God is presented as having joy and delight in creation, "And God saw everything that He had made, and indeed, it was very good" (Gn 1:31). Again, from the psalmist:

> The earth is the Lord's and all that is in it,
> the world and those who live in it;
> for He has founded it on the seas
> and established it upon the rivers (Ps 24:1).

The universe, according to the psalmist, is suffused with the glory of God. "The heavens are telling the glory of God, and the firmament proclaims His handiwork" (Ps 19:1). For Augustine and the Augustinian tradition nature and creation are so wounded by original sin that unless healed by grace they have no intrinsic value. Created reality, unless constantly healed by grace, tends toward nothingness. The conflict inherent in a theology that must accept both Augustine and the psalmist is well reflected by Gabriel Marcel:

> My most intimate and most unshakable conviction—too bad for orthodoxy if it is heretical—is that, whatever so many spiritual and learned men may have said, God in no way wants to be loved by us in opposition to the creature, but wants to be glorified through the creature and starting from the creature. That is why I cannot bear so many spiritual writings. That God, who is set up against all that is created and who is in some way jealous of his own handiwork, is but an idol in my eyes. It is a relief for me to have written this. And I declare that until I retract this I shall be insincere whenever I seem to state anything contrary to what I have just written.[4]

There are within Christianity different understandings of creation. There is Augustine and there is Irenaeus. For Irenaeus, God's creation manifests God's wisdom and goodness; God's creative relationship to the world is described as one of dispensation. For Irenaeus, creation emerges from God's loving wisdom as a realm of becoming and as such possesses a dynamic character. The goal of creation is creation: "The glory of God is the human being fully alive."[5] Thomas Aquinas would later develop similar notions in his *Summa,* notwithstanding Augustine's influence. For Aquinas, God's original blessing is creation; nature must be perceived in a positive way, and grace respects the role of the natural order and the secular values that go with it.

Creation in the Old Testament

In the Old Testament we find a rich and varied understanding of creation.[6] The accounts of creation in Genesis affirm a fundamental religious insight into the relationship between God and the world. Israel's belief in creation arose out of its experience of God within history and is shaped by this experience. The understanding of God as Creator of the world follows from the experience of God as Creator of Israel. The Exodus, the Covenant, the Settlement provided the models for the understanding of God as Creator of the world.

It is from the experience of the Exodus that Israel's idea of total dependence on the almighty Lord emerges: "Has any god ever attempted to go and take a nation for himself from the midst of another nation, by trials, by signs and wonders, and by war, by a mighty hand and an outstretched arm, and by terrifying displays of power, as the Lord your God did for you in Egypt before your very eyes?" (Dt 4:34).

The almighty God shaped Israel in the same way a potter shapes a statue out of clay. But God's shaping of Israel is not done once and for all. It is an ongoing process. God establishes a creative covenant with Israel: "The Lord spoke to you out of the midst of the fire...He declared to you his covenant" (Dt 4:12-13). Creation and covenant derive entirely from God's freedom. Yet there is a demand for a response on the part of Israel, a response that implies obedience, faith, trust and worship.

The creation of the world through God's Word brings about all reality under the lordship of God. All that is, is in a relation of obedience to God. The dependent status of creatures is evident in the idea of existence as obedience to a God-given command:

> The heavens are thine, the earth also is thine;
> the world and all that is in it, thou hast founded them
> (Ps 24:1).

> Know that the Lord is God!
> It is he that made us, and we are his (Ps 100:3).

Under the formal aspect of being creatures, all men and women are equal: "The rich and the poor have this in common; the Lord is the maker of them all" (Prv 22:2-3). Coming from God, creation is essentially good: "And God saw everything that he had made, and indeed, it was very good. For everything created by God is good, and nothing is to be rejected provided it is received with thanksgiving; for it is sanctified by God's word and by prayer" (Gn 1:31; 1 Tim 4:4-5). Creation is therefore a gift. Creation as such, then, is covenantal, emerging from a faithful and free God. As God's free act, creation is revelatory and inspires men and women to glorify it.

> Sing to the Lord, bless his name;
> tell of his salvation from day to day.
> Declare his glory among the nations,
> his marvelous works among all the peoples!
> For great is the Lord, and greatly to be praised;
> he is to be revered above all gods.
> For all the gods of the peoples are idols;
> but the Lord made the heavens (Ps 96:2-5).

In the Hebrew scriptures God the Creator does not exist in a relation of competition to creation. God is in constant and faithful relation to creation, giving guidance and life in human history. God undergoes an "Exodus" from Godself. Even the revelation of the Lord's name—"I am who I am" (Ex 3:14)—while pointing to God's transcendence demands a real presence—"I will be with you" (Ex 3:12).

While God as Creator is almighty and brings about reality by the power of the Word, yet since this Word is a personal Word it has authority over creation in a dialogical manner. It is a word of promise, of radical demand, yet in need of response, a word or invitation, a call. God's authority in the act of creating is in need of the acknowledgment of creation itself. This aspect has been stressed by Emil Brunner:

> Because in the full sense God can be Lord only of such a subject who in free personal decision acknowledges Him as Lord, He wills this independence of the creation...He wills to be their Lord because only in His being known as Lord is He really Lord in the complete sense.[7]

Because God creates in a personal way and not as an abstract power, what God has created must stand in a relationship to God. As Claus Westermann writes:

> The text is making a statement about an action of God who decides to create man in his image. The meaning must come from the creation event. What God has decided to create must stand in a relationship to him. The creation of man in God's image is directed to something happening between God and man. The Creator created a creature that corresponds to him, to whom he can speak, and who can hear him—God created

man in his image, corresponding to him, so that something can happen between God and the creature. This is presented here in narrative form: the possibility of something happening between God and man consists in this, that God gives man a command and man can only relate himself to this in freedom. He can abide by what has been commanded or he can reject it. In both cases he sets himself in either a positive or negative relationship to him who commands. The freedom of this relationship arises only from the command; without the command there would be no freedom.[8]

In summing up the Old Testament doctrine on creation, one can say that everything is understood as having been created by God; that God the Creator can be trusted, for he is the reliable one; that creation is the ground for a reflected dependence, trust, thankfulness, and obedience to God (Is 17:2; 22:11; 40:26ff.; Ps 103:22; 119:73).

In the Hebrew scriptures, creation becomes the ongoing trust that God will intervene redemptively in our lives: "Yet, O Lord, you are our Father; we are the clay and you are our potter; we are all the work of your hand. Do not be exceedingly angry, O Lord, and do not remember iniquity forever. Now consider, we are all your people" (Is 64:8f.), and "O Lord, God of Israel...you have made heaven and earth. Incline your ear, O Lord, and hear...save us, I pray you, from his hand [the hand of the enemy], so that all the kingdoms of the earth may know that you, O Lord, are God alone" (2 Kgs 19:15f., 19). And, lastly, creation in the Old Testament is acknowledged as the presupposition for and the foundation of a fruitful relationship to God, that of prayer, worship, obedience, and trust.

The Old Testament in a variety of places has affirmed that God created out of love, out of God's own free will (Ps 102:26-28; 103:19). Yet there remains the question whether creation is also the full and definitive expression of the *Hesed* of God, of his ongoing, merciful love of humanity, always ready to forgive. For God, to create is also to save. The creative power of God is almighty and irresistible and brings reality to existence—"'Can I not do with you, O house of Israel, just as this potter has done?' says Yahweh. 'Just like the clay in the potter's hand, so are you in my hand'" (Jer 18:6). God as Creator is a God of life and not destruction (Ps 135:6-9). God has shown Godself to be father in creation; the same father who saved Israel from bondage and has given her the land. In the Song of Moses (Dt 32:1-43) we find the passionate dimension of God's fatherhood as Creator: "Do you thus repay the Lord, O foolish and senseless people? Is he not the father who formed you? Did he not make you and establish you?" By being called Father, God is honored as the Creator: "Is not he your father, who created you, who made you and established you?" (Dt 32:6). "Have we not all one father? Has not one God created us?" (Mal 2:10). In the Jewish scriptures God's father-hood is related not only to care for Israel but also to care as Creator for all that there is. Israel appeals to God as Father in the light of its experi-ence of God as Creator who determines Israel's life in every aspect.

The Old Testament understanding of creation is presented as an organizing concept; it does not simply state something about a situation but affirms that whatever is relates to an originating principle. Such an understanding of creation does not simply present itself to our mind for intellectual acceptance. It implies a conversion on our part, a *metanoia*. Augustine marked the turning point of his journey when he grasped fully the fact of creation:

> Consider all things that are of a lower order than yourself, and I say that they have not absolute being in themselves, nor are they entirely without being. They are real insofar as they have their being from you.[9]

Creation in the New Testament: The New Creation

The New Testament's view of creation is essentially that of the Old Testament.[10] But for the New Testament writers the emphasis is on the new creation, the coming of the Kingdom of God, a time of re-creation in and through Christ.

> He is the image of the invisible God,
>   the firstborn of all creation.
> For in him were created all things in heaven and on earth,
>   the visible and the invisible,
>   whether thrones or dominions or principalities or
>   powers;
>   all things were created through him and for him.
> He is the head of the body, the church.
> He is the beginning, the firstborn from the dead
>   (Col 1:15-20).

The resurrection is proclaimed as a new creation because through it death has been defeated. Jesus Christ, the firstborn from the dead, is also the firstborn of creation in the sense that the created world is modeled on him.[11] Those who are reconciled in Christ emerge as a new creation. "So if anyone is in Christ, there is a new creation; everything old has passed away; everything has become new! All this is from God, who reconciled us to himself through Christ and has given us the ministry of reconciliation"

(2 Cor 5:17-18). Richard Clifford has recognized that this text alludes to Isaiah 43:18-21. Here the prophet "describes the new act of God in the language of both creation and redemption. Galatians 6:15 uses new creation similarly."[12]

Clearly, when referring to creation the Christian scriptures have a different agenda than that of the Jewish scriptures. In Jewish thought there is a temporal conception of a coming world, a world that fulfills the present, yet the Kingdom of God is experienced as operative in this world. This rule of God is perceived in hope and expectation for a change for Israel. As Schillebeeckx writes:

> The more radically this world deviates from God's creative ordinance and contradicts it, the less talk about the Kingdom of God is talk about this world, because this world as people experience it is simply not "in order." In that case, the Kingdom of God increasingly becomes something which is not experienced in this world. Only in this way does the Kingdom of God appear as an alternative to this world, an alternative to the reality of which will only be revealed in the last days. This gave rise to the apocalyptic world of two levels, where everything that was to take place among men had been prepared for from eternity in a heavenly world.[13]

Notwithstanding the experience of a world where God's rule is not fully realized, Israel remains faithful to its understanding of God as Creator and Conservator. Recognizing this, Christian theology seeks a deeper grasp of the apparent New Testament dualism and its rejection of this world. While the world is created good by God (Jn 1:10), yet there is a need for salvation and illumination. The world is obscured by the sins of human beings, yet it is also the object of God's mercy and love. As John writes, "God so loved the world..." (3:16). Jesus himself is named "the savior of the world" (Jn 4:42). Some of the Kingdom of God can be realized on earth. In the humanity of Jesus Christ that Kingdom has appeared and made itself present. Despite the difference between this world and the Kingdom of God, we are not bound to a two-story universe. While the final consummation of the Kingdom, of the life of grace, is in the future, yet it is also now present in this world.

A salvation history that would have nothing to do with creation history would be without meaning. God, the transcendent world-maker, is the agent and author of both processes. As world-maker, God is the Lord of all—the moon and the stars, the beasts on earth and humankind are all God's subjects. In a Christian context that unity of history and salvation history cannot be perceived without acknowledging the intrinsic connection between God the Creator and Jesus Christ the Redeemer. This connection can be understood in a variety of ways. The early Christians identified Jesus the Christ in some way with the Creator; Jesus as Christ was seen as the divine agent, God's instrument in the creation of the world.[14] The New Testament claims that Jesus is the divine Word (Jn 1:1ff.) by whose power and authority the world was created and constituted. Christ is the beginning of the creation (Col 1:15), but at the same time, he is heir to everything there is (Heb 1:2) in that all things were created through him and for him (Col 1:15).

For the New Testament, creation is redeemed and brought to completion in Jesus Christ. Creation awaits with eager expectation the revelation of the children of God, for creation was made subject to futility not of its own accord but because of the one who subjected it, in hope that creation itself would be delivered from slavery to corruption and share in the glorious freedom of the children of God (Gn 3:17-19; 6:11-13; Rom 8:18-30).

The New Testament emphasis on the new creation has led to a Christocentric understanding of God and a separation of creation from redemption. And yet, within the context of both Jewish and Christian traditions, there has never been a question of rejecting soteriology. As Gabriel Daly affirms: "Creation is not a mere backdrop to Redemption but is taken into a process that is continuously both creative and redemptive."[15]

Creation and Salvation

The issue of redemption in the Christian tradition has emphasized history as the basic theological reality.[16] For much of Christian theology history has become the framework for salvation and for redemption. The priority of history as an interpretative framework for redemption devolved to the priority of salvation over creation.[17] God's immanence in this tradition is reserved to the field of history, of human interaction, and the character of God is understood to be most fully revealed in the words and deeds of Jesus Christ. Emphasis on history, on politics, leads also to a radical form of anthropocentrism that pits human beings against nature. Such a view is expressed by John Macquarrie: "Our first step toward an interpretation of the doctrine of creation is to take man himself rather than nature as the paradigm of creaturely beings."[18] Such an emphasis on the centrality of the personal and existential is counterproductive in our attempt to understand the character of God. More productive is Gabriel Daly's position:

> When we human beings affirm our authentic presence in the world and seek to exercise our graced freedom there, it is

nature that is doing it in us, for it is through natural processes that we have emerged into humanized nature. In us nature groans for redemption. We cannot have it both ways: we cannot assert that the human species is part of nature and at the same time place that species over against nature. If men and women need redemption, nature can properly be said to need redemption. I find in that thought the basis for a fruitful interpretation of the concept of "new creation."[19]

It is necessary that we approach the relation between creation and incarnation from another perspective. Belief in God the Creator should be the source of belief in the gracious and forgiving God who has revealed himself in the human person of Jesus. As we read in Hebrews 11:6, "Whoever would approach him must believe that he exists and that he rewards those who seek him." God is Creator both of everything that exists and also of salvation. Creation is truly the original blessing to be accepted or refused. In that perspective, as Daly affirms, "redemption is not discontinuous with creation; it is not a redesign initiative on God's part. Redemption is God's answer to the human refusal to cooperate with God's creative purposes."[20]

As original blessing creation is an object of faith, a theological reality. The creation stories express a theological truth about humanity, about authentic human life in accord with a universal order. To accept God as Creator is to profess to accept God as Lord; it is to accept dependence upon God. It is to accept existence as gift, in gratitude; it is to accept God as the faithful one. There can be no acceptance of creation and of Creator without self-involvement. Knowledge of God through creation demands not simply a form of contemplation but an active doing; it involves a righteous person.

Creation and the Lordship of God: Creation ex Nihilo

To believe in God the Creator is not to offer a scientific explanation for the world; it is to accept good news about the world. Within the Jewish-Christian tradition a concept of creation as pure gift has gradually developed. In this tradition to be created, to be a creature—to be therefore not-God but a finite being—is truly a grace. In this tradition God alone is Creator, and everything else is creature and creation. In the tradition of the priestly writings, the verb *bara,* which may have originally meant "incise" or "engrave," was adopted to denote the special work of God in creating and redeeming. Only God can be the subject of *bara.* When this verb is used there is never any mention of a material from which something is "created." Creation is something absolutely new; God's creative activity has no human analogy. Creation in the Judeo-Christian tradition cannot have any preceding condition; it cannot follow on anything else. In its uniqueness it is in every respect "for the first time."

Irenaeus underlined the difference between the biblical concept of creation and that of the Greek tradition. Writing against the Gnostics, he asserted:

> They do not believe that God (being powerful, and rich in all resources) created matter itself, inasmuch as they do not know how much a spiritual and divine essence can accomplish...While men, indeed, cannot make anything out of nothing, but only out of matter already existing, yet God is in this point preeminently superior to men, that he himself called into being the substance of his creation, when previously it had no existence.[21]

Against the Gnostics' extreme pessimism relative to matter, Irenaeus states his understanding of the nature of creation:

> If...He [the Creator] made all things freely, and by His own power, and arranged and finished them, and His will is the substance of all things, then he is discovered to be the one and only God who created all things, who alone is omnipotent, and who is the only Father founding and forming all things, visible and invisible, such as may be perceived by our senses and such as cannot, heavenly and earthly, "by the word of His power" (Heb 1:3): and He has fitted and arranged all things by His wisdom...He [is] the Creator. He the Lord of all; and there is no one besides Him.[22]

The notion of creation *ex nihilo*—or the production out of non-being—is common among the early Fathers of the church, and though it has Christological implications, it is primarily employed to avoid a theory of creation as emanation. Such a theory would seem to draw the creatures out of God's own substance. By implication, creatures would then be divine by nature. St. Augustine insists that God does not generate things from God's own nature, but rather makes them from nothing, precisely from "no thing." Here "no thing" does not function as a kind of principle. Rather, creation *ex nihilo* insists that something began to be where there was nothing before. So creation *ex nihilo* is dependent on the power of the agent alone.

In Gregory of Nyssa we find a position different from the general patristic understanding. When Gregory affirms that the genesis of all things is from God, he means that, according to the scriptures, God created the world out of Godself; that is, by an emanation, which Gregory sees as an act in time and of will, not of God's nature.[23] The Fathers in opposing the Arians had emphasized the distinction between the Logos emanating of necessity eternally from the Father and the world created volitionally from nothing.[24] The volitional and temporal act of creation *ex nihilo* is interpreted by Gregory of Nyssa as an act of emanation not out of necessity but as volitional and temporal. If creation is from God and yet it is out of nothing, does this mean that for Gregory the essence of God is nothingness? Basically, Gregory is relating creation to the ineffable and incomprehensible nature of God, implying the negation of all that can be spoken of or thought of relative to God. For the early Fathers, the justification for the doctrine of *creatio ex nihilo* is founded upon considerations of power and rulership rather than questions of being as such.

In St. Anselm the doctrine of *creatio ex nihilo* is dealt with at a more explicitly ontological level. For Anselm, creation is from God considered as agent, yet creation is from nothing by way of material causality; that is, there is no material substrate. St. Anselm moves his understanding of the doctrine further. He perceives creation as a donation "from nothing." "Nothing" is understood as privation, an absolute privation, for in creation there is no pre-existent subject of privation. Nothing is expected or anticipated, for there is no subject who can expect or anticipate.[25] Privation in this context can better be understood within the analogy of gift. The element of gratuity implies that there is no ground in the recipient for this gift. Creation is the reception of something not due. It is absolute reception since there is no subject to receive. So creation is, before the fact, strictly an affair of the Creator, yet after the fact it is the totality of the creature itself.

From these various sources the world was created neither out of pre-existent matter nor out of the divine being but by the free will of God. God's freedom is not primarily power but love, which means self-communication. God creates out of love. Such a creation is considered by Anselm to be truly a gift, because it is in no way due—it is purely gratuitous and thus our gift.

This basic understanding of creation is to be found in Thomas of Aquinas: "To create is properly speaking to cause or produce the being of things."[26] To create is "to produce being absolutely, not as this or that being."[27] If creation pertains to the being of things, then there can be nothing previous to creation. It is only figuratively that one can speak of "before creation," for "nothing" here means the complete absence of being. For Aquinas, to create does not imply succession or even motion. As Aquinas affirms: "In every change or motion there must be something existing in one way now and in a different way before. For the very word 'change' shows this. But where the whole substance of a thing is brought into being there can be no same thing existing in different ways."[28] There is nothing "before" creation, but creation makes the most radical difference for the creature. Creation is the radical establishment of the creature itself. Again, Aquinas: "Creation is not a change but the very dependence of the created act of being upon the principle from which it is produced."[29] The point of the doctrine of *ex nihilo* is that everything owes its origin and continuation to God. The universe is absolutely dependent upon God for its existence.[30] Yet the reasons for creation have to lie in God's goodness and love. It is because God is good that we exist, for, as the tradition has affirmed, it is of the nature of goodness to communicate itself: *Bonum diffusivum sui.* Writing about the reason for the incarnation, Aquinas affirms: "The very nature of God is the essence of goodness—hence what belongs to the nature of goodness befits God. But it belongs to the nature of goodness to communicate itself to others."[31]

The affirmation *creatio ex nihilo* is an exclusive formula. While the preposition *ex* ("out of") excludes matter of any kind, the formula does not intend to say that creation has it roots in nothingness. Creation has its roots and reason in the reality of God characterized by freedom and especially by love. Love must mean the self-communication of the good. Creation manifests God's boundless power as it communicates God's love. Creation out of God's goodness, as an act of self-communication, and creation *ex nihilo* are in no way incompatible. The biblical tradition is the proclamation that there is only one who is truly God, a God who loves unconditionally. The theological maxim *creatio ex nihilo* arose when the idea of creation by sheer loving will was combined with the biblical insistence on God as the Creator of all.

In order to safeguard the divine freedom and the totally free and unreserved gift of creation, theologians have argued that God has such a fullness of inner life that God could have refrained from creating the world and from offering Godself to that creation without diminishing God's own joy. God freely chose to become Creator, but God could equally have chosen otherwise. To affirm that creation is an act of self-communication poses seriously the question of God's causal relationship to creation, a question that ultimately affects the whole issue of the character of God. Who is this God who creates in such a way? Creation poses fundamental questions about God's agency in the world, about God's relation to the world. Behind the various models of God that have emerged lie the different ways of conceiving the creative activity of God.

One basic understanding of God the Creator has expressed itself in a monarchial model. Here the biblical model of God as king and ruler led to an emphasis on the doctrine of divine omnipotence and omniscience.

In such a model there is a strictly unilateral relationship: God affects the world, but the world does not affect God, who is eternal, unchanging, and impassible. God, as sovereign ruler, is entirely self-sufficient and independent of the world. The monarchial model focuses on God's power, understood as power over "the other," and affirms the radical transcendence of God. Creation is not identical with the being of God or part of God's being; creation is not consubstantial with God. Creation is brought about without adding to or subtracting from the being of God.

For Aquinas, creation is simply the relation of creature to Creator: "Creation in the creature is nothing but a certain relation to the Creator as to the principle of its being."[32] From the side of God creation is an act of efficient causality; from our side it is a relation of dependence. God does not depend on the creature; the creature depends on God. God's relation to the creature does not constitute God's being; the creature's relation to the Creator constitutes its very being. But for Aquinas this does not mean that God is not closely related to the creature. God is present to the creature by God's very essence, by the pure act that God is. "God is said to be in all things by essence; not indeed of the things themselves, as if he were of their essence; but by his own essence; because his substance is present to all things as the cause of their being."[33] For Aquinas, such immanence of God emphasizes that God creates not simply out of power but also out of love. Only a God who is pure act and absolutely transcendent can create in pure freedom, liberality, and love.

Creation and Science

The question of whether or not God is absent from creation raises issues such as the relation of the immanence of God to God's transcendence and the nature of God's agency. The absolute and radical transcendence of God, even as Creator, does not necessarily lead us to an apathetic deity but to pure liberality. In fact, only a God who as Being itself is absolutely transcendent and independent of the world can give in pure graciousness, since in giving, God neither gains nor seeks benefit. The absolute dependence of the creature simply conveys the truth that all things come from God. Once we affirm that God creates out of goodness and is not absent from creation, but that God's transcendence is the measure of God's immanence, we have challenged the classical affirmation that God as Creator is immutable and unchangeable.

In the period when the monarchial model was predominant the created world was understood in terms of a static and hierarchical universe. The cosmos was accepted as a fixed order whose fundamental structures were unchanging. The Creator God was also seen as unmoving and unchanging. The eighteenth century brought about another view of the world—a world perceived as machine. The Creator was understood as the "clockmaker," and creation as controlled by the laws of cause and effect. This Creator is remote from creation, impassible, the rational architect of the universe.

Many of the basic assumptions of eighteenth-century science have come under severe criticism with the emergence of contemporary physics and biology. Many of the basic assumptions of the earlier sciences—for example, that reality is determined by fixed laws and that change is never substantial—have been challenged. Contemporary physics and cosmology join evolutionary biology, molecular biology, and ecology in showing the interdependence of all things. The rise of the biological sciences and the emergence of the evolutionary theory have led theologians to face again the question of God's causality in creation. Evolutionary biology has revealed a world that is fantastically complex.

> The intricate structures of DNA and protein molecules are dependent on myriads of interatomic forces. Molecular structures, in turn, contribute to the higher levels of organization, which lead to the emergence of sentience, purposiveness, consciousness, and self-consciousness. In nature, information is as important as matter and energy. Perhaps there is some parallel in the theological concept of Word or logos, which can be thought of as a form of information, the communication of meaning and message when correctly interpreted. But if nature is a message from God, it is not easily decoded.[34]

In the area of physics the universe is no longer understood in static categories but in terms of becoming, of continuing process. "Here astrophysics adds its testimony to that of evolutionary biology and other fields."[35] The understanding that an evolutionary process involves an interplay of chance and necessity poses a major challenge to earlier systems of theology and science.[36] Novelty in an evolutionary process is due to co-randomness. Jacques Monod affirmed the implications of the role of chance in this way: "Pure chance, absolutely free but blind, is at the very root of the stupendous edifice of evolution."[37] But as many reactions to Monod's position have made evident, chance alone does not govern the whole process of evolution. There are laws and structures. It is the interplay of chance and law that governs the process of becoming. As John Polkinghorne affirms: "The role of chance is to explore and realize that potentiality present in the pattern and structure of the physical world."[38] Scientists have been astonished at the incredible results of such an interplay. For Arthur Peacocke, "the way in which what we call 'chance' operates within this 'given' framework to produce new structures, entities and processes can then properly be seen as an eliciting of the potentialities that the physical cosmos possessed *ab initio*."[39]

The emphasis on chance in the evolutionary process leads necessarily to some substantial changes in our understanding of God's causal relation to creation, of God's presence and sustained action in the world. So, Daly writes, "we can rejoice in a God who is apparently happy to be creative at microscopic and macroscopic levels, through the instrumentality of an elegant interplay between chance and necessity."[40]

Peacocke recognizes that we can affirm that "God is the basic ground, the source itself for both law and chance. That God acts to create in the world through what we call 'chance' operating within the created order, each stage of which constitutes the launching pad for the next."[41] Such a causality on the part of the Creator must be characterized as genuinely innovative and adaptive, that is, as open-ended. Yet what seems apparent is that "chance" is loaded in favor of life. The Creator God who favors life allows the potentialities of the universe to emerge through chance. David J. Bartholomew has agreed that "chance offers the potential Creator many advantages which it is difficult to envisage being obtained in any other way."[42] He goes further, venturing that a world of chance is not merely consistent with a theistic view of nature but almost required by it. "It is more congenial to both faith and reason to suppose that God generates the requisite degree of randomness much as we do, by deterministic means. We emphasize again that this does not imply or require fore-knowledge of the consequences at the micro-level on God's part. He is concerned with macro-effects."[43]

Emphasis on the rule of chance leads us to understand God's causal relationship to the world in ways that may seem unfamiliar. A God who works through chance cannot be understood as ruler omnipotent, omniscient unchanging monarch, or as the "clockmaker" who designs a perfectly accurate world. Polkinghorne reflects:

> When one thinks of those eighteen thousand million years which elapsed from the big bang until conscious beings appeared, one can see that God is patient, content to achieve purposes through the slow unfolding of process. In that realization lies the small contribution that natural theology can make to that most agonizing of theological questions, the problem of the apparently wasteful suffering of the world.[44]

No interventionist understanding of God will do. God's activity must be located in the very nature of creation of which God is the

Guarantor; Creator God is not a cause among causes but the sustainer of this particular world. In a universe where chance plays an important role, the Creator accepts the vulnerability that accompanies chance. If a world characterized by chance is risky, one where human freedom is a given is even riskier. Just as we must emphasize God's immanent creative presence in the natural world, we must proclaim God's immanence in the world of human freedom and responsibility. Such immanence of God in the human personal world has always been affirmed in the Christian tradition as divine providence. Macquarrie defines the doctrine of providence as asserting "that the same God who gave the world being continues to govern its affairs."[45] Such governance is an energy that, creating and sustaining, respects human freedom. Again, such energy must be characterized by self-limitation, by kenosis.[46] Providential causality that respects human causality and freedom precludes us from perceiving God as an interventionist.[47]

Since a providential understanding of God demands an understanding of God as personal, the issue of providence becomes the issue of the nature of God's presence in causality. Such causality, as we will later indicate, does not need to be interventionist. Writing about prayer, Vincent Brummer affirms:

> By our actions we cause contingent events by bringing about conditions necessary for them which would otherwise be subject to chance. But if human persons can intervene in the course of nature in this way, why cannot God do so as well? Divine action in the world need therefore not take the form of miraculous intervention in violation of the natural order, any more than human action need do so.[48]

In divine personal causality where immanence and presence are essential, omnipotence and omniscience have to be qualified. Peacocke remarks:

> The way of regarding these essential attributes of God that most commended itself was seeing God as having a self-appointed vulnerability towards the events and processes of the world in the creation of which there had been a self-emptying (kenosis) by God's own self. If, as we argued, the source of the being of the world is other than itself, then we inferred that the "best explanation" of that world is a creator God who must be at least personal and who possesses a mode of rationality creative of and exploratory in new possibilities in the world.[49]

When it comes to establishing a model of God's agency one must be humble. For Daly, "Recognition of our inability to understand God's action in causal terms is an integral and scandalizing feature of faith."[50] Models of God and God's agency are not conceptually precise, but they are powerfully evocative. We have already seen that the Christian tradition carries a variety of models of God as Creator. These models emphasize the lordship of God, God's omnipotence. Such models are not compatible with a world characterized by chance and order. In a contemporary approach to creation God's immanence must be emphasized. Christianity has always affirmed the immanence of God, primarily within human beings but also in nature. Such immanence has been attributed to God as spirit and the process of immanence to a kenosis of God. An emphasis on God as spirit in creation suggests that God the Creator is not primarily the omnipotent controller of the universe but its immanent source of complexity, diversity, and generosity. God's immanence as spirit emphasizes a relationship at the deepest level of life, of unity.

Creation and the Kenotic Presence of God

While God's immanence can be construed as the presence of God as Spirit, the process of such a presence can best be described as one of kenosis. Creation involves a costly process. Creation is an act of kenotic love; in creating, God limits self and allows a cosmos to emerge with its own autonomy. God, in God's creative causality, makes room for human freedom and autonomy to emerge and for a natural order to be characterized by open-endedness and flexibility. David J. Bartholomew makes the point that "God chose to make a world of chance because it would have the properties necessary for producing beings fit for fellowship with himself."[51] That this should be the case should not surprise those who claim to find in Jesus Christ the fullness of fellowship with God. What characterizes the life of Jesus is self-offering and self-limitation. The God revealed in the self-limitation that is the incarnation is the same God who creates. Creation demands on the part of the Creator the same kenosis the incarnation demanded. Creation demands as much sacrifice as the building of the Body of Christ. The Creator has to work from inside creation, suffering its pains of growth and chancy development.

Christianity is committed to the affirmation that God is present to and acts in creating. Its fundamental question is about the mode of that presence and causality. That God is present to and cares for creation is a firm belief for Christianity; even the presence of evil cannot contradict it. But the mode of God's presence and care is quite another thing. It is my contention that the mode of presence and causality has to be kenotic. Peacocke says much the same:

The role of "chance" in creation impels us also to recognize more emphatically than ever before the constraints which we must regard God as imposing upon himself in creation and to suggest that God has a "self-limited" omnipotence and omniscience. For, in order to achieve his purposes, he has allowed his inherent omnipotence and omniscience to be modified, restricted and curtailed by the very open-endedness that he has bestowed upon creation.[52]

Kenosis, which in the Christian tradition has been understood to characterize the incarnation, must also inform the mystery of creation. We must approach creation from the simplest and most radical affirmation: "God is love" (1 Jn 4:8). God's love is ecstatic love and draws God to create a real "other." Creation emerges out of the ecstatic love that is God's intrinsic being. To call God ecstatic love is to see God as a kenotic being, and to see God as essentially a kenotic being is to qualify God's omnipotence. Kenosis implies self-limitation, self-denial, self-sacrifice. Ecstatic love is the abdication of power; it is the refusal of self-expansion.

Transcendence must qualify and characterize God in every aspect. As agent, God is total agency, complete self-giving, utter generosity of sharing; in God nothing is held back, nothing is given by measure. The trinitarian nature of God indicates this. Yet in creation the gift has to be limited if there is to be a passing from the infinite to the finite. How can the infinite, which is infinite giving, give less than itself, give less than the infinite? Does the very nature of the infinite exclude "otherness"? Does infinite being exclude all *ekstasis,* all going beyond itself? Or does it imply the fullness of this generosity?

In the Christian context the nature of our God must be found in the statement that "those who want to save their life will lose it" (Mt 16:25). The perfection of the divine nature resides not in its infinite self-satisfaction but in its self-giving love. Of course there is nothing other than God, or independent of God, to which God can give Godself. Yet may not God bring into being that which, being other than God (though always dependent upon God), can be the object of God's love and share in God's own nature? The idea of creation as a form of divine self-giving, a love that goes out of itself to bring about fully responsive reality, demands that Godself be put at the disposal of creatures and limited in relation to them. Creation as the effect of God's boundless and ecstatic love implies a self-limitation of God.

Christian theology, being witness to the trinitarian mystery, has always distinguished between an act of God inward and an act of God outward; that is, between the inner life of God and an act of God in creation, incarnation, and redemption. If we say that there is a "within" and "without" for God, and that God goes "out of Godself" in creating, then we have to accept a self-limitation of the infinite relative to God's creation. In order to create that which is outside of God, there must be within God the possibility of finitude within Godself. Through self-limitation God has created the world "in Godself," giving it time in eternity, finitude in God's infinity. Creation is God's act in God and out of God.

There must be a place for finitude in God before God can create that which is "other" than God. The *nihil* is within God. God's creative act is anchored in God's preceding self-restriction. Creation is an act not of self-expansion but of self-limitation. While it is true that creation does not mean a diminishing of the divine life, through creation God enters a new, limiting relationship. Through creation God brings about an "other" who is free. In creating, God has surrendered God's triumphant self-sufficiency and brought about God's own need. God has done this freely, out of love. Because of God's transcendence, God is free from the world that has been brought about; God is also radically free for the world.

We can define a basic principle of self-limitation, a kenosis that applies to God in relation to finite being. The nature of God's being as personal agent is a letting-be, an enabling to be. Letting-be is also self-giving or self-spending so that God's creative work is a work of love and self-giving. Creation is not so much an exercise of power as it is an exercise of love and generosity, an act of self-limitation.

Creation is never really from nothing, *ex nihilo,* but out of God. There is a sacrificial nature to creation; it is intrinsically a self-humbling, self-restraining, self-limiting act. "The creation of heaven and earth," writes Bulgakov, "...is a voluntary self-diminution, a metaphysical kenosis, with respect to divinity itself."[53] In order to understand how a unique God brings about an "other" *as* an "other," some dimension of self-limitation must be attributed to God. This is even more clearly the case when the "other" is given the specific possibility of freedom and personal relation. In creating, not only does God allow for the existence of a reality "other" than God, but God actually gives a created being the possibility of choosing to respond to the Creator. Creation, by being given independence from God, has, in a real way, made God vulnerable. Creation is the work of authentic love, not simply the effortless expression of the divine will. God's creative activity sets no limits to its own self-giving. It seeks constantly to enlarge the creature's capacity to receive. In creating, God holds nothing back.

Seen from God's side, creation may be considered as a sort of yielding, a making room for an "other." In order to create a world "outside," God must have made room for finitude in Godself. The "nothingness" in the *creatio ex nihilo* comes to be because God withdraws God's overwhelming presence and restricts God's power. This self-restricting love is the reason for the self-emptying of God in creation and the self-emptying that Philippians 2 sees as the mystery of the incarnation. In creation, as in the incarnation, God has taken the form of a servant.

The astonishing awareness that God has limited Godself in creation was dramatically expressed by the sixteenth-century Kabbalist Isaac Luria. Luria writes of the divine contraction *(Tsimtsum)*, of the withdrawing of God, an inversion of God. God's "contraction" becomes a creative force that makes room for creation.[54] Creation emerges as empty space, as God-forsaken space, as space set free for creation's own creativity. How empty a space the kenotic God has made available can be grasped when we consider the role of chance and the risks God takes in creation. For Peacocke:

> The attribution of "self-limitation" to God with respect to his omnipotence is meant to indicate that God has so made the world that there are certain areas over which he has chosen not to have power (for example, human free will, as generally recognized by theologians). Similarly, the attribution of "self-limitation" to God in regard to his omniscience is meant to denote that God may also have so made the world that, at any given time, there are certain systems whose future states cannot be known even to him since they are in principle not knowable (for example, those in the "Heisenberg" range and certain non-linear systems at the macroscopic level). If there is no particular point in time of which it could truly be said of those systems "this will be its future state," then it could not be known at any instant, by God or by us, what the future state of such systems will be. It seems that God has made the world so that, in these systems, he himself does not know their future states of affairs, since they cannot be known.[55]

If events in the subatomic range can be said to be unpredictable, this must be equally true of events in the human context of personal freedom. In a kenotic creating of the world, God willingly relinquishes God's absolute power or omniscience over events.

Such an approach to creation implies the radical rejection of extrinsicism. The infinite is immanent in the finite not by absorbing or destroying it but by taking on its finitude and existence. The infinite exists in and through the finite, but is never identical with it. The mode of God's immanence is not identity, but transcendence, and God's transcendence consists in the fact that God does not remove the difference between God and what is "other," but rather accepts the "other" precisely as different. God frees human beings to be human and the world to be secular. As Walter Kasper writes, "The intensity of creation's independence grows in direct and not inverse ratio to the intensity of God's action."[56]

In creation God determines God's own being as interactive; in so doing God actualizes God's own nature in particular, contingent ways as the One who is love. The relationship of God to the world must be a reciprocal, dialogical one. God cannot be understood as unilaterally significant to the world. The world and human history are also significant to God. Creation is a work of divine humility, and through this humility God is made vulnerable to creation; God is not, cannot be indifferent. While creation is marked by God's own imprint, namely, the image of God, God in a real but different way is marked by the world.

Creation and the Suffering of God

God's activity in creation is precarious. If creation is the work of love, then its shape cannot be predetermined. God is determined to be God only in relationship to God's creation. That is the risk of God's infinite love. Eternal love can become suffering love precisely because it has laid itself open to refusal. As J. Moltmann writes:

> God is not *unchangeable* if to be unchangeable means that he could not in the freedom of his love open himself to the changeable history of his creation. God is not *incapable of suffering* if this means that in the freedom of his love he would not be receptive to suffering over the contradiction of man and the self-destruction of his creation. God is not *invulnerable* if this means that he could not open himself to the pain of the cross. God is not *perfect* if this means that he did not in the craving of his love *want* his creation to be necessary to his perfection.[57]

Moltmann goes on, "God takes man so seriously that he suffers under the actions of man."[58] In the suffering of love we voluntarily open up to the possibility of being affected by another. While we may rightly deny that God is capable of suffering out of deficiency, we may not therefore assert that God is incapable of suffering out of the fullness of God's being, out of love. Contrary to Greek thought, God suffers not out of imperfection but out of the plenitude of God's love.

While God transcends history, history is important and makes a difference to God. There is therefore a helplessness in God that is corollary to the character of creation and incarnation. This helplessness is freely chosen and not ultimate. Divine omnipotence may be defined as the ultimate triumph of God's unchanging will of love. The key word here is *ultimate*. God has freely accepted temporal helplessness in the interest of open personal relation with God's creatures. There is real interdependence and reciprocity between God and the world. This interdependence does not spring from the limitation of God's essential being but from voluntary self-limitation.

Because creation is an act of self-limitation, God in some mysterious way has accepted a disadvantage, to be at the mercy of creation. Simone Weil has underlined this paradoxical nature of God's love: "A victim of misfortune is lying in the road, half-dead with hunger. God pities him but cannot send him bread. But I am here and luckily I am not God. I can give him a piece of bread. It is my one point of superiority over God."[59] Divine creativity involves risk, the risk of being denied. The creating God is not, according to Hans Küng, "a God of solitude, but a God of partnership, of the covenant. He is not an apathetic, unfeeling, impassible but a sympathetic, compassionate God."[60] God's power resides in the ability to evoke a response while respecting the integrity of "the other." In that process God is open to refusal and therefore to suffering.

Suffering, in God, does not spring from the limitation of God's essential being but from the voluntary self-limitation and self-expression entailed by God's love for others. The suffering of God does not imply the limitation of God's essential nature; rather it signifies God's strength to self-limit. To say that God suffers is to say that God is actively engaged in dealing with a history that is real to God. At no point does God overwhelm human freedom. The genuine freedom of the created to do what God has not willed is guaranteed by the self-limitation of God in bringing freedom into being. It is thus that freedom is real, that the future is open, that history is history. God acts in the future through our freedom and is limited by our freedom. The future is undecided and thus unknowable, in principle even to God. God, as the eternal One, does not merely establish time by creating it but freely assumes it as a specification of God's own self. As D. Dawe writes:

> In creation, God accepted the limitation of co-existence with
> man and the world, which have their own creativity and free-
> dom. Hence as long as there is a real human history in which
> men are acting freely and as long as God is concerned with
> men, there is some aspect of the divine being that is only
> potentially perfect. If God has a relationship with creation,
> and the created order has some measure of freedom, then

there is an element of openness or incompleteness in the divine being.[61]

God is Creator precisely in relation to a created world. To understand God fully as Creator one must modify the Aristotelian conception of God as unchangeably self-sufficient impassible being. The concept of the impassibility and immutability of God is in fact ambiguous. Classically understood, it means that God is not moved by anything outside of God. Yet God is not eternally Creator; nor was God eternally incarnate. God was free to become the Creator and to move outside of Godself. As John O'Donnell writes:

> The Christian God is not the absolute, the impassible God of classical philosophical theism, rightly rejected by atheists. The Christian God is the God who suffers in time, who enters our history in the event of Jesus Christ. To think of God in the light of this event is to think of a God whose being is in coming. God's coming to man proceeds from his sovereign freedom of overflowing love. In this sense God's coming is grounded in his transcendence. But since God's being itself is his coming, we cannot think of God without his creation or without man. Man is not accidental or external to God but through the unfathomable mystery of his love part of God's own self-definition.[62]

God's freedom to act is anchored in love and is therefore characterized by unchangeableness. The unchangeable quality in God is God's will to love, God's unswerving faithfulness to God's covenant. This divine immutability is not to be understood in terms of something static but as dynamic and historical. This implies the dynamic capacity for infinite responsive change in the interests of God's fixed purpose of love. In the holy "mutability" God has the ability to remain integrated in the fulfillment of the fundamental purpose of love. God's selfhood endures unimpaired, no matter how deeply and intimately God becomes involved with creation, with God's people. If anything is immutable in God, it is the completeness of God's love for us, which must include responses to our ever-changing needs.

The change that is denied to God is a change that rests on the incompleteness of the subject, whose potency is not yet fully actualized. If God is God, then such a mutability is impossible. But does change always involve imperfection, a transition from potency to act? The whole question here consists in the understanding of perfection. How may God's perfection be properly conceived of? How can God be predicated as the perfect reality and yet be open to change and growth? *Immutable* and *changeless* may be useful words to describe the being of God; they do not provide a useful understanding of God as personal agent, of God in God's relatedness. The Bible describes God as involved with creation, and creation as a kenotic act of God cannot be understood through the language of stasis. Political thought is dominated by a highly personal conception of the doctrine. This personalism is best characterized by the attribute of freedom ascribed to God. God is not determined by metaphysical necessity; God is determined by God's faithful love.

God's becoming is not the fulfilling of a need because of which God must be dependent on others, but rather the communication of God's richness by which, in complete freedom, God chooses dependence on another. God does not change nor is God changed for God's own fulfillment. We are saying too little if we praise God as a mover who always remains unmoved. God changes as God causes the being and becoming of the realities God has created, and God does so in a fully divine way without compulsion, in freedom and in love. The immutability of God is a dialectical truth like the unity of God. Karl Rahner has attempted to explain this dialectic in the following way: Although God "is immutable in and of himself, he himself can become something in another."[63] Rahner recognizes that this possibility is not rooted in an imperfection, "but [is] the height of his perfection. This perfection would be less perfect if he could not become less than he is...The absolute, or, more correctly, the absolute One in the pure freedom of his infinite unrelatedness, which he always preserves, possesses the possibility of himself becoming the other, the finite."[64] This possibility is the possibility of kenosis; "the other" is established as God's own reality through a dispossession of self, through a giving away of self. While in creation this kenosis is not complete, not full, and therefore "the other" established by God is not fully himself, yet creation is still the becoming of God in "the other." God, as personal agent, is changed and affected existentially, not structurally, by the creation of "the other." The change is dialogical; God's personal being is enriched or depleted by the character of our relationship with God. God has willed to be God not only interiorly but also for us, and this decision affects God's own being.

Peter Hodgson writes: "God will not be the same God upon the consummation of all things and their return to the Father as he was prior to the act of creation. In this sense he will have 'become' something 'other' and will have experienced something 'more' than was the case when God was God for himself alone."[65] Creativity at whatever level is affirmation of the Other, a giving of being, a sharing. *Actio fit in passo;* that is, the activity of the agent is in "the other," is "the other" as brought into being, "the other" who is a center of action and creativity.

Freedom is real. Things have come to be through a process of evolution. One cannot hold on to a God who is conceived as omnipotent and in control of everything. It is also unacceptable to perceive a world history laid down from eternity and manipulated by God. Our freedom at some point leaves God genuinely helpless. There is an intimate connection among freedom, luck, and helplessness.

Clearly a concept of creation that respects human freedom demands that God's attributes be reconsidered. In the past theologians concentrated on the doctrines of divine omnipotence and divine infinity. If creation unfolds in an evolutionary way and emerges in forms of autonomy, God's attributes of omnipotence and infinity must be in some way limited. One of the first things the scriptures say about God is that God is love. But if God is truly omnipotent, and the idea of God involves omnipotence, then there is no force outside of God that can limit God; omnipotence can be limited by nothing other than love. The power of God must be the power of love, which is therefore the power over Godself, the power of self-limitation. This self-limitation, this kenosis, must be the precondition for the emergence of free self-conscious persons. Such an act of self-limitation is consistent with and expresses the biblical affirmation that the character of God is marked by love. For in the context of human love (human love being our only access to divine love), love is most manifest in self-limiting for the sake of "the other." In the Judeo-Christian context such a love can be affirmed of God.

Yet God's omnipotence, as Walter Kasper has so clearly expressed, and the revelation of God's love are not contraries. God does not strip away God's omnipotence in order to reveal God's love. On the contrary, it requires omnipotence to be able to surrender Godself, to give away Godself; it requires omnipotence to be able to take Godself back in the giving and yet preserve the independence and freedom of the recipient. Here we have reached the key point: God's self-emptying, weakness, and suffering are not the expression of a lack, as they are in finite being; neither are they the expression of fated destiny. If God suffers, then God suffers in a divine manner. Divine suffering is an expression of divine freedom; suffering does not befall God, rather God freely allows it to touch Godself. God does not suffer as creatures do, from a lack of being; God suffers out of love and by reason of God's love, which is the overflow of God's being.

Love is supremely manifest in self-limiting and costly action on behalf of another. Authentic love is precarious; it risks rejection. Love requires involvement. The primary attribute of God in the scripture is that God is a God of love. The right order of priority in understanding the attributes of God is surely to take God's love as central and modify our ideas of omnipotence. While omnipotence can be limited by nothing else, it is limited by love. Love places restraints on power. God's omnipotence is not simply over creation but over Godself. As W. H. Vanstone writes:

> The infinity of the universe must be understood, with awe, as the expression of the consequence of the limitlessness of the divine self-giving: for the divine aspiration to give must ever enlarge the bounds of that which is to receive. Nothing must be withheld from the self-giving which is creation: no unexpended resources of divine power or potentiality: no "glory of God" or "majesty of God" which may be compared and contrasted with the glory of the galaxies and the majesty of the universe: no "eternity of God" which might outlive an eternal universe. It is to be understood that the universe is not to be equated with "that which science knows," nor even with "that which science might, in principle, come to know": the universe is the totality of being for which God gives himself in love.[66]

Creation and the Omnipotence of God

Creation may be termed an act of God's omnipotence, but this power is not power as we understand it in human affairs. Power is commonly understood as domination—the control of things, events, and persons. MacGregor writes, "God does not wield power over his creation; on the contrary, he exercises it in the creative act, and the exercise of it is the exercise of his love."[67] God's omnipotence is characterized by the fact that God's power is to be comprehended as effective even in apparent weakness. In God, power and love are simply two sides of the same reality. Because God's creative power is the power of love, God's creating is a letting-be. Love not only permits "the other's" otherness but actually makes it possible and requires it. The desire to be certain of "the other," to guarantee "the other's" response, is a violation of otherness and love. This can amount to little more than an attempt to control and hence to reduce "the other" to an instrument of one's interests and purposes. So Vanstone observes:

> The activity of God in creation must be precarious. It must proceed by no assured programme. Its progress, like every progress of love, must be an angular progress—in which each step is a precarious step into the unknown; in which each triumph contains a new potential of tragedy, and each tragedy

may be redeemed into a wider triumph; in which, for the making of that which is truly an "other," control is jeopardized, lost, and, through activity yet more intense and vision yet more sublime, regained; in which the divine creativity ever extends and enlarges itself, and in which its endeavour is ever poised upon the brink of failure. If the creation is the work of love, then its shape cannot be predetermined by the Creator, nor its triumph foreknown: it is the realization of vision, but of vision which is discovered only through its own realization: and faith in its triumph is neither more nor less than faith in the Creator Himself—faith that He will not cease from His handiwork nor abandon the object of His love. The creation is "safe" not because it moves by programme towards a predetermined goal but because the same loving creativity is ever exercised upon it.[68]

A kenotic understanding of the Creator God is best supported and framed in a process approach, as found in the work of Alfred North Whitehead and Charles Hartshorne. Process theology, influenced by process philosophy, is an attempt to rethink the doctrine of creation especially as this doctrine affects our understanding of God's relation to the world. For process philosophy, reality is not understood primarily in the category of substance but as a flux of events. Here being is conceived temporally and characterized by possibility. Temporality is the place for the shaping of finite being. To Langdon Gilkey, process thought has offered "a magnificent vision of process as characterized by both actuality and possibility, destiny and freedom, permanence and change, order and novelty..."[69] For process theology God is understood as the ground for the creative interrelations between actuality and possibility, between novelty and order. Being in its totality arises from God, for God is at once Creator and preserver of the finite creation in all its aspects. Yet God alone does not create the present; rather, divine creativity establishes a self-creative process. God creates by giving to all reality in its possibility the power of self-creation.

In process theology the immanence of God entails God's own temporality. God participates in passage. God's temporality, however, does not entail contingency, because God's being does not emerge out of an actualizing process. Gilkey notes:

He is the ground of being of *all* process and thus as the condition for each moment is present in each moment—and thus transcendent to its moving moments. As the power of being of each moment, he is in each moment and yet above it, not carried away by it into non-being but present and effective there out of the necessity of his own being. He is *a se* as the continuing, creative and so temporal ground of temporality.[70]

God's kenotic immanence is such that the distinction between actuality and possibility applies even to God. For God, the future is not actuality but possibility. God knows the future as future and not as actual. The future is open, and there can be no specific foreknowledge. Process theology offers the most coherent reasons for affirming that God can be the subject of change. Gilkey writes: "As creative power God is related to actuality as actuality and to possibility as possibility. Consequently, as possibility becomes actuality, as change and process occur, God's creative and providential relations to process themselves change, and God's experience and knowledge of his world change."[71] As creation evolves and changes, so does God; God's relation to the world is not a fiction of the mind but is real and essential.

While Whitehead's perception of creativity as the very nature of reality may be difficult to harmonize with the traditional understanding of creation *ex nihilo,* his concept of the kind of causality necessary in the process of creativity can be of real value for a kenotic understanding of creation. Whitehead's concepts of persuasive agency and of relationality are of particular relevance. Process theology affirms that God has power, but it is understood as the evocative power of love and inspiration.

The basis of process theology is the co-creativity of God and God's world. Such a co-creativity involves more than the authentic and responsible causality of secondary causes. The very elements of reality at a subatomic level participate in the co-creation of the world—God's creative presence is everywhere present offering occasions. God is seen to invite all created reality to its ultimate purpose.

In such a model of creation, divine causality cannot be characterized by domination or determinism. God does not interfere in creation, but in a patient, subtle manner sustains the universe, which God still influences through a continuous and flexible creativity. God's power is to be perceived as shared and mutual. The God of process theology is a God-in-relation. God is supremely in relation to all things, luring all reality to actuality, and simultaneously supremely influenced and moved by the world.

God's kenotic immanence and presence to creation means, in Peacocke's words, that God "suffers in, with and under the creative processes of the world with their costly, open-ended unfolding in time."[72] One can speak of the suffering God not only in the context of the cross but in relation to creation. It is thus that one speaks of salvation in relation to creation. As E. Schillebeeckx writes: "The experience of creation, a historically variable experience of fortuitousness and contingency, seems to me to be the permanent breeding ground for any experience of the saving nearness of God, and also for example the special experience that is to be found in Jesus and in the liturgy."[73] To create in a kenotic way is to prepare the way for salvation. Creation envisages salvation as its gracious crown. Seen from within the context of creation, salvation is not merely rescue. And such a salvation is not without cost.

Creation is indeed an original blessing that always comes to human beings, because of their freedom, with the possibility of refusal, and the possibility has, of course, become an actuality. As a species we have, on a significant scale, refused to cooperate with the Creator. In theological terms, redemption is not discontinuous with creation; it is not a redesign initiative on God's part. Redemption is God's answer to the human refusal to cooperate with God's creative purposes.[74]

Creation is cruciform; it is advanced not only by thought and action but by pathos, by suffering. So, for Holmes Rolston, "The God met in physics as the divine wellspring from which matter-energy bubbles up, as the upslope epistemic force, is in biology the suffering and resurrecting power that redeems life out of chaos."[75]

While redemption within the framework of the cross has been perceived primarily as redemption of sinful humanity, seen from the context of creation redemption has an ecological dimension. It has become clear that nature needs to be redeemed because of humanity's sinfulness.

Nature has been redeemed across the last several billion years, but the current threat is the greatest that nature has yet faced. Unless we can in the next millennium, indeed in the next century, regulate and control the escalating human devastation of our planet, there will be little or nothing to worry about after that. To recall the Pauline lament, the creation is being subjected to futility, and it cannot be set free from this degradation until the human race rises to its glory, imaging God and governing in suffering love. Does nature need to be redeemed? It can, it must, and let us work and pray that such redemption is at hand.[76]

Creation and Human Responsibility

In much contemporary theology concern for creation has been reduced to the anthropological and personal dimension; nature is considered profane and abandoned to science. This concept of secularization has been called into question by the growth of ecological consciousness. In an earlier theology humanity stands above nature as the image of God, while nature is understood instrumentally as an object of human use and abuse. But in our view of creation God can no longer be seen as a reality outside or apart from the reality of nature. The "new heaven and the new earth" of the scriptures cannot refer simply to the "new person." The new creation implies the first creation, which does not simply have a protological significance but also an eschatological one. A kenotic understanding of creation implies, even demands, a sacramental view of nature. As Peacocke has made clear:

> The created world is seen by Christians as a symbol because it is a mode of God's revelation, an expression of His truth and beauty which are the "spiritual" aspect of its reality; it is also valued by them for what God is effecting instrumentally through it, what He does for men and through it. But these two functions of matter, the symbolic and instrumental, also constitute the special character of the use of matter in the particular Christian sacraments. Hence, there is in each particular sacrament the universal reference to this double character of created physical reality and, correspondingly, meaning can be attached to speaking of the created world as a sacrament or as sacramental.[77]

As sacramental, creation requires a different attitude than that of stewardship. Humanity's role in relation to creation must take on a priestly character.[78]

Conclusion

A theology of creation is a theology about God and about God's creatures. While these two realities can never be separated, in this chapter I have looked at the nature and character of the God who creates. In a Christian context it is impossible to ignore the fact that God must be confessed as Creator. The God-Creator of the scriptures is manifested and characterized in many ways. This God is transcendent and immanent, a God who acts in history, nature's God. God creates and redeems. To confess God as Creator is to emphasize God's immanence, not simply God's transcendence; it is to question the depth of God's immanence and of God's presence in a world characterized by chance, order, and human freedom. The mode of God's action in the world reveals the character of God. One may deny that God acts in the world or one may affirm that God intervenes directly and sporadically in creation; both affirmations say something about the character of God. Christianity is committed to the confession that God is present to and acts in the world. Yet an unrestrained interventionism, while fulfilling deep and pre-reflective religious instincts, presents serious problems for a larger understanding of creation.

Creation demands a process of self-limitation on the part of God—a kenosis. Creation, as science continues to make evident, is dynamic and characterized by becoming. Our universe is an unfinished universe, one involved in an evolutionary process characterized by trial and error, struggle, and suffering. A kenotic approach emphasizes divine immanence while safeguarding transcendence; it can express the meaning of creation *ex nihilo* and of creation as an act of self-communication. A kenotic understanding of creation views God not as the cosmic clockmaker, not as the absolute monarch, but as the husbandman in the vineyard of the world, fostering and nurturing its continuous growth throughout the ages. This is God as "the Great Companion, the fellow-sufferer who understands."[79] Kenosis provides the primary reason for the mystery of creation. A kenotic approach to creation holds together both immanence and transcendence. It perceives creation to be "*in* God and *of* God." God the Creator is the God in whom "we live, and move and have our being" (Acts 17:28).

CHAPTER NINE

Jesus Christ and Authentic Humanness

T he kenotic Christologies of the nineteenth century were attempts within the orthodox framework of Chalcedon to emphasize the truth of the "truly human." These Christologies intended to deal seriously with emerging concepts of personality in the area of psychology and the new emphasis given to the historicity of the Jesus of the gospel in exegesis. The contemporary cultural issue, as we have seen, is the question of authentic humanity.

In this century there has also been an emphasis on the humanity of Jesus. This is evident in Karl Rahner's important essay "Current Problems in Christology," which considers the formula of Chalcedon and re-emphasizes the integrity of Jesus' humanity as it is united with the divinity.[1] For many theologians such an emphasis related to an emphasis on discipleship. Vatican II also stressed the humanity of Jesus. It did so in the context of its understanding of the church's mission. The preface of *Gaudium et Spes* declares: "It is man himself who must be saved; it is mankind that must be renewed. It is man therefore, who is the key to this discussion, man considered whole and entire with body and soul, heart and conscience, mind and will."[2] Chapter IV of *Gaudium et Spes* repeats with greater emphasis what it had already stated in the preface:

> All we have said up to now about the dignity of the human person, the community of mankind, and the deep significance of human activity, provides a basis for discussing the relationship between the Church and the world and the dialogue between them. The Council now intends to consider the presence of the Church in the world, and its life and activity there, in the light of what it has already declared about the mystery of the Church.[3]

Gaudium et Spes sees the paradigm of humanity revealed in the person of Jesus. It presents Jesus Christ as the revealer of the truth about humanity and humanization. He is presented as the true answer to the question about humanization.[4]

The Historical Jesus

Such an emphasis on the humanity of Jesus was made within the framework of the Chalcedonian dogma; that is, in Jesus we have someone who is truly human, truly divine, truly one: one person and two natures. Here the fundamental issue is that of discovering the authentic humanity of Jesus, of determining the range of possibilities and limitations for one who is at once divine and human. This is a dogmatic concern, but it is not unrelated to what has occurred in the area of New Testament exegesis. The concern of New Testament exegesis is to recover the historical Jesus. The variety of interpretations regarding his earthly existence converges with more dogmatic understanding concerning the authenticity of Jesus' humanity. Dogmatically, one can refer to the earthly Jesus; exegetically, this earthly Jesus cannot be recovered. The "historical Jesus" is simply "the Jesus whom we can recover and examine by using the scientific tools of modern historical research."[5] According to the dogma of Chalcedon it is the same Jesus, the earthly Jesus, who is truly divine, truly human, truly one, the Second Person of the Trinity. Yet if this Person was truly human, he has, arguably, left historical traces that can be recovered subject to the limitations of a scientific historical approach. Exegetes are attempting such a retrieval, and the titles of their books reveal what they believe the historical Jesus to have been, for example, a marginal Jew or a Mediterranean peasant.[6]

In Christology, while dogmatic and historical concerns are not to be thought identical, they clearly cannot and ought not be separated. Faith in Jesus as God-man does not simply emerge out of historical research. Certain historical discoveries about Jesus could certainly make faith in Jesus untenable. A kenotic understanding of Jesus' humanity seems to best respect both the ontological and historical concerns.[7]

In the mystery of the incarnation God, through an act of self-emptying, a kenosis, brings about the reality that is Jesus, a personal, human reality. Since Jesus is brought into being as person, the mystery of the incarnation is not a one-sided mystery, exclusively of God; Jesus' freedom and acceptance are crucial elements. The symbol of the incarnation points to God's self-communication, God's kenosis, but it also points to Jesus' kenosis.

Jesus is savior from within. The appearance of Christ within human history is not simply a breakthrough from above. It does not simply touch from outside. Jesus as the Son of God emerged within history like any other person: "Born of a woman, born under the law" (Gal 4:4). Jesus as the Christ, as the Son of God, was fully involved in the universal historical situation, which Paul describes as a state of accursedness, and which modern authors have regarded as one of alienation.

There is a self-communication from the divine and the human elements of the incarnation. In this sense the incarnation is process, and it has a dynamic character. It is not a question of the Logos simply being implanted in a human reality at conception or at any other time. Conception and birth represent the beginning of the incarnational process, not a completed process. Personhood cannot be understood simply as a substance injected into a body at conception. Personhood arises; it is brought about in the deeds and decisions of life; it is essentially historical. Personhood implies and demands an embodied existence in the world, an ongoing exercise of acceptance, the acceptance of freedom. Such an acceptance may never be understood as a once-and-for-all act; it is essentially historical, always in process. The mystery of the incarnation extends across the life history of Jesus and over human history. In Jesus the divine is revealed in terms of the human. God's presence, therefore, is still withheld in some fashion. The drama of incarnation is not yet completed; it has an eschatological dimension. The entire life of Jesus, his ministry and death, are elements of God's incarnational act. Jesus' acceptance is sealed on the cross in an ultimate act of trust and acceptance of the Father's will. The Father's acceptance is consummated in the resurrection of Jesus.

Jesus as Historical Person

Jesus' personhood, and therefore his Christhood, are realized progressively. There is growth and development. What is being affirmed here is that Jesus in all his reality is marked by history. Not only does God enter into history, but God also accepts it and embraces it. John writes, "The Word became flesh and made his dwelling among us" (Jn 1:14). The Savior is immersed in the full human condition. In the language of the Bible, *flesh* does not simply mean the material part of the person but the whole person as viewed in its wretchedness. God became not simply man but a wretched human being, fully subject to the human condition. God's way is the way of "enfleshment."

If we deny Jesus' historicity we attack the full humanity of Jesus.[8] A classical formulation can be stated as follows: Christ is not a historical "person"; his person is the divine person, who assumes in himself all history, but who is not "exhausted" in time. History, however, cannot be understood as accidental, extrinsic, adventitious to human existence.[9] History is not simply an epiphenomenon of a human nature that remains static and totally unaffected; the human nature itself is historical. As historical, Jesus' existence is carried out in a situation defined and characterized by history. This situation makes some things possible and others impossible. It is essential to Jesus' humanity that his history be the result of his personal decisions. These decisions, conditioned by time and space, historical in their essence, are of necessity the source of Jesus' history.[10]

From classical Christology we have inherited the teaching that Jesus was simultaneously *viator et comprehensor,* earthly pilgrim and possessor of the heavenly vision. In this view the pre-existent Second Person of the Trinity is understood as having chosen his own situation from all eternity. But if Jesus is characterized essentially by history there cannot be any pre-existent choice of the circumstances of his own life; these are brought about in time and space. Pre-existent choices would nullify genuine human destiny and history, and Jesus' history would be robbed of its actual source, the personal decisions of the man. It is not possible for Jesus to be simultaneously completed and on the way to completion, a pilgrim. These two are mutually exclusive. Any attempt to bring these two states together leads to a dualistic Christology. In an enhypostatic Christology the question of Jesus' full humanity becomes problematical, since the attributes of divinity are not simply different from those of humanity but are at times incompatible, the subject of both sets of attributes being the same subject, the Second Person of the Trinity.

Jesus' Knowledge

Traditional Christology has attributed unlimited knowledge to Jesus. Given beatific vision from the first moment of conception, he was also granted possession of all acquired and infused knowledge.[11] He possessed a clear grasp of his identity as the Second Person of the Trinity and a detailed knowledge of all that would happen to him during his lifetime. Such declarations appear mythological and are in real conflict with the New Testament's description of Jesus' ministry, where development in understanding, profession of ignorance, real suffering, and even abandonment are attributed to him.[12] According to B. Vawter, Jesus

> is shown as a man bearing the stamp of his times, as modern research into ancient religion and culture demonstrate clearly, and with ever-increasing precision. We almost have the impression that the only original thing about him was his own personality and the unique manner in which the influence of his milieu was concentrated in him—though every single human being is in his own way a unique sounding-board for his milieu.[13]

Theology during and after the Middle Ages conceived the psychology of Christ as man not merely in ontological terms but also on the basis of the perfection that on a priori grounds was considered befitting a divine person. We place greater emphasis on the words of scripture

(Heb 4:15) as cited in the Council of Chalcedon: "similar to us in all things save sin."[14] To think of Jesus as truly a man is to think of him as a historical being, growing in wisdom, grace, and maturity in a determinate social and cultural milieu.

Human reality as conditioned by history projects itself into the future. It is a self-creative task, a dynamic movement made up of inward decisions and commitments and of outward behavior, actions, and relations. Jesus was faced with the challenge of realizing his own humanity. That such self-realization can occur only within a human community is an opinion that has led to a new emphasis on and evaluation of language. Self-consciousness, it is argued, arises only in the presence of and in dialogue with an "other," with a "thou." Human life is authentically human when it occurs in dialogue; "subjectivity is always 'intersubjectivity,' and humanity, always co-humanity, and responsibility, the necessity of giving a response."[15]

Jesus must be understood in his human uniqueness—understood as being not contingently but necessarily in relation, as being at the center of an infinitely complex network of relations. Without this complexity, he is not to be understood. It was as a Jew, not as a man in general, believing in the divine in general, that Jesus trusted God. Jesus cannot be emancipated from his Jewishness, as he cannot be emancipated from history. It follows that Jesus' mind was formed by the tradition he inherited and the particular culture in which he lived.[16] As a human person Jesus is part of a flow of connectedness. Such movement is dynamic; it involves change. The human person is a mystery because its humanity is not a possession, not something already attained. We do not come into existence ready made. We have our being through a long period of growth and development.

We most truly experience this in the realm of knowledge and will. Yet the idea of the human, the foundation of the classical theory regarding Jesus' knowledge, is profoundly Hellenistic in nature. Human perfection is measured in terms of clear knowledge, of vision. From this standpoint history is perceived as accidental to human existence, as extrinsic to its substance. That which is permanent is of the highest importance. Development, movement, and growth are imperfections.

As a person is marked and conditioned by history, so knowledge and freedom are historical experiences. Knowledge and freedom affect and are affected by the personal openness of human reality to the future. Because it is historical, all human knowledge is basically contextual; dependent on temporary processes, it is therefore developmental in nature. In human existence a lack of knowledge is not merely that, but it is also the source for the venturing of one's own future. The whole range of implicit consciousness, of questions, of provisional interpretations and decisions, is an essential part of this venturing. R. Pesch writes: "Risk is of the essence of the self-perfecting of the finite person in the historical freedom of decision. Risk is involved; committing oneself to what is not totally visible, the hidden origin and the veiled end—a certain manner of not knowing is essential to the free act of a man."[17] If Jesus were omniscient he could not be perfectly human.[18] His immediacy to God does not exclude that process of learning, and of risk.

Kenotic Christology has shown that to have its being from and with God determines the nature of every creature, and the more completely a creature is from God—and therefore united with God—the more it exists in its own particularity. The hypostatic union, therefore, far from excluding real humanity in Jesus Christ, emphasizes the contrary: Christ possesses the perfection of real human existence to the highest possible degree. The communion of Jesus with God can in no way be conceived in a non-temporal way, which would impede the development of his selfhood. Jesus' understanding and knowledge, his acceptance of his mission, his love of God, were shaped by the social context, by the inherited tradition within which he found himself. Such a process is not excluded by Jesus' immediacy to God. Jesus' awareness of the "not yet decided" future is a condition of his human openness and freedom.

In classical Christology it is affirmed that Jesus knew from the beginning what his destiny was to be; his death and resurrection in all their historical details and their redemptive efficacy were known and willed from the beginning. Such an interpretation deprives Jesus of authentic humanity, of the value of his sacrifice, and masks the revelation of God's love for us. Jesus on the cross still trusts in God and throws himself upon the loving power of his Father by unselfishly letting go of his own life. A full knowledge of the future, of his own resurrection, would render Jesus' sacrifice of self meaningless. Jesus faced his future as a mystery and his death with dread yet in faith and hope. He went up to Jerusalem and to his death possessed of a human understanding and with human emotions. He did not act out a script that he already knew by heart. Obedient to his vocation as he perceived it, Jesus entered into events the shape of which was clearly perceived. While his death did not come upon him totally by surprise, yet his knowledge of it was a human knowledge.

Jesus' Self-Understanding

In what way or ways can we inquire into Jesus' self-understanding as a historical person conditioned by time and space and in process of self-completion? More specifically, how may we inquire into his knowledge of his relationship to God? Did he know himself to be, and did he call himself the Messiah–Son of God? Can there be such a separation between the order of being and the order of identity? As Vawter argues,

> To say that Jesus in his earthly life knew and judged himself to be God's natural Son and very God is to assert the unprovable, and from the perspective of the New Testament, the improbable. Had Jesus known such a thing he could hardly have contained his knowledge, yet the gospels are witness that his most intimate disciples did not recognize his essential relation to God prior to his resurrection.[19]

Contemporary theologians are not willing to give an unconditional yes to these questions.[20] Since Jesus is fully human involved in the complexity of a developing human nature, the answers are themselves necessarily complex.

Such a process of self-understanding—and self-consciousness in interaction with others, in openness to what others have to say—is a part of a person's history. Self-awareness is realized in the process of a journey from inarticulation to articulation. "The uniqueness and identity of a person is not constituted by an abstract self-consciousness, but by the particular character and unity of his life history."[21]

Rahner has attempted to construct a Christology based on the dimension of Christ's consciousness. As he sees it, the unity of Jesus' humanity to the Logos is so radical that it must be conscious of itself, for the higher the intensity of being, the more intelligible it is, the more present to itself. The presence of being to self in Jesus is not the source of an objective knowledge but of unobjectified, unthematized consciousness. While the infinite horizon of the human spirit is fulfilled in Christ, Jesus still has a need for experiential fulfillment in the context of a genuine human history.[22]

Jesus' Freedom

To have limited knowledge is an essential part of being human, since history is essential to the same humanness. Limitations also apply, paradoxically to freedom. Authentic freedom demands the possibility of choice in the context of unknown factors and finalities; we must entrust ourselves to a variety of situations and possibilities and to a future that is often unknown. Human freedom is always freedom within a situation, within a context. Freedom, if it is to be authentic, implies the possibility to determine for ourselves a certain course of action within a context relative to various external conditions. Decision, in fact, is an integral and foundational element of freedom. We posit ourselves by making decisions. It is clear that the ability to decide is not a matter of mere spontaneity. It is determined by inner motivation and by social and contextual conditions.

Pesch discusses the generally accepted opinion that Jesus was not free like other men but in some way pre-programmed. It is, he argues,

> a false alternative—Jesus was not free like other people; he was freer to do or not do what he himself wanted, he lived in a liberated freedom, which he preached and passed on. Jesus was not pre-programmed like other people: a wider range of possibilities was open to his freedom because the institution of freedom is not a process which can be pre-programmed, but an endless task which demands inventive spontaneity, creativity, talent for innovation. His task made him free because it bound him completely to the cause of freedom. The "must" under the shadow of which his whole life, his journey to death was passed (Mk 8:31) was a tie to the will of the Heavenly Father who wanted men to be free. Freedom grows at the same rate as the tie to freedom, the tie to God as the source and guarantee of freedom.[23]

There cannot be for Jesus a pre-established plan that he merely fulfills or a pre-existent choice of the circumstances of his life. This would be to nullify the reality of his freedom. For Jesus, the future cannot be an open book. He cannot have knowledge of the infallibility of his success. The future is always ambiguous and Jesus' freedom was and is conditioned by that ambiguity. The outcome of our free decisions is always uncertain this side of death. The early church understood Sonship as expressing and symbolizing Jesus' relationship to God, and we can accept this designation as referring to the humanity of Jesus in its process of completion in obedience and self-surrender to the Father. It is in terms of this self-surrender, which is the nature of his Sonship, that we may speak of Jesus' radical freedom. Radical freedom has been defined as a "freedom which has its source in openness to the free, manifests itself in acts of liberation, and issues in a fulfilled subjectivity."[24] Jesus' life was one of radical openness or obedience to God. His freedom was and is radical because in a fundamental way God's freedom is the reason and condition of Jesus' freedom. For Kasper, "Only the bond with the infinite and absolute freedom of God as the ultimate ground and meaning of man makes the latter free from all claims to absoluteness and thus also free for engagement in the world."[25] Jesus, because of and not in spite of his unity with the Father, embodied the essence of human freedom. This embodiment is expressed in terms of his openness to the Father and in terms of his radical commitment to and communion with the outcast and the oppressed.

Jesus' Sinlessness

This is the context in which we must consider Jesus' sinlessness. The scriptures speak of the sinlessness of Jesus—of his untainted and ongoing openness to God and to the neighbor. In classical theology the doctrine of the sinlessness of Jesus (Jn 8:46, 14:30; 2 Cor 5:21; 1 Pt 2:22; Heb 4:15) has its foundation in the doctrine of the hypostatic unity: the basic affirmation that, for Jesus, there can be no separation from God. Jesus' life is totally centered on God, in doing the will of God. It is a life of community with the Father; a community of will and of mind. On this basis the theological tradition affirms not only a factual sinlessness but also an essential sinlessness.[26] Yet Jesus' sinlessness cannot be an a priori characteristic, because this would destroy his human reality. Sin is not a necessary characteristic of human nature; it is a possibility and a fact. Because he is human, Jesus shares with us the possibility of sinfulness.

Human fallibility is the underlying ontological constitution of human reality establishing herein the possibility of faulted existence. It is not, however, to be simply identified with fault. Human fallibility implies that human freedom is always contextual, conditional, and dialectical. Human freedom exists in the context of polarities; it is marked by conflict and by fragility.[27] Polarities and tensions are not in themselves sinful, although the roots of sin lie in an interior act of the will. Yet unfaulted human existence is empirically impossible because, in a sense, fallibility is simply the susceptibility of human existence, of human freedom to fail. This susceptibility, this fragility, while not the cause of sin, is the pre-condition, the possibility of sin. Sin is not necessary, but it is inevitable. It is not necessary because it cannot be identified with the fallibility of human existence, but it is inevitable because it always happens.

The sinlessness of Jesus cannot be understood in metaphysical relationship to his humanity. It is to be seen as a result of God's self-gift and of Jesus' own response within the full span of his life. Bearing this in mind, we can understand how it is possible to accept fully the affirmation of the scriptures that Jesus was tempted, because it is characteristic of human beings to be tempted. Temptation is not sin but the condition of moral freedom; temptation is the external pre-condition of sin. While sinless in his own individual life, Jesus could not escape being caught up in the disorder of society. The temptations in the desert enact this dimension. As P. Hodgson writes, "The situation for tension, anxiety, or disproportion becomes the occasion for sin only when it is falsely interpreted, which is not purely the product of human imagination but is suggested by a principle or force of evil antecedent to any individual human action."[28] The principal cause of temptation lies in a false understanding of the source of our anxiety.

Jesus, the Man for Others

Even when one has affirmed and accepted the full humanity of Jesus in all its finite and historically conditioned situations, one has still not said enough about Jesus. His humanity is authentic as personal humanity. When we seek out his identity, when we ask who is this Jesus of Nazareth, we discover identity in the reality of his personhood. Jesus is recognized as the person who lives only in and because of his relationship to God the Father and to the outcasts and the abandoned. A man or woman reaches maturity, discovers the meaning of human existence through an ever-growing, ever more authentic oblation and selflessness. It is our discovery of others, and our encounter with them that opens the closed world of our self-centered totalities. In the infinity of the wholly other, we are shown the unique mystery. Jesus does not belong to himself but to the other. He does not exist in and for himself but for the other; he has emptied himself for the sake of the other. It is in love and dedication that Jesus' personhood is consummated. To love means to exist for the sake of the other; the identity of the individual self is not lost but fulfilled, taken up into a higher unity. For Jesus, love took on the form of suffering, self-giving and existence for others, even unto death.

What characterizes Jesus' love for us is its limitlessness: there is no greater love than to lay down one's own life for the other. The cross remains the symbol of Jesus' all giving love; the agony of expressing the depth of such love. The sole restriction upon his expression of love is our limited capacity to receive it. The authenticity of his love implies a totality disproportionate to the limitations of those who are to receive it. Jesus dies abandoned, alone. He accepts the fact that his love contains no assurance or certainty of completion. His love involves the hope that the other may receive; it also involves the possibility of failure.

The precariousness of Jesus' love is experienced in the passivity of "waiting." As we see so clearly expressed in the gospel of Mark, the apostles never understand; they are blind. Jesus must "wait" for them, for their response of receiving, which is the completion of his own activity of giving. Jesus' love is given to others. Jesus gives to others power over himself; the power to make him angry, to cause him grief and joy, to frustrate or fulfill. There is vulnerability in Jesus' love. He surrendered into other hands the issue and outcome of his own aspiration. His life is marked by interdependence. Jesus is not presented as a dictator who deals arbitrarily with human misery from a position of strength that then creates new misery. Jesus transcends humanity by sharing in a humanity that is poor and suffering. His dominion is in no way similar to the domination of the world rulers throughout history. He rules through service, love, and suffering. All force, all power, will come to be judged by the way in which they respect the powerless. We may therefore conclude with Moltmann, "His power is the impotence of grace, the reconciling force of suffering, and the dominion of self-denying love."[29]

CHAPTER TEN

Kenotic Anthropology:
The Issue of Suffering

W hen one confesses that Jesus is Lord, that he is the Christ, there is an understanding that this Jesus has universal significance. For David Tracy, such an understanding implies that Jesus "is disclosive of all reality, is meaningful for our common existence, is central for human understanding of the limitless possibilities of human existence."[1] Jesus reveals what it means to be fully human. Christianity proclaims that in Jesus Christ the meaning for which all human beings strive has been attained in history, that unless one is human as Christ was human one cannot be human at all.

A Christian View of Humanity

Jesus Christ is not only the revelation of the Godhead but also the revelation of human identity. In him the question who is God and who is human is answerable not as two questions but as one. In *Gaudium et Spes*[2] the church associates itself with a new humanism. The divine is not forgotten, but it is understood as implicit in each person's growing responsibility for his or her brothers, sisters, and history. The question about God has become a question about God's presence in human life as Creator and Redeemer. Personal history is the "locus of the supernatural." G. Baum has said that

> Christianity may be called a humanism, to be precise, a Christological humanism. For in Christ is revealed to us who man shall be or, more carefully, who the transcendent dynamism is by which, gratuitously, all men are summoned and freed to become more fully human. Divine grace recreates in men the perfect humanity revealed in Christ. Christianity is humanistic in the sense that it reveals, celebrates, and promotes the entry of all men into greater likeness to Jesus Christ.[3]

According to kenotic Christology, what is remarkable about Jesus, the Christ, is his self-emptying for others. The special action of God in

Christ is that of self-emptying; kenosis is actually *plerosis,* a positive expression of God's glory and the ultimate significance of human existence. To the basic question posed by a hermeneutical approach to Christology—Is there a distinctive Christian view of humanity? or In what way is Jesus Christ the true revelation of authentic humanity?—one must answer that in Jesus kenosis is the revelation of that which constitutes a person's deepest nature, love surpassing itself and emptying itself. Jesus in his life and death has particularized a universal fundamental law: "Whoever would save his life will lose it; and whoever loses his life for my sake and the gospel's will save it" (Mk 8:35).

Creatureliness

The affirmation of humanity as created in God's image, and of Christ as the perfect image of God, emphasizes creation and creatureliness. As the first strophe of the Philippian hymn declares: "He who being in the image of God, did not use to his own advantage his right to be treated as God but he emptied himself taking on the condition of a slave" (Phil 2:6-7). The thought of this strophe becomes articulate in the context of an understanding of Adam, the first man, and the new Adam, Jesus Christ. The first refused to accept his creatureliness, while the second accepts it fully.

In accepting the affirmation that we are "created in the image of God," it is our creatureliness that needs to be emphasized. Creatureliness underlies the fact that our very humanness emerges as a reality that is contextual, embodied, and conditioned. The claim of "the other" is essential.

Creatureliness, by essence, implies the notion of gift and grace. There is always, at the root of all that is, a receiving and a giving. These can never be eliminated. The often radically posited difference between nature and grace should never have been allowed to become a significant one. Creatureliness is always collaboration, humanity co-humanity. There is an original social nature of being from which and by which each person becomes more a person. Singularity and particularity are consequences of historical and social existence. Hans Urs von Balthasar has an interesting observation about this as he meditates on the Genesis narratives:

> It is strange that human nature, obviously quite different from the animals which were already created two by two, has to long for the other. The other is not simply there, but is brought to him by God, a grace, which harms as well as fulfills. For Eve was taken from his side—he has her within him, and yet she is more than he is and cannot be arrived at from him—in sleep, in defenseless ekstasis, which, according to old

theologians, foreshadowed the cross. Why should not Adam's dialogue relationship to God, in which he received through grace a share in the nature of God, have just as much and even more—beyond his natural capacities—awakened him to and given him the power to attain that for which he has always been intended by God?[4]

Even in relation to God, Adam cannot be complete without encountering himself in "the other." This relational dimension of existence underlines the graciousness as well as the precariousness of the process of becoming human.

The essential thing is that the child, awakened thus to love and already endowed by another's power of love, awakens also to the nature of the self and to its true freedom, which is in fact the freedom of loving transcendence from narrow individuality. No one reaches the core and ground of his or her own being, becoming free to the self and to all beings, without having received love.[5]

Deprivation of graciousness and of social encounter constitutes a privation of humanity with, at the least, psychological consequences. The "I" cannot exist without the "you," and it cannot develop its inherent singularity without a significant "Thou." The dignity and integrity of personal humanness are determined by "the other." The self is constituted as a person in its encounter with another. This encounter, which constitutes the individual's own personhood, implies an unconditional invitation to acknowledge "the other," encountered as a person with his or her own dignity and integrity.

Creaturehood and Personhood

The decentering of self is not a harmonious and simple process. "The other," while essential to our personhood, is a threat to our self-integration. This predicament is not only the result of original sin, or of the fallenness of human existence, but it is also the product of our finite creatureliness. Human existence, to be fully personal, demands an openness to an "Other," who is at the source of personal existence. The personal encounter with the "Other," far from being simply the occasion for self-integration, involves an unsettling decentering of our being that opens us to plurality, indeed infinity. Therefore, personhood is open to and has its foundation in the ultimate reality of God. As Hodgson writes:

> Dependence upon and openness to the infinite God do not cancel human subjectivity but rather constitute it within embodied limits; the reality of God as absolute or perfect freedom belongs to the essence of human beings as finite freedom.[6]

To reject creaturehood is to reject our dependence upon other creatures and God, to seek to escape the very conditions that make existence and continuous creation possible. In a traditional religious sense to deny creaturehood is to deny relationship to an ultimate or absolute source. At the same time, the humility of creaturehood is sharpened by the realization of ultimate dependence on God through creatures.

The refusal of creaturehood involves the refusal to be interdependent, the avoidance of the limiting conditions of relationship; it denies the possibility of being shaped by something other than our own choice; it is the refusal of indebtedness. Creatureliness, and therefore contingency, historicity and finitude characterize human existence. An anthropology built on the concept of creation in the image of God must be marked by the same characteristics. Human beings are understood to be created in the image of God and re-created in the image of God, in Jesus Christ. This "given" possesses a nature, which is submitted to history and contingency and which has need of development and process. It is the person in society and in nature, in mutual reciprocity, who is the image of God.

Personal life emerges in the encounter of person with person or personal otherness with personal otherness. Emphasis on creatureliness stresses the pervasiveness of relationality in the structure of everything. The individual is constituted by relationships at all levels. To accept the status of creature is to accept limits as opportunities. To accept the necessity of receiving from others, of relating without acquisitiveness or manipulation, is a kenotic understanding of humanness.

Within a kenotic Christology, anthropology will be developed in a kenotic perspective. It will necessarily focus on the constitutive nature of self-emptying love. Such an anthropology will avoid the idea of a self-positing ego and the error of the radically autonomous subject. The genesis of the self will occur in encounter mediated by a linguistic world. The genesis of the human self will be characterized by exocentricity. Unlike previous idealistic anthropologies, a kenotic approach does not take the fact of self-reflection as the original given of human subjectivity but understands human subjectivity as the consequence of a becoming. The human being as self-conscious ego is constituted through a relation to "the other." Christian anthropology concerns itself with personhood. Personhood as we perceive it from a kenotic perspective suggests a category that cannot be reduced to a traditional notion of the individual. True personhood is achieved through such a becoming, and its context is structured in co-humanity. There can be no authentic personhood without participation in the outward historic life of co-humanity. The self as a person exists in and through deeds and words that reveal it to others. Thus person is sacramental.

The kenotic theme may be found in the personality theories of such people as R. D. Laing and H. Fingarette.[7] These authors tell us that human unfolding and becoming is a painful act. They affirm the paradox that self-realization and self-divestment are mutually reinforcing. A more satisfactory development of a kenotic concept of person is to be found in the works of John Macmurray.[8]

Person as Relational: John Macmurray's Position

It is Macmurray's fundamental contention that a dialogical and act-centered understanding provides the best interpretation of reality. To accept subjectivity as a starting point for dealing with reality threatens to destroy the bridge between subject and object, knower and known. Within the tradition inherited from Descartes, the self is pure subject considered in its moment of reflection while directing its activity to the acquisition of knowledge. Descartes established a dichotomy between the self, constituted by thought, and the body, constituted by extension and understood in purely mechanical terms with the rest of the material universe. The self in reflection can withdraw into itself and into contemplation; it does not act or involve itself with the life of the world, which it perceives as object. For this reason the traditional point of view is not only theoretical but also egocentric. The self in reflection knows the world in isolation. It thus ensures that it will relate to the world only with its imagination and only as a spectator. The traditional theoretical point of view protects the self in reflection from challenge, growth, and change by providing it with a habitation other than the real world. This is the ideal world of the mind, in which the self is guaranteed to discover truth. While the self remains the self in reflection, it remains in a static and impersonal framework. As long as this framework is maintained, a dynamic relationship between the self and "the other" in the real world of real action will not only be unnecessary and undesirable but impossible.

Macmurray contends that the adoption of the "I think" as the starting point of philosophy leads to the impossibility of doing justice to religious experience. "For thought is inherently private; and any philosophy which defines the Self as the Thinker, is committed formally to an extreme logical individualism. It is necessarily egocentric."[9] But religious experience demands that God be seen as a "Thou," as an "Other" who can be related to in a personal way. Otherwise God becomes simply an object of thought, of understanding.

It is Macmurray's aim to leave aside Descartes's starting point and to begin with the fact of existence and the affirmation that "to exist is to have a being which is independent of thought."[10] To exist is not simply to be independent of thought but it is "to be part of the world in systematic causal relation with other parts of the world."[11] In place of Descartes's *cogito,* Macmurray begins with the experience, concept, and phrase "I do." The self is primarily conceived as agent, as doer. And, since primarily conceived as agent, the subject is not isolated but is in relation with others, not "I" alone, but "you" and "I." The idea of an isolated agent is self-contradictory. Any agent as agent is necessarily in relation to "the other." Apart from this essential relation the doer does not exist. Further, "the other" in this constitutive relation must be personal. Persons, therefore, are constituted by their mutual relations to one another.[12]

Person as Agent

If action is primary, thought is secondary, serving the ends of action. Thought is a derivative of experience. When the self is considered as person with action the primary mode of being and thought included as secondary and subordinate, the correlative of the person cannot be the material world nor the organic world. Neither provides the necessary poles for an action that is constitutive of the person. In other words, the self as agent cannot exist in a personal sense in isolation. The personal is constituted by personal relatedness. As a person, I begin to exist as one pole in the complex "you and I." According to Macmurray, "the unit of personal existence is not the individual but two persons in personal relations...we are persons not by individual right, but in virtue of our relation to one another. The personal is constituted by personal relatedness."[13] The process of becoming a person is heterocentric, not egocentric. "The other" is the center of interest and attention.

When the person's primary mode of being is that of agent, the person is also a subject. As subject, however, the person becomes separated from "the other" and withdraws into itself. In subjective withdrawal it is possible to see "the other" objectively. The person is doer and thinker, agent and subject, but the thinker's subjectivity arises as a consequence of an initial encounter and exists for the sake of action. There is both a positive and a negative dimension to the person. For Macmurray, the form of the personal is conceived as a positive that contains and is constituted by its own negative.

The self is at the same time both agent and subject.

> The unity of the Self is neither a material nor an organic, but a personal unity. The logical form of such unity is one which represents a necessary unity of positive and negative modes. The Self is constituted in this capacity for self-negation. It must be represented as a positive which necessarily contains its own negative.[14]

The unity of the person is contrapletal.[15]

The action of the agent involves two aspects: "I move" and "I know." Without knowing there is no action, only happening or personal activity. Moving and knowing are contrapletal. It is not enough to say that the self is agent; one must be able to say that the self is an intentional agent and therefore a thinking agent. The self that reflects and the self that acts are the same self; action and thought are contrasted modes of activity. Nonetheless, it does not follow that they have equal status in the being of the self. In thinking, the mind alone is active. In acting, the body indeed is active, and the body involves the mind in its action. When we turn from reflection to action we do not turn from consciousness to unconsciousness. Action is always intentional; personal action realizes an intention.[16]

Every action involves a transcending of the person's individuality from the self to "the other." As an agent, I transcend myself, my individuality, in my action. However, my transcendence is not my withdrawal into an inaccessible realm of individuality. It is an action with another by which "the other" knows me as a person in relation. Rationality and intentionality are the capacities for self-transcendence. The center of interest resides in another person.

Person as Non-person

By intention, however, I can isolate myself and reduce "the other" to the impersonal. Within the relationship with another person, which is constitutive of my existence, "I can isolate myself from you in intention so that my relation to you becomes impersonal. In this event, I treat you as an object, refusing the personal relationship. This is always possible because the form of the personal involves its own negation. Impersonality is the negative aspect of the personal; since only a person can behave impersonally, just as only a subject can think objectively."[17] Personal knowledge always involves a transcendence of self within its own individuality.

"I can know another person only by entering into personal relation with him."[18] To treat "the other" as an object is also to treat oneself objectively, impersonally. Macmurray observes:

> Since Self and Other are primary correlates, our determina-
> tion of one of them must formally characterize the other
> also...How then is it possible for the Other to be known as
> non-personal? Only by a reduction of the concept of the Other
> which excludes part of its definition; only, that is to say, by a
> partial negation; only by downgrading the "You" and the
> "You and I" to the status of "It." If we do this, however, we
> necessarily reduce its correlate the "I" in the same fashion.[19]

The "I" and the "you" are constituted by their relation; self-knowledge is only possible when I reveal myself to you. "All knowledge of persons is by revelation—my knowledge of you depends not merely on what I do, but upon what you do; and if you refuse to reveal yourself to me, I cannot know you, however much I may wish to do so."[20] Self-revelation is primarily practical; it is "giving oneself away" in contrast to "keeping oneself to oneself." Although self-revelation is action centered, it requires definitive communication. The basic condition for communication is language. Human language reveals that human subjectivity exists only in intersubjectivity with another and for another. The form of the personal emerges as dialogical.[21]

Person as Intentional Agent

The self as person is an intentional agent. There is a difference between what is done and what simply happens; the former is an action, the latter an event.[22] Action can only be understood by reference to the intention of its author. "Actions are the realization of intentions; events, the effects of causes."[23] For each event there is a cause, for each act, a reason—"If we believe a change to be an event, and wish to understand it, we must ask, 'What caused it?'; if we think it an act, we have to ask, 'Who did it, and why did he do it?'"[24] Since action is intentional, the intender, who is the agent, while immanent to his or her action, necessarily transcends it. What has been done, the existent, is what has been determined, and the agent is the determinant. The agent has determined the past yet transcends the past. "His reality as agent lies in his self-transcendence."[25] The terms *transcendent* and *immanent,* which are strictly correlative, refer to the nature of persons as agents. Pure immanence, without transcendence, has no meaning. "Whatever is transcendent is necessarily immanent; and immanence, in turn, implies transcendence."[26]

Person and Freedom

The person as an agent who acts intentionally is characterized by freedom. The agent generates a past by actualizing a possibility. To act is really to determine the future. To be characterized by freedom is to be free to determine the future. "I am free" is the correlate of "I do."[27] The other does not represent a limitation of freedom but its very condition. Real freedom is possible only in solidarity, in being free for others. The freedom of the subject is merely a potentiality; it depends for fulfillment on the encounter between free persons. The social dimension is essential to freedom.

To grasp fully the nature of freedom requires the essential dimension of otherness. It is "the other" addressing me who alone can challenge my egoism, requiring me to take into account another center of meaning and value, another orientation into the world.

Creation, therefore, is the decentering of the self. Its focus is "the other," the neighbor in whose advent we know ourselves. We cannot responsibly avoid relationship. The advent of "the other" reveals that our freedom, insofar as it relates only to itself, is arbitrarily created and is determined by both the physical and the social voluntary. Writing about Genesis 1:26-27, Hodgson affirms:

> In the Genesis passage, human freedom is defined in terms of certain constitutive relationships; the relationship to God, in whose image we are created; the relation to the earth and its living creatures, over which "A Dahm" is to have dominion; and the relation between man and woman as the primordial community in which human being can be free "for the other."[28]

Again, Hodgson writes that "the essence of the human being is created, embodied freedom limited by and reciprocal with the body (both individual and collective, organic and social), an incarnate, contingent, finite freedom, yet still a freedom."[29]

Person and Interdependence

While the person as agent is characterized by freedom, his or her development is dialogical. Development is interpersonal, just as communication is interpersonal. Persons in relation are correlative and mutually evocative. It is not the self that stands as the foundation of our life and thought but self and other. Personal life and dignity emerge not in reflection of the self upon itself, not in isolation from "the other," but in a collaborative movement acting and responding to "the other." The uniqueness and identity of a person are not constituted by an abstract self-consciousness. They are experienced only in the character and unity of his or her life history. The structure of our experience as human beings is such that it depends on the experience of what is other than ourselves. Dependence on what is not ourselves is the core of our reality. Macmurray, referring to the dependence of the child on the mother, writes: "If the 'terminus a quo' of the personal life is a helpless, total dependence on the Other, the 'terminus ad quem' is not independence, but the mutual interdependence of equals."[30]

We need one another in order to be ourselves. "This complete and unlimited dependence of each of us upon the other is the central and crucial fact of personal existence."[31] Absolute autonomy, individual independence is an illusion; the totally autonomous self is a nonentity. "It is only in relation to others that we exist as persons; we are invested with significance by others who have need for us; and borrow our reality from those who care for us. We live and move and have our being not in ourselves but in one another; and what rights or powers or freedom we possess are ours by grace and favor of our fellows."[32]

The basic fact of our human condition is that we are servants of one another, which implies that each of us values all others for themselves. No one outgrows dependence on others or being-for-others. Relational thinking does not posit an ontological difference between realities, including God. It assumes an ontological sameness insofar as the primary kenotic principle of becoming has its verification in all that actually is. In a relational world metaphysical sameness contains the possibility of an infinite degree of variation. From a relational perspective all that actually is is interdependent.

Kenotic love is at the source of personhood. To exist as a person is to be referred to others. Total self-reference brings about the negation of love; dissolution of personhood implies the inability to love. Love is the existential component of personhood. The capacity to love is the capacity to place another within the reality of self-existence in such a way that real modification occurs for each. One can indeed say that the essence of the person is love. Hegel affirms this: "It is in the nature or character of what we mean by personality or subject to abolish its isolation or separateness. In friendship and love, I give up my abstract personality and in this way win it back as concrete personality."[33] He considers true personhood an entering into community with "the other" or a surrendering to "the other." One becomes a person by loving oneself in "the other." In the process of self-emptying the self is enriched and embodied in its presence to others. The person is the bringing together of universality and particularity, the possibility of at once eliminating and possessing distinction.

Personhood and Kenotic Love

In the kenotic way the crucial decision regarding God is made in our relationship to one another. The place for trusting surrender to God is in the love of our neighbor. When we love kenotically, "the other" is radicalized. The New Testament affirms that one who loves one's neighbor has fulfilled the Law. This is the ultimate truth: God has been one's neighbor.[34] In the kenotic life, everyone is our neighbor, whoever happens to be at hand, unconditionally, without discrimination.[35] This is why a kenotic love involves the enemy. As Kierkegaard writes,

> He who in truth loves his neighbour loves also his enemy.
> The distinction, friend or enemy, is a distinction in the object
> of love, but the object of love to one's neighbour is without
> distinction. One's neighbour is the absolutely unrecognizable

distinction between man and man; it is eternal equality before God—enemies, too, have this equality.[36]

There is a permanence to such love, an independence from changes occurring in the neighbor. Such a love is different from other loves:

> You can also continue to love your beloved and your friend no matter how they treat you, but you cannot truthfully continue to call them beloved and friend when they, sorry to say, have really changed. No change, however, can take your neighbour from you, for it is not your neighbour who holds you fast...It is your love which holds your neighbour fast.[37]

Kenotic love is love of the unworthy, the worthless, the lost. The love of neighbor does not arise from nor is it proportional to anything we possess or acquire. Such a love, Outka suggests, "is based neither on favoritism nor instinctive aversion. Its presence is somehow not determined by the other's actions; it is independent both in its genesis (he need not know who I am) and continuation (he may remain my enemy). One ought to be 'for' another, whatever the particular changes in him for better or for worse."[38] There can be no exclusiveness, no partiality, no elitism. Kenotic love is characterized, essentially, by its universality; it is the foundation of interdependence. Interdependence is a way of being, of existing without mastery, without force, without difference in status. In interdependence whatever is superior demonstrates its superiority by its power to empty itself. The abundance of interdependence in reality is revealed in the humiliation of the exalted and the exaltation of the lowly.

Love of Neighbor

The interdependent life is one of radical mutuality and reciprocity, of receiving and of giving, so completely for and from "the other" that nothing is left of self-centeredness. The deepest center of the self is always beyond the individual ego. Human suffering at its deepest level is not the self-suffering of isolated monads.

For-otherness constitutes the person as person. A self turned toward others finds its fulfillment. The issue of authentic selfhood turns on the issue of love for neighbor. We are authentic selves only in direct proportion to our ability to be affected by and related to others. The substance-self of the classical tradition is at best an abstraction. I am the person I am precisely because of my relationship to this history, this family, these friends. I am a profoundly relative, not substantial, being. Whether I know it or not, I am the person I am because this friend, person, idea, has entered my life.

While for-otherness is constitutive of personhood, so is from-otherness. That we derive from others, that we live from others, is fundamental. It is through being loved that we learn to love; we have to receive in order to be able to give. A breakdown in this basic from-otherness may lead to a radical breakdown of self. Since we are neither autonomous nor self-sufficient, we have to receive in order simply to be. Interdependence is the basic structure and dynamic of personal existence. The interdependent life is made up of mutuality, exchange, and reciprocity.

Personhood and Suffering

To be a person means to live for others and to live from others. The fact of our derivation is fundamental. We have to be shaped by others to be who we are. We are always incomplete and never self-sufficient. And so we are intrinsically vulnerable, a fact that leads to the basic issue for any anthropology, the question of suffering.

Suffering occurs because personal existence is interdependent. Suffering results from the malfunctioning of interdependence, which necessarily includes within itself the twofold possibility of fulfillment and suffering.

Suffering in its widest sense means being acted upon. It means to bear, to undergo. There is a basic connotation of passivity in suffering; receptivity is essential to suffering. And yet, despite the essential dimension of passivity in suffering, there is also an existential dimension of activity. In suffering there is not simply a contrast between activity and passivity. Suffering is not to be equated with evil. It is easy enough to identify the two, since suffering is directly or indirectly linked to all forms of evil. Suffering is the price we have to pay for our limitations and our finitude while evil resides in the world. So, according to Lavelle, "there is perhaps no evil in the world that does not bear some relationship to suffering; but evil is not to be identified with suffering; it is the will's attitude toward it that matters. Sometimes the will lets itself be overcome by the suffering in question; sometimes it imposes it on others; and sometimes it accepts it in order to alleviate, enter and transcend it."[39] Just as suffering should not be equated with evil, it is likewise wrong to equate it with pain.[40] Pain has a physical dimension that is not essential to suffering; while pain is endured passively, suffering involves us in an existential dimension of activity. In English one will usually say "I am in pain," while, relative to suffering, one will say, "I suffer." In a sense, pain concerns only part of ourselves while suffering involves the whole self and can penetrate to its essence.

By *suffering* we mean an anguish we experience not only as pressure to change but as a threat to our composure, our integrity, and the fulfillment of our intentions. It challenges our capacity to maintain ourselves and retain the poise of self-direction. According to Heidegger's understanding, suffering appears to threaten annihilation. Suffering discloses our own radical contingency, the fact that ultimately our situation is not of our own making, that it is beyond our control.

The major difference between pain and suffering is that suffering possesses a basic existential dimension. Suffering, as existential, is always an interpersonal phenomenon. Although we experience it as if it were totally within ourselves, both the locus and source of suffering are in relationship. While pain is primarily related to the body and can be inflicted by things, suffering is related to our personhood. We suffer primarily in our relation to others.

> The possibility of suffering measures the intimacy and the intensity of the bonds which unite us to another being. We do not suffer in our relations with those who are indifferent. In fact, indifference in some sense protects us against suffering. When indifference ceases, our capacity for suffering returns, and it is proportionate to our interest in and our affection for one another. It emerges as soon as the bonds which unite us to the other are threatened; it is then that the bonds of friendship testify to their existence and their depth.[41]

Suffering results from the breakdown of interdependence. Because suffering is essentially interpersonal, it has a necessary social dimension. That dimension of suffering has been called affliction. Affliction involves desolation. The infant's most despairing cry is not the one he or she utters when in pain, but the one we hear when the infant feels abandoned, when all cries seem to go unanswered and no familiar face appears. Abandonment and degradation, or the fear of abandonment and degradation seem involved in all forms of affliction. Degradation shows itself in the isolation that invariably accompanies affliction. Lack of solidarity with the afflicted is a common phenomenon. The dimensions of affliction are more fully understood when we realize the significance of our ongoing quest for the esteem of others.

Person, Suffering, and the World of Meaning

Since suffering is essentially interpersonal, it must be considered from within the dimension of human freedom, that is, from within the realm of the will. Suffering viewed from outside the realm of human freedom is clearly absurd. Within the context of freedom, suffering can be given a meaning. As human beings, we are aware of the limitations of our existence, of the uniqueness and unrepeatability of our existence. We infer that the success or failure of our existence is as irrevocable as existence itself. Meaninglessness, lived futility, is as great a threat as death. Meaning transforms the whole person and gives a definite path to existence. Suffering as an interpersonal reality requires to be given meaning. There are two basic questions that need to be asked about suffering: What is its cause? How can it be eliminated? Both questions need to be asked simultaneously if we are to avoid masochism. Suffering always remains an attack on human life. It can never be glorified or sought. Taken by itself, suffering is meaningless.

We must also make a sharp distinction between suffering before which we stand powerless and meaningful suffering. Suffering can be so acute and so long lasting that the sufferer feels powerless to break away from it. In this case the person experiences a total loss of freedom. The prospect for the hopeless sufferer is nothingness; the future does not exist for this person. Certain forms of suffering are so radical that they lead to the abandonment of all hope, to the most extreme forms of apathy. According to Dorothy Soelle, "Feelings for others die."[42] In this condition, everything has become inessential and death is most welcomed. Extreme suffering turns a person in on the self completely; it destroys the ability to communicate.

Only that suffering which can be changed and from which we can learn can be meaningful. Potentially meaningful suffering is suffering that is not completely passive. What we do when we suffer is the active dimension of suffering. It is in this dimension that meaning can be given to suffering; this is the interpersonal realm. The active dimension of suffering involves the opening of the sufferer's horizons and the transcending of self to "the other."[43]

Suffering leads an individual to reality. So says Miguel de Unamuno: "Suffering tells us that we exist; suffering tells us that the world in which we live exists."[44] In suffering we reach our extreme limit, encountering the decisive questions of personal identity, the meaningfulness or futility of existence, or reality as a whole. Suffering proves to be the ongoing test of reality. Suffering challenges our basic trust in existence. Through suffering we begin to answer the question "Who am I?" Thus the possibility of a heightened self-consciousness may accompany suffering.[45] Lavelle has remarked of suffering: "It gives us an extraordinary intimacy with ourselves, it produces a form of introspection in which the spirit penetrates to the very roots of life, where it seems that suffering itself will be taken away. It deepens consciousness by emptying it of all the preoccupying and distracting objects that had hitherto sufficed to fill it."[46]

What is most important about the experience of suffering is that it leads us to the acceptance of self as limited and "the other" as other. It leads to the fundamental acceptance of interdependence, the for-other-ness and from-otherness of personal existence. We do not experience directly the radical dimension of our finitude. What we experience directly are particular expressions of our finitude: suffering, the death of someone close to us, needs of "the other," and our need of them. We become more aware of the radical dimension of limitedness only after reflection upon these particular events. There is a movement from the particular to the universal, from the concrete to the more abstract. From immediate and specific experiences each of us universalizes about our total situation.

Suffering leads to reflection upon the depth of our existence. And because of its interpersonal dimension, suffering can reveal not only our finitude but also the dialogical nature of our existence. When suffering becomes an experience of self-transcendence, it may disclose to us the deepest dimension of our existence: being in community, supported by love. So Viktor Frankl described his experience in a Nazi concentration camp: "In a position of utter desolation, when man cannot express himself in positive action, when his only achievement may consist in enduring his suffering in the right way—an honourable way—in such a position man can, through loving contemplation of the image he carries of his beloved, achieve fulfillment."[47] Marcel recognizes a similar truth: "A complete and concrete knowledge of oneself cannot be egocentric; however paradoxical it may seem I should prefer to say that it must be hetero-centric. The fact is that we can understand ourselves by starting from the other, or from others, and only by starting from them."[48] Suffering can lead to a recognition of the vicariousness of interpersonal existence. Since suffering is caused by the breakdown of interdependence, that interdependence may be restored vicariously by someone not responsible for the original breakdown. This is because vicariousness is a fundamental characteristic of interdependence. Personal life is vicarious because it involves living from and for others. Vicariousness is not something esoteric; rather, it is the fundamental principle of all personal life. Interdependence is broken by self-centering. Vicariousness involves self-giving. Vicarious suffering is only one category of the larger and more general principle of vicariousness. It does not stand alone but presupposes the give and take of ordinary relatedness.

The acceptance of fundamental interdependence is a basic element of love. To love is to accept one's dependence upon "the other." To love is also to accept another who makes his or her own decisions. In loving one makes the history of another's freedom one's own history. The refusal to accept another person's freedom to be and to decide is a failure in love. Love at its most profound level is the acceptance of "the other" without regard for our own well-being; this demands a radical self-emptying. Here love and suffering cohere. Interdependence abused is traumatic and leads to suffering. It is the cessation of self-giving that leads to the breakdown of interdependence. The restoration of inter-dependence involves the restoration of self-giving.

A kenotic understanding of personhood makes it possible to grasp in depth the issue of human suffering. It also illustrates the resources humanity possesses to deal with suffering: vicariousness and compassion. Kenotic personhood implies radical solidarity; we are linked for better or for worse. Kenosis is, in itself, a fundamental feature of solidarity. Solidarity abused is traumatic; upheld and nurtured, it is transformative and salvific. When solidarity is restored, suffering can be transformed.

Personhood and Compassion

There is no love without compassion. One who is compassionate manifests human solidarity by crying out with those who suffer, by feeling deeply the wound of "the other." Compassion invokes our consciousness of the unity of the human race, the knowledge that all people, wherever they dwell in time and space, are bound together by the human condition. Nothing human is foreign to us. Paul Ricoeur writes: "My humanity is my essential community with all that is human outside myself; that community makes every man my like."[49] This sense of self is not based on an understanding of how and where we differ, but on how we are the same. Personal identity is found in the common experience of being human, in compassion, in suffering with others, in real love. Compassion does not lead to commiseration but to comfort, to being strong with "the other."

Shared suffering has the power to create communities of understanding and mutuality. This becomes possible if suffering has been given meaning and if it is communicated to and heard by "the other"; this sharing must occur in some form of dialogue, through communication. Language, as a sign, has an ontological as well as a descriptive purpose. It extends our vision of reality and initiates a process of fuller realization of self. These processes are intertwined. Self-realization is obscured in desolation. Meaninglessness can be avoided through the transcendence involved in the act of dialogue, which brings into consciousness a sense of the actuality of suffering and reveals possibilities that interact in the future determination of that actuality. Dialogue introduces additional possibilities for the determination of a deeper understanding. In dialogue we reach out together for whatever plenitude of meaning can be found in suffering. It is neither possible nor desirable to eliminate the phase of dialogue in the hope that suffering might more quickly be done away with. Without dialogue there can be no change;

causes of suffering can be eliminated but not suffering itself, since it is essentially interpersonal. In dialogue the sufferer finds solidarity, and solidarity is already victory over suffering.[50]

This solidarity is not merely a present reality. It has a historical dimension. If solidarity is understood as constituting an ongoing community of interpretation, it is also constitutive of a historical community of interpretation that transmits present interpretation to future generations. Past sufferings are not remedies for themselves; nonetheless, they give the ongoing community new hope in the present and future. Past memories are not simply recalled but are reinterpreted, reconceived, accepted, and lived within the present. These are dangerous and liberating memories.[51]

CONCLUSION

Toward a Kenotic Church

In a world where evil is so evident and suffering so omnipresent the fundamental question to be asked is whether God makes a difference. The Christian answer must be affirmative, and that it is in and through the person of Jesus that the difference God makes is revealed. Jesus is the grace of God, the new covenant, the new creation. Yet the fundamental question also relates to Jesus himself. What difference does Jesus Christ make? The answer must be: discipleship. This answer can only be fully understood within the perspective of a kenotic Christology.

In a kenotic theology of creation and incarnation God has truly "become flesh." Kenosis means abdication, and the abdication of God means the immanence of God. Transcendence is not extrinsic but intrinsic to human existence, not part of life's superstructure but rather the ground of its possibility. The supernatural is not alien to humans nor is it imposed upon them. So understood, the frontiers between God's work and the human task are not immovable. Human existence, and with it the total temporal structure in its very profanity, becomes both the objective expression of God's self-communication and the objective expression of the human response to that self-giving. God's kenotic immanence as Spirit respects the otherness of creation, its interdependence and freedom. God's kenotic presence and action in the world is characterized by its never being superior to or parallel with the world; it works within history, unobtrusively, even secretly. God is not a cause alongside other causes.

Such immanence takes the whole of creation as its sacrament; the transcendent is disclosed in and through creation. The Word is truly flesh. Such sacramentality is a consequence of God's kenotic activity; therefore no experience of God is possible unless mediated through an experience of the world, because God has emptied Godself in the world: God is Spirit-in-the-world. God is present to the world in stillness, weakness, and powerlessness.

Discipleship

Within a Christian vision of creation God transforms the world through discipleship. God's ultimate kenosis is the choice to be present in

179

the world in and through us. Within a Christian context the question about discipleship is at the same time a question about the church. For the church, if it is anything at all, is constituted by discipleship, is a community of disciples. Again, within a Christian kenotic vision of creation God transforms the world through God's church, the kenotic church. Discipleship in the church has as its foundation not an idea or principle but a person, Jesus Christ. This concrete and historical person is distinguished, as Bonhoeffer so clearly affirmed, by his being "the man for others." In the synoptic gospels Jesus has compassion for the marginal people; he is in their midst as a servant. Jesus does not exert his power but humbly calls the dispossessed to full personhood in the kingdom of God. Here they are no longer "nonpersons" but God's beloved and privileged people.

Church as Mission

Jesus' kenotic existence created a new, alternative community, a kenotic church. The word *church* literally means "a community that has been called out." Being called out is the essence of the *ecclesia*. To be called out means to be missioned. At Vatican II the church was perceived as having a missionary vocation.

Although all the conciliar documents have some bearing upon this sense of mission, essential contributions are contained in the dogmatic constitution *(Lumen Gentium),* the pastoral constitution *(Gaudium et Spes),* and the decree on the church's missionary activity *(Ad Gentes).* In these documents several themes related to the nature of mission are presented and the mission of the church is included within the larger framework of the mystery of the Trinity. No belief is more essential to the Christian faith than that of God as the mystery of salvific love, of God's universal salvific will. The church must, in consequence, be intrinsically part of the matter of salvation.

The origin of the mystery of salvation lies within the Godhead. It is manifested in the incarnation of Jesus and is present and operative in the gift of the Spirit. The person of Jesus Christ is at the heart of the church's mission. And the church is a sacrament of Christ's presence in history: "The Church, in Christ, is in the nature of sacrament, a sign and instrument, that is, of communion with God and of unity among all men."[1]

The decree *Ad Gentes* emphasizes that mission constitutes the basic nature of the church: "The Church on earth is, by its very nature, missionary."[2] And, "It is clear, therefore, that missionary activity flows immediately from the very nature of the Church."[3] Mission is not to be conceived as something that occurs at the periphery but rather at the center of the church's life.

The nature of the church may no longer be regarded as a rigid structure but rather as a body in dynamic relationship with God's salvific will.

The "divine" nature of the church is determined by its relation to God's salvific action in history and must be defined by functional symbols. The basic symbol, which is that of mission, responds directly to the question, Why the church? The nature of the church is determined by its mission to and for the world. *Mission* has roots deep within the New Testament. Symbolically, it suggests a quality to be desired for the church, the dual capacity to go deeper and to rise higher than the empirical and quotidian. *Mission* points to a dimension that goes beyond and is prior to the community itself: "What we have to learn...is not that the Church 'has' a mission, but the very reverse: that the mission of Christ creates its own Church. Mission does not come from the Church; it is from mission and in the light of mission that the Church has to be understood."[4] The strong sense of priority here immediately recalls both the salvific will of God and, within history, Jesus' sending out of the disciples.

The church does not exist for its own sake. Mission encompasses its whole nature. Mission came first; mission called the church into being. The church must serve and express its mission; if it fails to do this it fails to be the church. We must not envisage a "first moment" in which the church comes into being as a distinct community of faith and grace followed by a "second moment" in which the church decides to be the instrument of the divine will. God's salvific will originates and consummates mission; God's salvific will is constantly moving the church across cultural boundaries and national frontiers. This fundamental conviction regarding the salvific will of God remains the most urgent challenge to the contemporary church. All claims to exclusivity or religious triumphalism will eventually be brought face to face with this universal vision of God. Such a vision requires of us a dynamic and developmental view of world history. God moves humanity forward. God's salvific will is progressive, inclusive, in nature; not Israel alone, not the church itself, but *all* nations—and indeed the cosmic powers—are caught up in and comprehended by this salvific will. The ultimate word is not death but life, the final action not frustration but fulfillment.

The church as mission sacramentalizes God's salvific will in human history. Such sacramentality occurs precisely in its visible, organized, and institutional forms in history; as such this sacramentality is concrete, practical, and existential. It also calls for a critical relevance; sacramentality demands visibility so that action becomes a necessary element of the church's nature, and ministry the substance of the church.

Church as Ministry

Ministry is the substance of the church because the church's essence is mission.[5] This is true not only in the theoretical sense that the purpose of the church in history is its role of ministry to the world. It is also true in the existential sense that ministry creates the church to be what it actually is as historical reality; the church's existence is determined by what it does. Jesus' ministry was service:

> So Jesus called them and said to them, "You know that among the Gentiles those whom they recognized as their rulers lord it over them, and their great ones are tyrants over them. But it is not so among you; but whoever wishes to become great among you must be slave [*doulos*: a word denoting abasement] of all. For the Son of Man came not to be served but to serve, and to give his life as ransom for many" (Mk 10:42-48).

In John's gospel we read,

> "You call me teacher and lord—and you are right for that is what I am. So if I, your lord and teacher, have washed your feet, you also ought to wash one another's feet. For I have set you an example, that you also should do as I have done to you" (Jn 13:13-15).

The ministry of the church must be understood in the light of the self-sacrifice of Jesus and of his compassionate ministry to the marginalized and the oppressed. In his ministry Jesus makes it clear that anyone who would follow him is called to live as he did; self-giving for the sake of others is to be the way of discipleship. The kenotic ministry of Christ's church is characterized by its communal dimension and complete restructuring of all personal relationships, by the absolute value given to compassion, by its transformative nature and redemptive solidarity, and lastly, by its true ecumenicity.

Church as Unitive Communion

While ministry is the prime characteristic of a church that is essentially missionary, it cannot be forgotten that the church is essentially a community. We have affirmed in our approach to the mystery of the Trinity that God is unity in communion and that it is the role of the Holy Spirit to bring such unity about. The eternal "sending" of the Godhead issues from the overflowing kenotic love that characterizes the Godhead, and the ultimate salvific "sending" of the Godhead is the Holy Spirit. The Holy Spirit creates the community of faith as a missionary community. The mission of the church originates in God's own mission and is confirmed in the specific mission of the Holy Spirit. The church is not a completed edifice of the Spirit's making but a dynamic reality in the world, perpetually in the service of others. "You are God's own people that you may declare the wonderful deeds of Him who called you out of darkness into his marvelous light" (1 Pt 2:9).

The kenotic activity of the Holy Spirit in creation, incarnation, and salvation moves always to the same end: the fostering of unity. The Spirit's function is to gather together that which is separated: creation, humanity in general, individual men and women. This gathering is achieved through incorporation into that which is deepest in God. The Spirit, the bond of love between the Godhead and Christ, also binds every relationship between God and humanity. The Spirit is the bond between persons, the source of social as well as divine unity. The Spirit is the source of all *koinonia,* of all communion. The Spirit is the creator of the particular *koinonia* we name church. The church is the sacrament not only of Jesus Christ but also of the Spirit. Through the kenosis of the Holy Spirit the church is established. By the kenosis of the Spirit the church is given gifts, charisma, and creativity. Pentecost makes manifest the activity of the Holy Spirit: creating communion in diversity, institution, and charism. Continuity and creativity compose the church and its dynamic. In community the Spirit makes room for Christian freedom, for unity in difference. The Spirit makes inconsequential our differences of race, religion, social status, and gender.

Communion in love is not uniformity but union in difference both among human beings in general and between each particular person and God. Union in the Spirit preserves and perfects humanity precisely in its finite individuality and otherness. The real positivity of the finite world precisely in its radical "otherness" before the infinite God is grounded in the inner trinitarian otherness that unites the Godhead with Christ in the Spirit. The community created by the Holy Spirit is respectful of the manifold differences in human existence. Unique aspects of individual personality that contribute to a person's growth are welcomed and nourished in a Spirit-filled community. The infinite worth of the finite human creature is thus established and preserved. It is not destroyed horizontally either by the sacrifice of the individual for the common good or by the transferral of significance from the individual to the family, the nation, or humanity in general. It is not destroyed vertically by the dissolution of the finite human spirit into the infinity of the Godhead or by the self-absolutizing of the finite into the infinite. Communion and respect for otherness are the authentic marks of a Spirit-filled community, where each person makes room in love for the freedom proper to others. To enter into genuine union is to respect "the other's" true freedom and uniqueness. It is the "go-between," God the Holy Spirit, that makes possible this shared existence, this dynamic emancipatory coherence. The church is called to make manifest the community and unity of the

Trinity. The Trinity is a community where there is neither superiority nor subordination. The kenotic church is characterized by the same *perichoresis,* the dynamic process of making room for another around oneself.[6] Perichoresis emphasizes relatedness and communion.

The vision of the church at Vatican II was that of communion. Indeed, the Roman Synod of 1995 affirmed that this vision was the Council's most important teaching. Both communion and community derive from the Greek *koinonia. Koinonia,* in turn, comes from *koinos,* "common," and the verb *koinoun* means "to put together." *Koinonia* and its Latin cognates *communion* or *communicatio* indicate the action of having in common, of sharing in and participating in. Robert Kress reminds us that the real sense of these words is one of participation, solidarity, and responsibility.[7] *Communion,* unlike *community,* is an active word.[8] It involves active and mutual communication. Moltmann's understanding is that "we give one another life and come alive from one another. In mutual participation in life, individuals become free beyond the boundaries of their individuality."[9] Yet without kenosis we cannot have communion, nor can we experience the unity that respects diversity. Communion as perichoresis is achieved through self-emptying yet going out to "the other," fully respecting the otherness of "the other."

Church and Power

In such a kenotic communion there can be no opposition between power and authority, on the one hand, and love and freedom, on the other. A kenotic ecclesiology does not preclude structure, order, authority, or the bestowing of ecclesiastical office. While none of these realities is to be identified necessarily with power, power is most frequently involved in them. The issue of power in relation to the church has always been an important one. In a kenotic church, power becomes a dominant issue. Power is usually understood as the capacity to influence someone prior to or apart from the exercise of freedom. Power and powerlessness exist as dimensions of relationships and are therefore a part of the unavoidable complexity of human relations. Our society understands *power* as a value term, taking it to imply worthwhile significance. Within the kenotic framework there is the possibility of further complexity in the affirmation that power is a gift from God and that powerlessness is an evil; for example, "Power in some mode or other is part of God's creation, and while it may be true, as Rahner asserts in his superb article on power, that only in a world lacking the gift of integrity can influence be exerted on another person or group apart from their freedom, still power is not simply, of itself, evil."[10] God is given the attribute of almighty. We do call God the almighty, alone truly powerful.[11] And as Christians we use the concept of power in the first articles of the creed.

Even so, power is a reality conflictual in nature, ambiguous in its experience, analogical as a concept. Somehow power must mean the ability to change reality, our own or another's. Yet the nature of power is affected by its subject. One can speak of the power of knowledge, of love. The power of knowledge and the power of love are clearly distinct; they are experienced differently and they affect reality in different ways. Power as physical force is clearly distinct from power as spiritual force. Power that limits human freedom is surely to be understood differently from that which elicits consent. Power that involves physical force is often coercive and abusive of another's freedom. Power, even when God-given and legitimate, is "something to be gradually modified and absorbed by love. It should be used to bring about its own abrogation, though this is only absolutely possible eschatologically."[12]

The complexity of power—divine and human—is manifest in Jeremiah's experience of God. Jeremiah utters a powerful protest, "Lord, you have seduced me, and I am seduced; you have raped me and you have prevailed." Abraham Heschel observes:

These terms used in immediate juxtaposition forcefully convey the complexity of the divine-human relationship; sweetness of *enticement* as well as *violence* of rape...The call to be a prophet is more than an invitation. It is first of all a feeling of being *enticed,* of acquiescence or willing surrender. But this winsome feeling is only one aspect of the experience. The other aspect is a sense of being *ravished* or carried away by violence, of yielding to overpowering force against one's own will. The prophet feels both the *attraction* and the *coercion* of God, the *appeal* and the *pressure,* the *charm* and the *stress.* He is conscious of both *voluntary identification* and *forced capitulation.*[13]

In the New Testament, also, the nature of power is ambiguous in act and effect. Jesus' origins, lifestyle, ministry, and attitudes in general do not sustain an image of power and authority. His ministry is located among the poor and the powerless, social outcasts, the disreputable. He associates with lepers, sinners, and publicans. As revealed in the garden of Gethsemane where he accepts his cross, he has rejected any form of human power and ultimately even of divine power. The temptation narrative also culminates in his rejection of power. This episode has been interpreted as a dramatization of the Messiah's coming in triumphant power and of his ultimate victory. But such an interpretation accords ill with Jesus the rejected, abandoned Messiah.

Jesus' messianic program subverts the nature of power. The Messiah becomes a servant; power is no longer domination but service. This subversion is also evident in his use of the metaphor of the Kingdom of God to make evident God's gracious presence. In his parables and parabolic actions Jesus makes iconoclastic use of the metaphor of a kingdom, reversing it so that those at the bottom of the pyramid become the first in the Kingdom of God (Mk 10:14; Mt 19:30). The people without status are privileged members of the Kingdom of God.

Paul's discovery of the gospel was the discovery of the true character of divine power. In common with other Jewish disciples of Jesus, Paul would have expected God's Kingdom to be inaugurated by a "mighty act," but the death on the cross manifested not power but powerlessness (2 Cor 13:4). Its effect on Paul was one of radical conversion, a violent reversal analogous to that called for in Mark 10:42-45 and an abrupt realization that it is in his powerlessness on the cross that God's power is revealed.[14]

God's power in the gospels cannot be understood except in terms of powerlessness, its apparent opposite.[15] God's power is to renounce power. According to Mark, it is through God's power that Jesus is free to become powerless and submit to death. Dorothy Lee-Pollard sees in this paradox that

> The divine power by which Jesus in the Gospel heals and liberates others is the same power by which he is able to renounce the power to save his own life.
>
> So that breath-taking power to renounce power—to renounce what is most precious, what alone gives purpose and meaning to life, what lies at the core of one's identity—is precisely what reveals and actualizes the power of God. That is why the centurion recognizes who Jesus is in the blackness of despair of his own death.[16]

What is true of Jesus is also true of discipleship. God's power enables us to relinquish power. God can empower even the rich and powerful so that they are able to sacrifice wealth and power in the service of the poor.

Power, according to the paschal mystery, is not something to be retained or withheld; it is essentially relational and self-sacrificing. It is what Rollo May would call integrative power; it envisions mutuality and reciprocity. It is neither power over, power against, nor power for, but rather power with.[17]

The capacity to absorb and influence is as truly a mark of power as the strength involved in exercising an influence. Power is the capacity to sustain a relationship. This is the relationship of influencing and being influenced, of giving and receiving, of making claims and permitting and enabling others to make their claims.[18]

This model of power is relational where selves and groups emerge as realities. The magnitude of power consists in "the range and depth of relationships that we can sustain."[19] This includes relationships of receptivity, even of suffering; it is not the positing of will against will. Power is relation, and therefore the greater the power the greater the relationality.

The goal of relational power is the creation and development of relationships. It does not either directly or indirectly intend to control "the other"; it intends the enlargement of freedom; it is a commitment to the relational "us," to mutuality. Relational power, the capacity to sustain relationships, is not the business of management control or domination. Relational power is costly, however, for such power often involves suffering. In the Christian tradition the exact symbol of such a price paid is the cross, and the proper symbol of relational power is the suffering servant. Every true Christian reality passes through the crucible of kenotic love. Authority and power must necessarily do so.

Power which has been filtered through kenosis is never power from above but always power *with*. God's creative power never breaks in from the outside; it does not assent to the destructive facets of the human exercising of power. It is a power of love that challenges, releases, gives life. "Behold I stand at the door and knock" (Rv 3:20); God does not force the door of our heart.[20] Jesus' own *exousia* is characterized by precariousness and is experienced in the passivity of waiting: "His power is the impotence of grace, the reconciling force of suffering, and the dominion of self-denying love."[21]

The church's power must also be characterized by kenosis. Within history its power, expressed in hierarchical terms, militates against the Christic and sacramental nature of its own ministry. Hierarchical power is power as mastery, as domination even; it implies that power is something within the individual person that causes changes in others. It is unilateral not relational power. A kenotic church, on the other hand, manifests a transformation of hierarchical into relational power;[22] mission and ministry call for such transformation. Self-limitation on the part of the church as institution is the one sure way by which space can be created for authentic discipleship.

A Compassionate Church

A kenotic church is a compassionate church. Compassion stands in opposition to unilateral power. The church's ministry must be characterized, as was the ministry of Jesus, by compassion. Compassion is the basic characteristic that informs all divine activity; it is to be understood as a metaphor which provides a kenotic understanding of the church. It is the hermeneutical key for interpreting the church's mission.

God reveals Godself in the history of Israel and in Jesus' ministry as a compassionate God. In Israel, God is characterized as both a compassionate father and a compassionate mother. The intimacy and the loving attachment are related to the womb. Like the womb, divine compassion is life-giving; compassion creates the possibility for rebirth. God's compassionate love is a vital creative force. By compassion Jesus is brought to minster to the blind and the deaf. His miracles are signs of the inbreaking of God's compassionate reign. The disciples are called to compassion: "Be compassionate as your Father is compassionate" (Lk 6:36; Mt 5:48). He offers the parable of the Good Samaritan to his disciples as an ideal upon which they should model themselves. The Samaritan "was moved to pity at the sight" of the wounded traveler (Lk 10:25-37). A more literal translation of "moved to pity" would be "moved in his spleen." Compassion is not only a question of understanding suffering but also of feeling "the other's" suffering in one's own life.[23]

Compassion is not simply a feeling; it is primarily the capacity to enter into the joys and sorrows of another. The referent of compassion is always "the other." Compassion moves the church beyond the confines of self-centeredness. Such symbols as the Exodus, Emmanuel, the incarnation, and the crucifixion allow the church to be perceived as compassionate. Its power is compassionate power. Compassion is other-centered and self-sacrificing. It is grounded in a kenotic causality that exists both in nature and in the divine nature.

The church is the self-expression and self-realization of the Holy Spirit—historically and socially embodied. The church is to be known by— *necessarily* to be known by—its compassion: historical and visible compassion, concretely realized in the mystical body, the people of God, and visibly expressed in action, rites, and words. The presence of compassion in our midst is a sign of the inbreaking of God's reign. Compassion in Jesus, as in Jesus' followers, is a harbinger of the reign of God.

The Church and Salvation

The church's compassionate existence is directly connected to its salvific mission. In Jesus it is revealed that compassion is more salvific than power. Compassion leads to solidarity with and for "the other." Compassion is inextricably interwoven with hope and justice. Compassion does not remain within the area of intentionality and demonstration; it demands efficacy. Such compassion has as object and goal emancipatory solidarity. To identify with the crucified and compassionate Christ in the contemporary world is not to conjure up an emotional experience of remote and ancient suffering. It is to place ourselves alongside the wretched of the earth today, those deprived of all earthly hope, the poor and the oppressed, those who have been abandoned. Solidarity with "the other" is always related to some form of kenosis, of letting go. While kenosis is a way of describing the divine being and the divine action of Jesus Christ, it also describes what the believer must do. Kenosis is an affirmation of ultimate salvation—not through power but through "the other." Kenosis, the revelation of who God is and of ourselves as we are to be, can be accepted and enacted only within a kenotic community. The church community of those who recall Jesus must embody Jesus' vision and way of life. In the absence of the ecclesial community's solidarity with the oppressed, the gospel becomes impossible to believe. The kenosis of God in Jesus Christ cannot be believed unless it is experienced in the kenotic community. The mediating of this revelation can be found only within the common actualities of Christian living:

> The church is called to life through the gospel of Christ's self-giving. Hence it is fundamentally born out of the cross of Christ. At its center is "the word of the cross" and the Eucharist with which the death of Christ is proclaimed. It is from the cross of Christ that there develops the fellowship of the godless with god. What makes the church the church is the reconciliation "in the blood of Christ" and its own self-giving for the reconciliation of the world.
>
> The church of Christ is therefore at the same time the church under the cross. The fellowship of Christ is experienced in common resistance to idolatry and inhumanity, in common suffering over oppression and persecution. It is in this participation in the passion of Christ and in the passion of the people that the "life" of Christ and his liberty become visible in the church. Christian fellowship proves itself in temptation and resistance.[24]

The partnership, the interdependence brought into being by God's presence in self-emptying, serves to reconcile the world through solidarity with the suffering and the oppressed. The one truly effective way to redeem people is the way of sociological incarnation, that is, by immersion in the wretchedness from which we need to be liberated. This solidarity by immersion becomes emancipatory, because it is ultimately humanizing. As disciples of the crucified and self-emptying Christ, we are drawn into his self-surrender, into his solidarity with the lost, his public suffering (cf. 1 Cor 1:26-31).

Church and Liberation

A kenotic theology is especially to be realized through ministry among the poor. As proclaimed by Paul, the helplessness experienced by Jesus on the cross nonetheless embodies the power of God: "For God's foolishness is wiser than human wisdom and God's weakness is stronger than human strength" (1 Cor 1:25). The church's faithful ministry among the poor is grounded in the kenosis of God, which itself manifests power in weakness. It is a ministry of expectation, often unrealized expectation; to the eyes of the world it often looks like failure. It is a ministry that cannot be measured in terms of worldly success. As kenotic, the church is called to do battle with the causes of social sin and to be in solidarity with the poor. Here the church has much to learn from liberation theology.

God's works are accomplished in stillness and weakness, that is, in witness. The humility of the incarnation and the humble origins of every creature characterize God's work. It calls for a certain affinity with God to notice and appreciate these things; weakness has an inner affinity with the living God, an affinity that power does not have.

A kenotic church can do no other than make a preferential option for the poor when it identifies itself with the roots of Jesus' ministry. We cannot be with the poor except in continual struggle and protest against poverty. Solidarity with the poor is essential:

> In the language of liberation theology...God as liberator acts in history to liberate all through opting for the poor and the oppressed of the present system. The poor, the downcast, those who hunger and thirst, have a certain priority in God's work of redemption. Part of the signs of the kingdom is that the lame walk, the blind see, the captives are fed, the poor have the gospel preached to them. Christ goes particularly to the outcasts, and they, in turn, have a special affinity for the gospel. But the aim of this partiality is to create a new whole, to elevate the valleys and make the high places low, so that all may come into a new place of God's reign, when God's will is done on earth.[25]

A kenotic church must stress that the preferential option for the poor is also an articulation of the sustaining presence of the Spirit as it is experienced by us in the world. If we within the church also experience an apparent absence of the Spirit this may be a form of self-emptying, the way in which God creates space for the poor to find a new identity as privileged persons. Such an experience involves the recognition that it is the marginalized who can best understand the kenotic presence of God's Spirit. The poor are the ones who can imagine a logic radically at odds with the rationale of power and domination. It is they who are best able to perceive that God is not absent, but hidden from the world.[26]

Church and World

In fulfilling its kenotic nature the church must reenact the compassion of the prophets. Its compassion must be universal. It shall not discriminate between those who are members of the church and those who are not; it shall not choose between friends and enemies. Its compassion must be unconditional and inclusive. It must never be ethnocentric, denominational, nationalistic, or chauvinistic in any way.[27]

The kenotic community engendered by the Spirit can be neither exclusive nor hermetic. The Lucan account of Pentecost supposes an intentional universality of the gift of the Spirit. The message entrusted to the apostles is destined for all, given to all as the point where the divine enters and is received. No person or community has a monopoly on the Holy Spirit: "The wind (Spirit) blows where it chooses and you hear the sound of it, but you do not know where it comes from or where it goes" (Jn 3:8). No person or institution can possess the Spirit, for it blows where it pleases. The bestowal of the Spirit—whether upon Jesus or upon a community—is always for a universal purpose; it is for the benefit of all.

Church and Incarnation

Ecclesial documents largely emphasize the incarnation as the theological point of departure for our understanding of evangelization as well as our understanding of the church as an instrument of God's word in the world. What God has done in and through Jesus of Nazareth is paradigmatic of what the church is called to do among people of different times and places, having priority over such methods as "adaptation," "indigenization," "contextualization," or "inculturation."

As one instrument of Jesus' incarnational mission, the church, reaching out to the whole world in its vast diversity, must also empty itself of its ephemeral historical accretions and cultural attachments. Let the church open itself to ways of understanding and modes of expression that it did not have previously, and let it humble itself in order to gain experience and to celebrate new life among the nations. The church, in other words, is to become completely at home among each people in the same radical and authentic way that Jesus was at home fully accepting the limitation of the human condition in all things except sin.

The mission of the church as understood at Vatican II is that of evangelization through inculturation. Through kenosis, and only through kenosis, is it possible to become all things to all people; this is the only way to be at home in a strange land, the only way to love people who belong to other civilizations. Through kenosis one is open to others. Kenosis grants us the capacity to accept strong personal ties and demanding encounters. It is the precondition for dialogue and inculturation.

The church in its historical reality is always expressed ambivalently and contingently. There cannot be an idealistic approach to Jesus' humanity. The church in the concreteness of its ministry relates to our ongoing quest for ultimate reality. Its universal significance is not to be recognized apart from the continuing effects of its ministry in the world or from its sacramentality. A kenotic church demands an ecclesiology "from below." An ecclesiology from below directs itself to the historical church; it plainly states that all true ecclesiological language must originate in the historical setting and praxis of the church.

Conclusion

Bernard Lonergan has argued that the church is to be understood as self-constitutive. "The Christian church is the community that results from the outer communication of Christ's message and from the inner gift of God's love."[28] In a kenotic perspective, the inner gift of God's love is the gift of God's kenotic love experienced as a transformative movement toward "the other." Such love is conducive to and necessary for the formation of community. When the inner gift of God's kenotic love is matched by the outer gift that is Jesus Christ, the community that emerges is called the church. The church emerges when the inner gift of God's kenotic love is known and named through Christ's kenosis; that is to say, when a community can confess that the crucified Jesus is truly Lord. In that common confession, prior to any other words or deeds, the church has already come into existence. The church-consciousness of the first Christians is the consequence of the gift of the Holy Spirit: the substance of God's kenotic love manifested, revealed, named in the person of Jesus Christ. "No one can say 'Jesus is Lord' except by the Holy Spirit" (1 Cor 12:3).

The mission of the Holy Spirit consists in actualizing the mystery of the kenotic creation and incarnation. The mediation by the Holy Spirit of these kenotic self-communications of God is simultaneously the interior transformative communication of these God-given realities. The consequence of the self-emptying love of God manifested on the cross is this transformation of the hearts of men and women. Thus Paul asserts that his individual existence is, at the same time, homologous with the pattern of the crucifixion/resurrection pattern.[29] The Christian community is called into being to communicate the gospel of the cross; as it is shaped by the message of the cross, so it must take on a cruciform life in order to accomplish its mission. For all this, its mission is not death, much less death on the cross. Its mission is life, life eternal. The crucified Jesus is the risen Jesus. Life emerges out of death. What kind of life is it that can become eternal life, authentic life? It is life as gift, given and received. In the gospel of John such a life is described by one word: love. Such a life is not a possession to be held onto but to let go of. "Unless a grain of wheat falls into the earth and dies, it remains alone; but if it dies it bears much fruit" (Jn 12:24). It is a life best lived when it is given, intensified when it is shared. The abundance of such a life is not found in the exercise of power over others but in the empowerment of others, not in the striving for more but in dispossession. Authentic life must go out of itself in order to preserve itself. Authentic life is the opposite of self-aggrandizement. Let us ask where "eternal life is to be found; or better, where it is hidden. The answer is 'In human suffering and degradation, in poverty and hunger, among the two-thirds who starve, in races that are brought low, in the experience of failure, in exposure to the icy winds of the nihil, in the midst of hell—there it looks for the God whose acting is the precondition of Christian obedience.'"[30]

The "remembering" of God's kenotic love for us in Jesus Christ is not and cannot be an empty return to a vacant past. Anamnesis is directed to the future and it demands action. The hoped-for redemption of the world from power-brokering and alienation cannot come to pass except through an active solidarity with the oppressed and suffering.

The Christian intention for life, the idea revealed in the person of Jesus, the Christ, constitutes no threat to human authenticity. On the contrary, in our world where "small" must necessarily be beautiful, this Christian project constitutes our only real hope for survival; the one area where Jesus reveals the fullness of human reality lies paradoxically in his self-emptying and his self-giving love. In the acceptance of "the other" as constitutive of himself, Jesus as the Christ, the revelation of Godself, does not simply present us with a static model of mature humanity. There is an eschatological dimension to this revelation—a "not yet" that does not limit imitation to repetition or restrict human development to a fixed pattern. We are yet to know what we are to become. The full depths of self-emptying are yet to be fully understood and realized. Our cultural and political situations are demanding of us now a global will for self-limitation.

There are many models of the church; a church for our time needs to be kenotic:

> It is essentially a movement in society rather than an institution...In its structure [it] is much more pluriform than the

contemporary Church...A principle feature...is its low "visibility" in society, for the Church sees itself as hidden within
society as a popularist movement rather than set over against
society in institutional form.[31]

Our contemporary situation requires that the church travel light and live
off the land—here the great metaphor for kenotic church is that of pilgrimage. The church is called to minister "on the road." In the gospels of
Mark and Luke, road *(hodos)* becomes language defining Jesus' salvific
mission. Pilgrimage is the metaphor that best describes the church in a
world where so many are physically and spiritually homeless. A kenotic
church should also be characterized as a place of pilgrimage: "Places of
pilgrimage are as a rule, more hospitable to the strange and the stranger
than institutions entrenched in one particular community."[32] In a place
of pilgrimage, pilgrims of all races and social strata leave behind their
particular cultural milieux; they become a new community on the way.
"Communitas is, as it were, at the opposite pole to the institutional life of
the church."[33] A kenotic church is always an apophatic church, always
anti-establishment, always offering an alternative vision, always on the
road to Jerusalem.

APPENDIX

Poetics and the Kenotic Hymn

By Geoffrey Hill

If commentators on Christian aesthetics and poetics had first grounded their understanding in Karl Rahner's "The Theology of the Symbol,"[1] they would have spared themselves and their readers a burden of metaphysical embarrassment. I do not exclude myself from these strictures, nor can I exempt Rahner himself. In "Poetry and the Christian"[2] he, too, writes with the profane folly common to the rest of us but rare in his own work, an odd lapse from his characteristic attention to the expression of the kenotic. The expression to which I refer does not originate with Rahner but, as he himself makes clear, with the Thomists' *reditio completa in seipsum,*[3] behind which stands—paradoxically—an Aristotelian "activity of the complete or perfect *[energeia tou telelesmenon].*"[4] Of this activity no finer understanding and exegesis than Rahner's have been brought into being this century. "Poetry and the Christian," on the other hand, is what he himself might have termed a *masquerade:*

> The more deeply great poetry leads man into the abysses which are the foundation of his being, the more surely it forces him to face those dark and mysterious acts of human self-realization, which are shrouded in the fundamental ambiguity in which man cannot certainly say if he [is] saved or lost.[5]

Within a limited space I cannot hope to give a cogent explanation for the seemingly irresistible gravitational force of mere verbal habituation into which "Poetry and the Christian," against Rahner's own best judgment, is drawn. One can point to Emerson's essay "Self Reliance,"[6] with its crucial emphasis on "the aboriginal Self...that source, at once the essence of genius, of virtue, and of life, which we call Spontaneity or Instinct."[7] Mill's treatise *On Liberty*[8] may also be cited, with its insistence that "because the tyranny of opinion is such as to make eccentricity a reproach, it is desirable, in order to break through that tyranny, that people should be eccentric."[9] Rahner's "dark and mysterious acts" seem little more than a recycling of Mill's licensed eccentricities; his "self-realization" utters a void reassertion of Emerson's vacuous "aboriginal Self"; the "abysses" re-echo the voice of Zarathustra, who had read Emerson.[10]

"The Theology of the Symbol," which presents a profoundly positive understanding of poetic kenosis, has not a word to say of poetry and the poetic. Herein is its power and, to use a profane word, its relevance. I can perhaps best account for the significance of "positive understanding" if I say that before I knew of Rahner's work I had found in Karl Barth the best defined *negative* ground on which a rectified Christian poetics might be established, one that would compromise itself as little as possible with Christian aesthetics, for these are scarcely to be distinguished from a "surrogate post-Christian religion of artistic gratification."[11] Barth writes, in his commentary on the Epistle to the Corinthians,

> The limit of my power over all is exactly where I have power over things, the point where it is not transformed into power over me. Where that happens, and that is happening in Corinth, things have just gained power over men. What passes for freedom is in reality slavery.[12]

For one looking at the question in the light of Barth's perception, if there is to be such a creature as the individual voice, or style, it can exist only as an expression of sustained vigilance along a line that may be understood as a continuum of Barthean "points." I would add that, judged against Barth's words, Emerson's "transcendentalism of common life,"[13] Mill's "real morality of public discussion,"[14] together with Tillich's "the courage to be,"[15] appear as types of Corinthian self-delusion.

However, I have already termed Barth's perception the *negative* ground of right distinction. Its positive correlative is to be seen in Rahner's argument for the reality of the symbol, or "symbolic reality":[16] "all beings are by their nature symbolic, because they necessarily 'express' themselves in order to attain their own nature."[17] The vitiating factor in aesthetic symbolism is that it came into being, and was established, as an arbitrary answer to the arbitrariness of Hobbesian nominalism[18] and that it is itself thoroughly Hobbesian, taking the symbol to be an "equivalent," not a real, expression. Christianized aesthetics, on this basis, do not gain reality; they remain Corinthian and occult.

The kenotic is antithetical to the occult. It is therefore peculiarly difficult and particularly necessary to confront the ill-fated aesthetic gestures of modern theologians and philosophers with the Pauline text of Philippians 2:5–11, the words of the "kenotic hymn." If the kenotic hymn is a poem, *since* it is a poem, poetry as we would hope to understand it is not utterly lost among the slavish originalities of Corinth, the chorus of profane "protest," the masquerades of confession. Fr. Richard argues that the *en morphe* of the hymn is "less a statement about personal nature than a statement about origin" (p. 59). I take this to be in accord with Rahner's "'primordial word' of religious speech";[19] it seems evident to me that neither is to be confused with the inwardness of an "aboriginal Self" and that each pertains to what Richard understands in terms of *character:* "An authentic Christology must affirm that Jesus' life is simultaneously characterized by power...and by powerlessness" (p. 63). If, as it must be, character is something other than personality, each true act of expression is the making of a character, kenotically conceived: an affirmation of selfhood which, even in the instant of expression, is self-forgetting. Other than William Tyndale's Englishing of Philippians 2:5-11, in 1526,[20] the purest kenotic poetry in English is that of George Herbert, simultaneously characterized by power and powerlessness, magisterial in its rhetorical command (Herbert had been Public Orator to the University of Cambridge), and yet recurrently and finally self-humbling:

> Sir, I pray deliver this little Book to my
> dear brother *Farrer,* and tell him, he shall
> find in it a picture of the many spirituall
> Conflicts that have past betwixt God and my
> Soul, before I could subject mine to the will
> of *Jesus my Master:* in whose service I have now
> found perfect freedom; desire him to read it:
> and then, if he can think it may turn to the
> advantage of any dejected poor Soul, let it be
> made publick: if not, let him burn it: for
> *I and it, are less than the least of God's mercies.*[21]

Notes

Introduction

1. Michael Green, ed. *The Truth of God Incarnate* (London: Hodder and Stoughton, 1977); Michael Goulder, *Incarnation as Myth: The Debate Continues* (Grand Rapids, Mich.: Eerdmans, 1979).

2. J. D. G. Dunn, *Unity and Diversity in the New Testament* (London: SCM, 1977), pp. 226-27.

3. Hans Küng, *The Incarnation* (Edinburgh: T & T Clark, 1987), p. 19.

4. Avery Dulles, "Incarnation 1973," *Commonweal*, vol. 99, no. 13 (Dec. 28, 1973), p. 329.

5. *Gaudium et Spes* (Pastoral Constitution on the Church in the Modern World), no. 22, in *The Documents of Vatican II*, ed. Walter Abbott (New York: Herder and Herder, 1966).

6. Ibid.

7. George A. Lindbeck, *The Nature of Doctrine* (Philadelphia: Westminster, 1984), p. 32.

8. *Gaudium et Spes,* no. 4.

9. Ibid., no. 10.

10. Clifford Geertz, *The Interpretations of Cultures* (New York: Basic Books, 1973), p. 312.

11. Ibid., p. 90.

12. Dietrich Bonhoeffer, *Letters and Papers from Prison* (London: SCM, 1967), p. 36.

13. Karl Barth, *Church Dogmatics*, trans. G. W. Bromiley (New York: Charles Scribner's Sons, 1956), 4/1: 192-93.

14. L. Gilkey, *Naming the Whirlwind: The Renewal of God-Language* (Indianapolis: Bobbs-Merrill, 1969), p. 250.

15. Ibid., pp. 375-76.

Chapter One

1. L. Gilkey, *Naming the Whirlwind: The Renewal of God-Language* (Indianapolis: Bobbs Merrill, 1969), p. 33.

2. Ibid., p. 34.

3. P. Berger writes, "By secularization we mean the process by which sectors of society and culture are removed from the domination of religious institutions and symbols. When we speak of society and institutions in modern Western history, of course, secularization manifests itself in the evacuation by the Christian churches of areas previously under their control or influence—as in the separation of church and state, or in the expropriation of church lands, or in the emancipation of education from ecclesial authority. When we speak of culture and symbols, however, we imply that secularization is more than a social-structural process. It affects the totality of cultural life and ideation and may be observed in the decline of religious contents in the arts, in philosophy, in literature and, most important of all, in the rise of science as an autonomous, thoroughly secular perspective on the world. Moreover, it is implied here that the process of secularization has a subjective side as well. As there is secularization of society and culture, so there is a secularization of consciousness. Put simply, this means that the modern West has produced an increasing number of individuals who look upon the world and their own lives without benefit of religious interpretation" (*The Sacred Canopy* [New York: Doubleday, 1967], pp. 107-8).

4. P. Berger, "For a World With Windows," *Against the World for the World*, ed. P. Berger and R. J. Neuhaus (New York: Seabury Press, 1976), p. 10.

5. Gilkey, pp. 37-73.

6. P. Tillich, *Theology of Culture* (Oxford: Oxford University Press, 1959), p. 43.

7. P. Berger, *Facing Up to Modernity* (New York: Basic Books, 1977), p. 70.

8. Tillich, pp. 43-44.

9. Ibid., p. 45.

10. R. Nisbet, "The Impact of Technology and Ethical Decision Making," *The Technological Threat*, ed. J. D. Douglas (Englewood Cliffs, N.J.: Prentice-Hall, 1971), p. 41.

11. Victor C. Ferkiss, *Technological Man: The Myth and the Reality* (New York: George Braziller, 1969), p. 250.

12. J. Ellul, *The Technological Society* (New York: Alfred A. Knopf, 1964), p. 43.

13. Hannah Arendt, *The Human Condition* (Garden City: Doubleday, 1955), p. 3.

14. S. Keen, *Apology for Wonder* (New York: Harper & Row, 1967), p. 117.

15. Hans Jonas, "Toward a Philosophy of Technology," *Hastings Center Report* (February 1970), p. 38.

16. F. Nietzsche, "Thus Spake Zarathustra," *The Philosophy of Nietzsche* (New York: Modern Library Press, n.d.), p. lxxii.

17. F. Nietzsche, *The Birth of Tragedy and the Genealogy of Morals* (Garden City, N.Y.: Doubleday, 1965), pp. 149-88.

18. R. Bultmann, "The Idea of God in Modern Man," *Theology into the Modern Age*, ed. Robert W. Funk (New York: Harper & Row, 1965), p. 96.

19. Gilkey, p. 58.

20. Jean-Paul Sartre, *Being and Nothingness*, trans. H. Barnes (New York: Philosophical Library, 1956), pp. 47-70, 73-218.

21. B. F. Skinner, *Beyond Freedom and Dignity* (New York: Bantam/Vintage Books, 1971).

22. B. F. Skinner, *Cumulative Record*, 3d ed. (New York: Appleton, 1972), p. 3.

23. Craig E. Wollner, "Behaviorism and Humanism: B. F. Skinner and the Western Intellectual Tradition," *Review in Existential Psychology and Psychiatry*, vol. 14, no. 3 (1975-1976), p. 158. According to W. Thompson, "Liberals like Zbigniew Brzezinski and Herman Kahn believe we can eliminate the tragic flaw in man: following Brzezinski, we can replace the chaos of politics with the system of management; following Kahn, we can hook up the brain to computers to create an electronic superman" (*Evil and World Order* [New York: Horizon Press, 1976], p. 2). For these men, faith in progress is so complete that they cannot help but believe that some technological miracle will deliver us from any impending disaster.

24. Wollner, p. 159.

25. *Time* (20 September 1971).

26. B. F. Skinner, *Science and Human Behavior* (New York: The Free Press, 1953), p. 119.

27. Heinz Otto Luthe, "What Is Manipulation?" *Concilium*, vol. 63 (New York: Herder and Herder, 1971), pp. 12-26.

28. Y. Leslie Gould, *The Manipulators* (New York: David McKay, 1966).

29. J. M. R. Delgado, *Physical Control of the Mind* (New York: Harper & Row, 1971).

30. H. Marcuse, *One Dimensional Man* (Boston: Beacon Press, 1964), p. 158.

31. Nietzsche, *The Birth of Tragedy*, p. 210.

32. Christopher Lasch, *The Culture of Narcissism* (New York: W.W. Norton Co., 1978), p. 34. See also, Shirley Sugarman, *Sin and Madness: Studies in Narcissism* (Philadelphia: Westminster, 1978).

33. Lasch, p. 232.

34. Ibid., p. 43.

35. Ernest Becker, *The Denial of Death* (New York: The Free Press, 1973).

36. R. Dawkins, *The Selfish Gene* (New York: Oxford University Press, 1976), p. 2.

37. Ibid., p. 3.

38. For more details, see R. Hogan "Theoretical Egocentricism and the Problem of Compliance," *American Psychologist* 5 (1975) pp. 533-40, and *Personality Theory: The Personological Tradition* (Englewood Cliffs, N.J.: Prentice-Hall, 1976).

39. J. W. Thibault and H. H. Kelley, *The Social Psychology of Groups* (New York: John Wiley and Sons, 1959); G. C. Homans, *Social Behavior: Its Elementary Forms* (New York: Harcourt, Brace & World, 1961).

40. D. Bakan, *Sigmund Freud and the Jewish Mystical Tradition* (Princeton: Van Nostrand Co., 1958).

41. P. Rieff, *The Triumph of the Therapeutic: The Uses of Faith after Freud* (New York: Harper & Row, 1966).

42. E. Fromm, *Man for Himself: An Inquiry into the Psychology of Ethics* (New York: Rinehart & Co., 1947), p. 7.

43. G. Nathan Adler, *The Underground Stream: New Life Styles and the Antinomious Personality* (New York: Harper Torchbooks, 1971); J. Hougan, *Decadence: Radical Nostalgia and Decline in the Seventies* (New York: William Morrow, 1977).

44. R. Ringer, *Looking Out for Number One* (New York: Funk and Wagnalls, 1978); B. N. Kaufman, *To Love Is to Be Happy With* (New York: Coward, McCann & Geoghegan, 1978); M. Newman and B. Berkowitz, *How to Take Charge of Your Life* (New York: Harcourt, 1978).

45. Y. R. Schacht, *Alienation* (London: George Allen and Unwin Ltd., 1971).

46. Ruben Alves, *Tomorrow's Child* (New York: Harper & Row, 1972), p. 20.

47. Tillich, p. 46.

48. R. Niebuhr, *The Children of Light and the Children of Darkness* (New York: Charles Scribner's Sons, 1944), p. 59.

49. M. Friedman, *To Deny Our Nothingness: Contemporary Images of Man* (New York: Delta Books, 1967), pp. 243-309.

50. E. Becker, *The Denial of Death* (New York: The Free Press, 1973), p. 87.

51. Ibid., pp. 276-77.

52. Ibid., p. 283.

53. Friedman, pp. 309-54.

54. Douglas John Hall, *Lighten Our Darkness: Toward an Indigenous Theology of the Cross* (Philadelphia: Westminster, 1976), p. 168.

55. Becker, p. 284.

56. R. Niebuhr, *Faith and History: A Comparison of Christian and Modern Views of History* (New York: Charles Scribner's Sons, 1949), p. 9.

57. George Grant, *Philosophy in the Mass Age* (Toronto: Capp Clark Publishing, 1966), p. 23.

58. Ibid., pp. vii-viii.

59. B. J. Callopy, "Theology and the Darkness of Death," *Theological Studies*, vol. 39, no. 1 (1978), p. 48.

60. Hall, p. 57.

61. Ibid.

62. Hans Urs von Balthasar, *Love Alone* (New York: Herder and Herder, 1969), p. 15.

63. Hall, p. 220.

64. Paul and Ann Ehrlich, *Population, Environment: Issues in Human Ecology* (New York: W. H. Freeman Co., 1970), p. 324.

65. E. F. Schumacher, *Small Is Beautiful: Economics As If People Mattered* (New York: Harper & Row, 1973).

66. E. Fromm, *To Have or to Be* (New York: Harper & Row, 1976), p. 10.

67. G. F. and J. R. Feibleman, *Understanding Human Nature* (New

York: Horizon Press, 1978); M. Stanley, *The Technological Conscience: Survival and Dignity in an Age of Expertise* (Yale: Yale University Press, 1978).

68. Schumacher, p. 30.

69. Ibid., p. 31.

70. Hall, p. 159.

71. Ibid., p. 183.

72. R. A. Falk, "On the Creation of a Just World Order," *On the Creation of a Just World Order*, ed. S. Mendlovitz (New York: The Free Press, 1975), p. 220.

73. Fromm, p. 9.

74. Niebuhr, *The Children of Light and the Children of Darkness,* p. 19. According to E. F. Schumacher, the Sermon on the Mount outlines the general direction for contemporary society:

> It may seem daring to connect these beatitudes with matters of technology and economics. But may it not be that we are in trouble precisely because we have failed for so long to make this connection? It is not difficult to discern what these beatitudes may mean for us today:
> —We are poor, not demigods.
> —We have plenty to be sorrowful about, and are not emerging into a golden age.
> —We need a gentle approach, a non-violent spirit, and small is beautiful.
> —We must concern ourselves with justice and see right prevail.
> —And all this, only this, can enable us to become peacemakers (pp. 157-58).

Chapter Two

1. D. Tracy, *The Analogical Imagination* (New York: Crossroad, 1981), p. 322.

2. Cf. J. Dunne, *Time and Myth* (New York: Doubleday, 1973).

3. On the Emmaus narrative a critical survey of the bibliography can be found in R. J. Dillon, *From Eye Witness to Ministers of the Word* (Rome, 1978).

4. For a fuller analysis of this text see X. Leon Dufour, *Life and Death in the New Testament: The Teachings of Jesus and Paul* (San Francisco: Harper & Row, 1986), pp. 32-35.

5. See W. Michaelis, "Pascho," *TDNT*, vol. 5, p. 904.

6. J. Moltmann, *The Crucified God* (New York: Harper & Row, 1974), p. 74.

7. P. Schoonenberg, "The Kenosis or Self-emptying of Christ," *Concilium*, vol. 1, no. 2 (1966), p. 35.

8. D. Soelle, *Suffering* (Philadelphia: Fortress Press, 1975), p. 163.

9. V. A. Harvey, *The Historian and the Believer: The Morality of Historical Knowledge and Christian Belief* (New York: Macmillan, 1966).

10. According to N. Perrin: "The central feature of the message of Jesus is, then, the challenge of the forgiveness of sins and the offer of the possibility of a new kind of relationship with God and with one's fellow man. This was symbolized by a table-fellowship which celebrated the present joy and anticipated the future consummation: a table-fellowship of such joy and gladness that it survived the crucifixion and provided a focal point for the community life of the earliest Christians—and was the most direct link between the community-life and the pre-Easter fellowship of Jesus and his disciples...We are justified in seeing this table-fellowship as the central feature of the ministry of Jesus; an anticipatory sitting at the table in the Kingdom of God and a very real celebration of present joy and challenge" (*Rediscovering the Teaching of Jesus* [New York: Harper & Row, 1976], p. 107).

11. K. Barth, *Church Dogmatics* (Edinburgh: T & T Clark, 1961), 4/2:184; see also 3/2:211.

12. See K. Rahner, "Resurrection," *Encyclopedia of Theology: The Concise Sacramentum Mundi* (New York: Seabury Press, 1975), pp. 1436-42.

13. Quoted by P. Hodgson, *Jesus—Word and Presence, An Essay in Christology* (Philadelphia: Fortress Press, 1971), p. 216.

14. See J. B. Metz, *Faith in History and Society* (New York: Seabury Press, 1980), p. 216.

15. See Moltmann, p. 113.

16. Ibid., p. 160.

17. According to R. Pesch, the foundation of the church's faith in the resurrection is not to be found in the historical Jesus, and not in the events that followed Jesus' death ("Zur Entstehung Des Glaubens An Die Auferstehung Jesu," *TQ* 153 [1973], pp. 201-28).

18. E. Schillebeeckx, *Christ: The Experience of Jesus as Lord* (New York: Seabury Press, 1980), pp. 726-29.

19. E. Schillebeeckx, *Jesus: An Experiment in Christology* (New York: Seabury Press, 1979), p. 643.

20. W. Pannenberg, *Jesus—God and Man* (Philadelphia: Westminster, 1968), p. 194.

21. J. Macquarrie, *Principles of Christian Theology* (New York: Charles Scribner's Sons, 1966), p. 283.

Chapter Three

1. E. Schillebeeckx, *Jesus: An Experiment in Christology* (New York: Seabury Press, 1979), p. 549.

2. See F. Hahn, *Mission in the New Testament*, Studies in Biblical Theology 47 (London, 1965); J. Jeremias, *Jesus' Promise to the Nations* (London: SCM, 1967).

3. C. F. D. Moule, *The Origin of Christology* (New York: Cambridge University Press, 1977), p. 131.

4. Schillebeeckx, p. 438.

5. See W. Kasper, *Jesus the Christ* (New York: Paulist Press, 1976), pp. 18-19.

6. R. Schnackenburg, *Lexicon Fur Theologie Und Kirch* (1964), vol. 9, cols. 851-54.

7. J. Jeremias, *New Testament Theology I* (London: SCM, 1971), pp. 53-55.

8. B. M. F. van Irsel, "'Der Sohn' in Der Synoptischen Jesusworten," *Nov Test Suppl* 3 (1964).

9. F. Hahn, *The Titles of Jesus in Christology, Their History in Early Christianity*, trans. H. Knight (London: Lutterworth Press, 1969), pp. 284-88; R. H. Fuller, *The Foundations of New Testament Christology* (London: Collins, 1965), pp. 164-67.

10. Fuller, pp. 165f.

11. Hahn, *The Titles of Jesus in Christology*, p. 281.

12. Ibid., p. 288.

13. W. Pannenberg, *Jesus—God and Man* (Philadelphia: Westminster, 1978).

14. Hahn, *The Titles of Jesus in Christology*, p. 289.

15. Ibid., p. 295. Cf. J. B. Metz, *Poverty of Spirit* (New York: Newman Press, 1968).

16. Hahn, *The Titles of Jesus in Christology*, p. 297.

17. See R. E. Brown, *The Birth of the Messiah* (New York: Doubleday, 1977), pp. 160-62; 298-310; 517-34.

18. Hahn, *The Titles of Jesus in Christology*, p. 299.

19. See Fuller, p. 166.

20. Hahn, *The Titles of Jesus in Christology*, p. 300.

21. Ibid., p. 203. Cf. Rom 4:4; Phil 2:6; Jn 1:14.

22. E. Schweizer, "UIOS," *TDNT*, vol. 8, pp. 387-88.

23. B. Vawter, *This Man Jesus: An Essay Toward a New Testament Christology* (New York: Doubleday, 1973), p. 132.

24. Kasper, p. 198.

25. K. Rahner, "Theios in the New Testament," *Theological Investigations*, vol. 1 (New York: Seabury Press, 1974), p. 112.

26. Ibid.

27. C. H. Dodd writes: "There is a reason for this realism of the parables of Jesus. It arises from a conviction that there is no mere analogy, but an inward affinity, between the natural order and the spiritual order; or as we might put it in the language of the parables themselves, the Kingdom of God is intrinsically like the processes of nature and of the daily life of men. Jesus therefore did not feel the need of making up artificial illustrations for the truths he wanted to teach. He found them ready-made by the maker of man and nature. That human life, including the religious life, is a part of nature is distinctly stated in the well-known passage beginning 'Consider the fowls of the air...'(Mt. 6:26-30; Lk. 12:24-28).

Since nature and supernature are one order, you can take any part of that order and find in it illumination for other parts. Thus the falling of the rain is a religious thing, for it is God who makes the rain to fall on the just and the unjust...and the love of God is present in the natural affection of a father for his scapegrace son. This sense of the divineness of the natural order is the major premise of all the parables" (*The Parables of the Kingdom* [London: 1935], p. 2).

28. R. Hammerton-Kelly, *God the Father* (Philadelphia: Fortress Press, 1979), p. 81.

29. See W. Pannenberg, *Theology and the Kingdom of God* (Philadelphia: Westminster, 1969); Norman Perrin, *Jesus and the Language of the Kingdom* (Philadelphia: Fortress Press, 1976); Rudolph Schnackenburg, *God's Rule and Kingdom* (New York: Herder and Herder, 1963).

30. Moule, p. 152.

31. See James D. G. Dunn, *Christology in the Making* (Philadelphia: Westminster, 1980), pp. 98-128.

32. Ibid., p. 106.

Chapter Four

1. The bibliography on Philippians 2 is enormous. The following titles seem to be among the most important: E. Lohmeyer, *Kyrios Jesus: Eine Untersuchung zu Phil. 2,5-11* (SHAW, 1928); E. Kasemann, "A Critical Analysis of Phil. 2:5-11" (1950) ET *JThC* 5 (1969), pp. 45-88; R. P. Martin, *Carmen Christi: Phil. ii, 5-11*, MSSNTS 4 (1967); M. D. Hooker, "Phil 2,6-11," in *Jesus und Paulus*, Festschrift fur W. G. Kummel zum 70 Geburtstag, ed. E. E. Ellis and E. Grasser (Göttingen: Evanderhoeck and Ruprecht, 1975), pp. 151-64; F. Manns, "Un hymne judeo-chretienne: Phil 2,6-11," *ED* 29 (1976), pp. 259-90; J. Murphy O'Connor, "Christological Anthropology in Phil 2:6-11," *RB* 83 (1976), pp. 23-50; G. Howard, "Phil 2:6-11 and the Human Christ," *CBQ* 40 (1978), pp. 368-87; C. J. Robbins, "Rhetorical Structure on Phil 2.6-11," *CBQ* 42 (1980), pp. 73-82; T. Nagata, "A Neglected Literary Feature of the Christ Hymn in Phil 2.6-11," *AJBI* 9 (1983), pp. 184-229; N. T. Wright, "*Harpagmos* and the Meaning of Phil 2:5-11," *JThS NS* 37 (1986), pp. 321-52; J. A. Fitzmyer, "The Aramaic Background of Phil 2:6-11," *CBQ* 50 (1988), pp. 470-83; and U. B. Muller, "Der Christushymnus Phil 2.6-11," *ZNW* 79 (1988), pp. 14-44.

2. On the question of preexistence in general see, Pierre Benoit, "Preexistence et incarnation," *Exegese et theologie* (Paris: Editions du Cerf, 1981-82), 4/4:11-61; Fred B. Craddock, *The Pre-Existence of Christ in the New Testament* (Nashville: Abingdon Press, 1973); Robert G. Hammerton-Kelly, *Pre-Existence, Wisdom, and the Son of Man: A Study of the Pre-Existence in the New Testament*. Society for New Testament Studies Monograph Series 21 (Cambridge: Cambridge University Press, 1973); Alan Segal, "Pre-existence and Incarnation: A Response to Dunn and Holladay," *Christology and Exegesis: New Approaches*, ed. Robert Jewett, *Semeia* 30 (Decatur, GA.: Scholars Press, 1985), pp. 83-95. Concerning Philippians 2 see the following: C. H. Talbert, "The Problem of Pre-Existence in Phil. 2:6-11," *JBL* 86 (1967), pp. 141-53; G. Bornkamm, "On Understanding the Christ Hymn (Phil.2:6-11)," *Early Christian Experience* (London: SCM, 1969), pp. 112-22; D. Georgi, "Der vorpaulinische Hymnus Phil 2,6-11," in *Zeit und Geschichte*, GS, R. Bultmann (Tubingen: Mohr, 1964), pp. 263-93.

3. See Martin.

4. See J. B. Lightfoot, *Paul's Epistle to the Philippians* (New York:

Macmillan, 1927), pp. 109-15; Lohmeyer, *Kyrios Jesus: Eine Unter-suchung zu Phil. 2,5-11*.

5. L. D. Hurst, "Re-enter the Pre-existent Christ in Philippians 2.5-11?" *NTStud* 32 (March 1986), pp. 449-57.

6. O'Connor.

7. Ibid., p. 31.

8. James Dunn, *Christology in the Making: An Inquiry into the Origins of the Doctrine of Incarnation* (Philadelphia: Westminster, 1980).

9. Hooker, p. 156.

10. See Kasemann, "A Critical Analysis of Phil. 2:5-11," pp. 45-88.

11. R. P. Martin, *Carmen Christi: Philippians 2:1-11 in Recent Interpretation and in the Setting of Early Christian Worship* (Cambridge: Cambridge University Press, 1967), p. 153.

12. Hooker, p. 156.

13. Ibid., p. 155.

14. Ibid., p. 162.

15. R. Scroggs, *The Last Adam: A Study in Pauline Anthropology* (Philadelphia: Fortress Press, 1966); C. A. Wanamaker, "Philippians 2,6-11: Son of God or Adamic Christology?" *NTS* 33 (1987), pp. 179-93; N. T. Wright, "Adam in Pauline Christology," *SBL* (1983 Seminar), pp. 359-89.

16. Martin Hengel, *The Son of God* (Philadelphia: Fortress Press, 1976), pp. 33-35.

17. See Kasemann.

18. Hooker, p. 162.

19. C. F. D. Moule, "The Manhood of Jesus in the New Testament," S. W. Sykes, *Christ, Faith and History* (Cambridge: Cambridge University Press, 1972), pp. 95-111.

20. Ibid.

21. Hooker, p. 164.

22. See M. D. Hooker, "Interchange in Christ," in *JoTh* 22 (1971), pp. 349-61. What the early Easter profession of faith suggests is explicit in some early hymns to and confessions of faith in Christ. In these hymns and confessions we find a Christology of exchange. A great exchange has taken place in the divine-human history. "For you know how generous Our Lord Jesus Christ has been: he was rich, yet for your sake he became poor, so that through his poverty you might become rich" (2 Cor 8-9). The

first letter of Peter brings out this connection between the two-stage Christology and the Christology of exchange. "For Christ also died for our sins once and for all. He, the just, suffered for the unjust, to bring us to God" (3:18). In connection with exchange Christology, the two-stage Christology carries a universal scope and dimension. This is underlined in 1 Timothy 3:16 when an older hymn is quoted: "He who was manifested in the body, vindicated in the spirit, seen by angels; who was proclaimed among the nations, believed in throughout the world, glorified in high heaven." Jesus Christ, heaven and earth in flesh and spirit are united. Cf. H. W. Bartsch, "Die koncrete Vahrheit und die Luge der Spekulation: Untersuchung uber den vorpaulineschen Christushymnus und seine gnotische Mythisierung," *Theologie und Wirklichkeit* 1 (Bern: H. Lang, 1974); J. F. Collange, *L'Epitre de Saint Paul aux Philippiens* (Cambridge: Cambridge University Press, 1972); J. T. Sanders, *The New Testament Christological Hymns* (Cambridge: Cambridge University Press, 1971).

23. Hammerton-Kelly.

24. Karl Joseph Kushel, *Born Before All Time? The Dispute Over God's Origin* (New York: Crossroad, 1993), pp. 253ff.

25. Commentaries on Mark include Vincent Taylor, *The Gospel According to St. Mark* (London: Macmillan, 1959); Ralph Martin, *Mark: Evangelist and Theologian* (Grand Rapids, Mich.: Zondervan Publishing House, 1973); Monica D. Hooker, *The Message of Mark* (London: Epworth Press, 1983).

On the structure of Mark see H. C. Kee, "Mark's Gospel in Recent Research," *Interpretation* 32/4 (1978), pp. 353-68; J. D. Kingsbury, "The Gospel of Mark in Current Research," *Religious Studies Review* 5/2 (1979), pp. 101-7; W. L. Lane, "The Gospel of Mark in Current Study," *Southwestern Journal of Theology* 21/1 (1978), pp. 7-21; N. Perrin, "The Interpretation of the Gospel of Mark," *Interpretation* 30/2 (1976), pp. 115-24; B. G. Powley, "Revisiting Mark," *Scripture Bulletin* 12/2 (1981), pp. 40-45; Sean P. Kealy, *Mark's Gospel: A History of Its Interpretation* (New York: Paulist Press, 1982); M. E. Boring, "Mark 1:1-15 and the Beginning of the Gospel," *Semeia* 52 (1990), pp. 43-81.

26. Norman Perrin, *A Modern Pilgrimage in New Testament Christology* (Philadelphia: Fortress Press, 1974).

27. See John Donahue, "A Neglected Factor of the Theology of Mark," *JBL* 101 (1982), pp. 563-921.

28. On the *Theios Aner* question see H. D. Betz, "Jesus as Divine Man," *Jesus and the Historian*, ed. F. F. Trotter (Philadelphia: Westminister, 1968), pp. 114-33; Theodore Weeden, *Mark: Traditions in Conflict*

(Philadelphia: Fortress Press, 1971), p. vii; William Lane, "*Theios Aner* Christology and the Gospel of Mark," *New Dimensions in New Testament Study*, ed. Richard Longenecker and Merrill Tenney (Grand Rapids, Mich.: Zondervan Publishing House, 1974), pp, 144-61; Jack Kingsbury, "The 'Divine Man' as the Key to Mark's Christology: The End of an Era?" *Interpretation* 35 (1981), pp. 243-57; Carl Holladay, *Theios Aner in Hellenistic Judaism: A Critique of the Use of This Category in New Testament Christology*, SBLDS 40 (Missoula, Mont.: Scholars Press, 1977).

29. Perrin, *A Modern Pilgrimage in New Testament Christology*, p. 110. On Christology in Mark see Leander Keck, "Mark 3:7-12 and Mark's Christology," *JBL* 84 (1965), pp. 341-58; Norman Perrin, "The Christology of Mark: A Study of Methodology," *JR* 51 (1971), pp. 173-87; Jan Lambrecht, "The Christology of Mark," *Biblical Theology Bulletin* 3 (1973), pp. 256-73; E. Trocme, "Is There a Markan Christology?" *Christ and Spirit in the New Testament*, ed. Barnabas Lindars and Stephen S. Smalley (Cambridge: Cambridge University Press, 1973), pp. 3-14; Eduard Schweizer, "Towards a Christology of Mark?" *God's Christ and His People*, ed. Jacob Jervell and Wayne Meeks (Oslo: Universitetsforlaget, 1977), pp. 29-42; Paul Achtemeier, "'He Taught Them Many Things': Reflections on Marcan Christology," *CBQ* 42 (1980), pp. 465-81; Jack Dean Kingsbury, *The Christology of Mark's Gospel* (Philadelphia: Fortress Press, 1983); F. Ferrario, "La Cristologia di Marco: Appunti su alcune piste della ricerca recente," *Bibbia e Oriente* 28 (1986), pp. 15-31.

30. On narrative in Mark see Robert Tannehill, "The Gospel of Mark as Narrative Christology," in *Perspectives on Mark's Gospel*, ed. Norman Petersen, *Semeia* 16 (Chico, CA: Scholars Press, 1979), pp. 57-95; Elizabeth Struthers Malbon, *Narrative Space and Mythic Meaning in Mark* (San Francisco: Harper & Row, 1986).

31. See Sharon Echols Dowd, *Prayer, Power and the Problem of Suffering* (Atlanta: Scholars Press, 1988).

32. See N. Perrin, *What Is Redaction Criticism?* (Philadelphia: Fortress Press, 1969), pp. 40-63.

33. See J. B. Tyson, "The Blindness of the Disciples in Mark," *JBL* 80 (1961), pp. 261-68.

34. L. T. Johnson, *The Literary Function of Possessions in Luke-Acts*, SBL Dissertation Series 39 (Missoula, MT: Scholars Press, 1977), p. 221.

35. P. S. Barbour, "Gethsemane in the Tradition of the Passion," *NTS* 16 (1969/70), pp. 231-51.

36. See L. Mahieu, "L'abandon du Christ sur la Croix," *MSR* 2 (1945), pp. 209-42; M. Rehm, "Eli, Eli Lamah Sabachthani," *BZ* 2 (1958), pp. 275-

78; J. Gnilka, "Mein Gott, Mein Gott, Warum Hast Du Mich Verlassen?" *BZ* 3 (1959), pp. 294-97; G. Joussard, "L'abandon du Christ en Croix dans la Tradition," *RSR* 25 (1924), pp. 310ff.; *RSR* 26 (1925), pp. 609ff.

37. J. Moltmann, *The Crucified God* (New York: Harper & Row, 1973), pp. 193-96.

38. E. Schillebeeckx, *Jesus: An Experiment in Christology* (New York: Seabury Press, 1980), p. 421.

39. J. Donaldson, "'Called to Follow': A Twofold Experience of Discipleship in Mark," *Biblical Theological Bulletin* 5 (1975), pp. 67-72.

On discipleship in Mark see Robert Tannehill, "The Disciples in Mark: The Function of a Narrative Role," *JR* 57 (1977), pp. 386-405; Paul Achtemeier, "'And He Followed Him': Miracles and Discipleship in Mark 10:46-52," *Semeia* 11 (1978), pp. 115-45; Ernest Best, *Following Jesus: Discipleship in the Gospel of Mark, JSNTSup* 4 (Sheffield: JSOT, 1981); John Donahue, *The Theology and Setting of Discipleship in the Gospel of Mark,* 1983 Pere Marquette Theology Lecture (Milwaukee, WI: Marquette University Press, 1983).

40. See Monica Hooker, *Jesus and the Servant: The Influence of the Servant Concept of Deutero-Isaiah in the New Testament* (London: SPCK, 1959).

41. W. H. Kelber, *The Kingdom in Mark: A New Place and a New Time* (Philadelphia: Fortress Press, 1974). On the Kingdom in Mark see Joel Marcus, *The Mystery of the Kingdom of God,* SBLDS 90 (Atlanta: Scholars Press, 1986); Frank Matera, *The Kingship of Jesus: Composition and Theology in Mark 15*, Society of Biblical Literature Dissertation Series 66 (Chico, CA: Scholars Press, 1982).

Chapter Five

1. Novatian, *The Presbyter,* trans. Russell De Simone, *The Fathers of the Church,* vol. 67 (Washington, D.C.: Catholic University Press, 1972), pp. 81-83).

2. Third Letter of Cyril to Nestorius, text in T. H. Bindley and D. F. W. Green, eds., *The Oecumenical Documents of the Faith* (London: Methuen, 1950), p. 212.

3. Peter Brown, *Augustine of Hippo* (London: Faber and Faber, 1967), p. 302.

4. Plato, *Dialogues*, cited by R. B. Edwards, "The Pagan Dogma of the Absolute Unchangeableness of God," *Religious Studies* 14 (1978), p. 309.

5. See R. M. Grant, *The Early Christian Doctrine of God* (Charlottesville: University of Virginia Press, 1966), p. 291.

6. Athanasius, *On the Incarnation*, in *Christology of the Later Fathers*, ed. U. Baillie and J. T. McNeil (Philadelphia: Westminster, 1954), pp. 107-8.

7. Cyril of Alexandria, "Scholia on the Incarnation," in *Five Tomes Against Nestorius*, ed. E. B. Posey (Oxford: James Parrer and Co., 1881), 12, p. 197.

8. Ibid., 13, p. 202.

9. Ibid.

10. P. Van Buren, *The Secular Meaning of the Gospel* (New York: Macmillan, 1963), p. 42.

11. D. Dawe, *The Form of a Servant* (Philadelphia: Fortress Press, 1964), p. 340.

Chapter Six

1. For a history of kenotic Christology see Lucien Richard, "Kenotic Christology in a New Perspective," *Eglise Et Theologie* 7 (1976), pp. 5-39.

2. For example, see G.Thomasius, *Christi Person und Werk* (Erlangen, 1853). The translation of Thomasius's work is to be found in C. Welch, ed., *God and Incarnation in Mid-Nineteenth Century German Theology* (New York, 1965). See also H. R. MacKintosh, *The Doctrine of the Person of Jesus Christ* (Edinburgh: T & T Clark, 1913).

3. J. Macquarrie, "Kenoticism Reconsidered," *Theology* 77 (1974), p. 121.

4. J. Moltmann, *The Crucified God* (New York: Harper & Row, 1973), p. 4.

5. Ibid., p. 205.

6. For an influential criticism of this formula, see F. Schleiermacher, *The Christian Faith*, ed. H. R. MacKintosh and J. S. Stewart (New York: Harper & Row, 1963), vol. 2, pp. 392ff. E. Brunner argues against the formula in the following way: "The doctrine of the Two Natures becomes the object of purely external, theoretical, semi-scientific discussion and explanation. Faith becomes intellectualized, and it is henceforth possible to discuss the Deity of Christ in the same way that a physical phenomenon could be discussed" (*The Mediator*, trans. O. Wyon [Philadelphia: Westminster, 1967], p. 341).

7. W. Pannenberg, *Jesus—God and Man* (Philadelphia: Westminster, 1968), p. 284.

8. Cf. T. DeRegnon, *Etudes de Theologie Positive sur la Sainte Trinite*, vol. 1 (Paris: Victor Retaux, 1892), p. 433.

9. R. Cantalamessa, "The Development of a Personal God," *Concilium*, vol. 103 (New York: Seabury Press, 1977), p. 61.

10. Ibid.

11. St. Augustine, *On the Trinity*, VII, 6.11.

12. Pannenberg, pp. 337-38.

13. Ibid., p. 295.

14. Ibid.

15. K. Rahner writes: "The Jesus of the Chalcedonian dogma, which was directed against Monophysitism and Monothelitism, likewise has a subjective centre of action which is human and creaturely in kind, such that in his human freedom he is in confrontation with God the inconceivable, such that in it Jesus has undergone all those experiences which we make of God not in a less radical, but on the contrary, in a more radical—almost, we might say, in a more terrible—form than in our own case. And this properly speaking not in spite of, but rather because of the so-called hypostatic union" ("The Position of Christology in the Church between Exegesis and Dogmatics," *Theological Investigations*, vol. 11 (London: Darton, Longman, and Todd, 1974), p. 198. P. Schoonenberg takes a similar direction in his Christology and affirms that one must speak of a human person when one speaks about Jesus Christ (see *The Christ* [New York: Herder and Herder, 1969]).

16. G. W. H. Lampe, "The Holy Spirit and the Person of Christ," in *Christ, Faith and History*, ed. S. W. Sykes (Cambridge: Cambridge University Press, 1972), p. 111.

17. P. C. Hodgson, *Jesus—Word and Presence: An Essay in Christology* (Philadelphia: Fortress Press, 1971), p. 65.

18. K. Rahner, "Incarnation," in *Encyclopedia of Theology: The Concise Sacramentum Mundi* (New York: Seabury Press, 1975), p. 695.

19. K. Rahner, "Current Problems in Christology," *Theological Investigations*, vol. 1 (Baltimore: Helicon Press, 1965), p. 161.

20. On this point E. Martinez writes: "Jesus did not proclaim himself—his whole life was a proclamation of the Father and the coming of the Kingdom of God his Father. Faith in God the Father who saves is what Jesus proclaimed and this shines through all the expression of his teaching. After Jesus' Resurrection the early Church did not change this emphasis: the disciples proclaimed the God who has raised up Jesus" ("The Identity of Jesus in Mark," *Communio* 4 [Winter 1974], p. 342).

21. See J. Knox, *The Humanity and Divinity of Christ* (New York: Cambridge University Press, 1967).

22. See J. Hick, ed., *The Myth of God Incarnate* (Philadelphia: Westminster, 1977).

23. Pannenberg, pp. 33-37.

24. K. Rahner makes the point in the following way: "This Savior, who represents the climax of this self-communication, must therefore be at the same time God's absolute pledge by self-communication to the spiritual creature as a whole *and* the acceptance of this self-communication by this Savior; only then is there an utterly irrevocable self-communication on both sides, and only thus is it present in the world in a historically communicative manner" (*Theological Investigations*, vol. 5 [Baltimore: Helicon Press, 1961], p. 176).

25. To concentrate too exclusively on the Christ-event and not on what the Christ-event reveals about God is to run the risk of reductionism. Such a concentration gives rise to the death-of-God theology.

26. See W. Kasper, *Jesus the Christ* (New York: Paulist Press, 1976).

27. P. Schoonenberg, *The Christ* (New York: Herder and Herder, 1969), p. 90.

28. Ibid.

29. See K. Rahner, "Current Problems in Christology," p. 117.

30. This is in opposition to W. Pannenberg: "Apart from Jesus' resurrection it would not be true that from the very beginning of his earthly way God was one with this man...Until his resurrection, Jesus' unity with God was hidden...because the ultimate decision about it had not been given" (*Jesus—God and Man,* p. 321). For Pannenberg, the resurrection is the ground of Jesus' personal unity with God. It is the resurrection and nothing preceding it that decides Jesus' divinity. Here the future has ontological priority.

31. Pannenberg, p. 336.

32. Ibid., p. 335.

33. Ibid., 336.

34. Ibid., p. 337.

35. K. Rahner, *Foundations of Christian Faith* (New York: Seabury Press, 1978), p. 128.

36. Ibid., p. 217.

37. K. Rahner, "The Concept of Mystery in Catholic Theology,"

Theological Investigations, vol. 4 (New York: Seabury Press, 1974), p. 62.

38. K. Rahner, "On the Theology of the Incarnation," *Theological Investigations*, vol. 4 (New York: Seabury Press, 1974), p. 117.

39. See K. Rahner and H. Vorgrimler, *Dictionary of Theology* (New York: Herder and Herder, 1965), p. 240.

40. Rahner, "Current Problems in Christology," p. 161.

41. Rahner, *Foundations of Christian Faith*, p. 197.

42. Rahner, "On the Theology of the Incarnation," p. 114.

43. Ibid., p. 116.

44. See Rahner, *Foundations of Christian Faith*, pp. 202-3.

45. Rahner, "On the Theology of the Incarnation," p. 117.

46. See K. Rahner, "Theological Observations on the Concept of Time," *Theological Investigations*, vol. 11 (New York: Seabury Press, 1974), p. 290.

47. J. Macquarrie, *Principles of Christian Theology* (New York: Charles Scribner's Sons, 1966), p. 274.

48. Rahner, *Foundations of Christian Faith*, p. 218.

49. Rahner, "On the Theology of the Incarnation," p. 117.

50. J. B. Metz, *Theology of the World*, trans W. Glen-Doepel (New York: Herder and Herder, 1969), p. 26.

51. Ibid.

52. See K. Rahner, "The Theology of the Symbol," *Theological Investigations*, vol. 4 (New York: Seabury Press, 1974), p. 237.

53. Cf. Pannenberg, p. 133.

54. Macquarrie, *Principles of Christian Theology*, p. 249.

55. Ibid.

56. Rahner, "The Theology of the Symbol," p. 224.

57. Ibid., p. 230.

58. Ibid., p. 229.

59. Ibid., pp. 229-30.

60. Ibid., p. 234.

61. Ibid., p. 237.

62. Ibid.

63. Ibid., p. 239.

64. Ibid.

65. Rahner and Vorgrimler, p. 240.

66. Macquarrie, "Kenoticism Reconsidered," p. 121.

67. Pannenberg, op. cit.

68. See P. Schoonenberg, "He Emptied Himself, Phil 2:7," *Concilium,* vol. 11 (1966), pp. 53-66.

69. D. Dawe, *The Form of a Servant* (Philadelphia: Fortress Press, 1964), p. 194.

70. Macquarrie, "Kenoticism Reconsidered," p. 121.

71. Ibid., p. 123.

72. Ibid.

73. W. Kasper, *The God of Jesus Christ* (New York: Crossroad, 1976), p. 194.

Chapter Seven

1. D. G. Dunn, *Christology in the Making* (Philadelphia: Westminster, 1980), p. 262.

2. See the discussion of the issue of immutability in Chapter 5.

3. Cf. Jurgen Moltmann, *The Crucified God* (New York: Harper & Row, 1974); Eberhard Jungel, *God as the Mystery of the World*, trans. Darrell L. Guder (Edinburgh: T & T Clark, 1977); Karl Barth, *Church Dogmatics*, IV/I-IV/3 (Edinburgh: T & T Clark, 1958); and Paul Fiddes, *The Creative Suffering of God* (Oxford: Clarendon Press, 1988).

4. For Moltmann, the cross became "the material principle of the doctrine of the Trinity" (Moltmann, p. 24). The cross reveals the eternal Son as "delivered up" and "abandoned" by the Father and reveals the Father who becomes fatherless by the death of the Son. The cross becomes the cross of the "Crucified God." For Moltmann, the cross must be understood as a divine event. "If the cross of Jesus is understood as a divine event, i.e. as an event between Jesus and his God and Father, it is necessary to speak in Trinitarian terms of the Son and the Father and the Spirit" (ibid., p. 346).

5. E. Jungel, "The Relationship between 'Economic' and 'Immanent' Trinity," *Theology Digest* 24, no. 2 (1976), pp. 180-81.

6. Moltmann, p. 277.

7. Barth, II/2: pp. 164-65. Barth writes of the Father: "It is not at all the case that God has no part in the suffering of Jesus Christ even in his mode of being as the Father. No, there is a *particular* truth in the teaching

of the early patripassians. This is that primarily it is God the Father who suffers in the offering and sending of his Son, in his abasement. The suffering is not his own, but the alien suffering of the creature, of man, which he takes to himself in him. But he does suffer it in the humiliation of his Son with a depth with which it never was or will be suffered by any man—apart from the One who is his Son...This fatherly fellow-suffering of God is the mystery, the basis, of the humiliation of his Son; the truth of that which takes place historically in his crucifixion (Barth IV/2: p. 357).

8. These various theologies of the cross are influenced by the theology of Luther. They appeal to the exegesis of Mark 15:39. The true confession and revelation of Jesus as Son of God takes place at the foot of the cross in the act of dying. Mark seems to affirm that Jesus' divine Sonship is expressed in suffering and in dying. In light of Mark's gospel no one can really perceive the God of Jesus Christ as an apathetic God.

9. P. Hodgson, *New Birth of Freedom: A Theory of Bondage and Liberation* (Philadelphia: Fortress Press, 1976), pp. 336-37.

10. Jungel, "The Relationship between 'Economic' and 'Immanent' Trinity," p. 182.

11. E. Jungel, *The Doctrine of the Trinity: God's Being Is Becoming* (Grand Rapids, Mich.: Eerdmans, 1976), p. 182.

12. This aspect of the inner life of God has been developed by S. N. Bulgakov. He writes: "The Sonship is already an eternal kenosis...because the Word seems to become wordless (in Himself) and makes Himself the Word of the Father...If, on the side of the Father, there is self-negation in begetting of the Son, the Son is thoroughly emptying Himself when He accepts the passive state of the One who is begotten" (quoted by N. Gorodetzsky, *The Humiliated Christ in Modern Thought* [London: SPCK, 1938], p. 162).

13. J. O'Donnell, *The Mystery of the Triune God* (New York: Paulist Press, 1989), p. 65. He refers to H. Urs von Balthasar, *Theodramatik* III (Einsiedeln: Benziger, 1980), pp. 297-305 and *Herrlichkeit* III, 2, Teil 2 (Einsiedeln: Benziger, 1969), p. 208. See von Balthasar's essay *Life Out of Death: Meditations on the Easter Mystery* (Philadelphia: Fortress Press, 1985).

14. Moltmann, p. 255.

15. K. Rahner, *The Trinity* (New York: Herder and Herder, 1970), p. 23.

16. H. Wheeler Robinson, *The Christian Experience of the Holy Spirit* (London: Nisbet Co., 1942), pp. 89-90.

17. C. E. Raven, Gifford Lectures, *Natural Religion and Christian Theology*, vol. 2, *Experience and Interpretation* (Cambridge: Cambridge University Press, 1953), p. 157.

18. Cf. Robinson, pp. 192-98.

19. The 1986 encyclical *Dominum et Vivificantem* affirms the coming of the Holy Spirit at the cost of Christ's death: "The Holy Spirit as Love and Gift comes down, in a certain sense, into the very heart of the sacrifice which is offered on the cross...He consumes this sacrifice with the fire of the love which unites the Son with the Father in the Trinitarian communion. The Holy Spirit is revealed and at the same time made present as the Love that works in the depths of the Paschal Mystery, as the source of the salvific power of the Cross of Christ, and as the gift of new and eternal life" (*Origins*, vol. 16, no. 4 [June 12, 1986], p. 4). The encyclical seems to be moving into pneumatology by way of the theology of the cross. The encyclical can even affirm "the pain of God," which now "in Christ Crucified acquires through the Holy Spirit its full human expression" (ibid.).

20. "In his intimate life, God 'is love,' the essential love shared by the three divine Persons: Personal love is the Holy Spirit as the Spirit of the Father and the Son. Therefore he 'searches even the depths of God,' as uncreated love-gift. It can be said that in the Holy Spirit the intimate life of the triune God becomes totally gift, an exchange of mutual love between the divine Persons, and that through the Holy Spirit God exists in the mode of gift. It is the Holy Spirit who is the personal expression of this self-giving, of this being-love. He is person-love. He is person-gift. Here we have an inexhaustible treasure of the reality and an inexpressible deepening of the concept of person in God, which only divine revelation makes known to us" (*Dominum et Vivificantem* [Origins, vol. 16, no. 4 (June 12, 1986), p. 81]).

21. Ibid.

22. William Hill, *The Three-Personed God: The Trinity as a Mystery of Salvation* (Washington, D.C.: The Catholic University of America Press, 1982), p. 286.

23. Ibid.

24. As Walter Kasper writes: "The Spirit thus expresses the innermost nature of God—God as self-communicating love—in such a way that this innermost reality proves at the same time to be the outermost, that is, the possibility and reality of God's being outside of himself. The Spirit is as it were the ecstasy of God; he is God as pure abundance, God as the overflow of love and grace" ("The God of Jesus Christ," trans. M. J. O'Connell

[New York: Crossroad, 1984], p. 226). See also H. Urs von Balthasar, "Der Heilige Geist als Licht," *Spiritus Creator, Shriftin zur Theologie* 3 (Einsiedeln: Johannes V., 1967), pp. 106-22.

25. Hans Küng, *The Incarnation* (New York: Crossroad, 1987), p. 450.

26. Ibid.

Chapter Eight

1. On the theology of creation see Robert C. Neville, *God the Creator: On the Transcendence and Presence of God* (Chicago: University of Chicago Press, 1968); John Reumann, *Creation and New Creation: The Past, the Present and Future of God's Creative Activity* (Minneapolis: Augsburg Publishing House, 1973); Jurgen Moltmann, *God in Creation: A New Theology of Creation and the Spirit of God* (San Francisco: Harper & Row, 1985); Zachary Hayes, *What Are They Saying about Creation?* (New York: Paulist Press, 1980); Langdon Gilkey, *Maker of Heaven and Earth: The Doctrine of Creation in the Light of Modern Knowledge* (New York: Doubleday, 1959).

2. G. von Rad, *Theology of the Old Testament* (Edinburgh: Oliver and Boyd, 1962).

3. Charles Darwin, *The Origin of Species*, 6th ed. (London: Watts, 1950), pp. 408.

4. Gabriel Marcel, *Journal Metaphysique* (March 5, 1933), quoted in Robert Bultot "The Theology of Earth Realities and Lay Spirituality," *Concilium*, no. 19 (1966), p. 54.

5. Irenaeus, *Against the Heresies*, 4.20.7; 3.20.2.

6. See Bernard Anderson, *Creation Versus Chaos: The Reinterpretation of Mythical Symbolism in the Bible* (New York: Association Press, 1967); Reumann, *Creation and New Creation*; Claus Westermann, *Creation* (Philadelphia: Fortress Press, 1974); and Richard Clifford, "The Hebrew Scriptures and the Theology of Creation," *TS* 46 (1985), pp. 507-23.

7. Emil Brunner, *The Divine Human Encounter* (London: SCM, 1949), pp. 40, 45.

8. Claus Westermann, *Creation*, trans. John S. Scullion (London: SPCK, 1974), p. 56.

9. Augustine, *Confessions*, trans. R. S. Pine-Coffin (Baltimore: Penguin Books, 1961), p. 147; cf. W. F. Hambly, "Creation and Gospel, a Brief Comparison of Gen. 1:1-2, 4 and John 1:1-2, 12," *Studia Evangelica*, 5 (1965), pp. 69-74.

10. W. E. Pilgrim, "Luke-Acts and a Theology of Creation," *Word and World* 12 (January 1992), pp. 51-58.

11. See Richard Clifford, "The Bible and the Environment," in *Preserving the Creation: Environmental Theology and Ethics*, ed. Kevin Irwin and Edmond N. Pellegrino (Washington, D.C.: Georgetown University Press, 1994), pp. 20ff.

12. Ibid., p. 21.

13. Edward Schillebeeckx, *Christ: The Experience of Jesus as Lord* (New York: Seabury Press, 1980), p. 554.

14. See John G. Gibbs, *Creation and Redemption: A Study in Pauline Theology* (Leiden: Brill, 1971).

15. Gabriel Daly, "Foundations in Systematics for Ecological Theology," in Irwin and Pellegrino, p. 42.

16. See Gabriel Daly, *Creation and Redemption* (Wilmington, Del.: Michael Glazier, 1988).

17. J. D. Levenson, *Creation and the Persistence of Evil* (San Francisco: Harper & Row, 1988).

18. John Macquarrie, *Principles of Christian Theology* (London: SCM, 1977), p. 212.

19. Daly, "Foundations in Systematics for Ecological Theology," pp. 48-49.

20. Ibid.

21. Irenaeus, *Against the Heresies*, 2.30.9.

22. Ibid.

23. See H. A. Wolfson, "The Identification of Ex Nihilo with Emanation in Gregory of Nyssa," *Harvard Theological Review* 63 (1970), pp. 53-60.

24. This can be found in Athanasius and is well-expressed in John of Damascus, who writes: "Generation is beginningless and eternal, being the work of nature [that is, not of will] and coming forth as the Father's own essence, [...] while creation in the case of God, being the work of the will, is not co-eternal with God, but it is not natural that that which is brought into existence from nothing should be co-eternal with that which is beginningless and everlasting" (quoted by Wolfson, p. 53).

25. Anselm writes: "Although it is clear that before they were made, those things which have been made were nothing—with respect to the fact that they were not then what they are now and there was not anything from which they were made—nevertheless they were not nothing with

respect to their Maker's thought [*rationem*], through which and according to which they were made" (Anselm of Canterbury, vol. 1: *Monologion, Proslogion, Debate with Guanilo, and Meditation on Human Redemption,* ed. J. Hopkins and H. Richardson [Toronto: Edwin Mellen, 1975], p. 18).

26. Thomas Aquinas, *Summa* I.45. 5. ad 1.

27. Ibid., I, 45, 5.

28. Thomas Aquinas, *Contra Gentiles* II, 17.4.

29. Ibid., II, 18.2.

30. Creation *ex nihilo* is a doctrine of the church. Vatican I in its *Dogmatic Constitution, Dei Filius,* affirms the following: "This one and only true God, of His own goodness and almighty power, not for the increase of His own happiness, nor for the acquirement of His perfection, but in order to manifest His perfection through the benefits which He bestows on creatures, with absolute freedom of counsel, 'from the beginning of time made at once (*simul*) out of nothing both orders of creatures, the spiritual and the corporeal, that is, the angelic and the earthly, and then (*deinde*) the human creature, who as it were shares in both orders, being composed of spirit and body'" (no. 19).

The fifth canon that follows this text affirms the following: "If anyone refuses to confess that the world and all things contained in it, the spiritual as well as the material, were in their whole substance produced by God out of nothing; or says that God created not by an act of will free from all necessity, but with the same necessity by which He necessarily loves Himself; or denies that the world was made for the glory of God, *anathema sit*" (texts found in *The Christian Faith in the Doctrinal Documents of the Catholic Church,* ed. J. Neuner and J. Dupuis [New York: Alba House, 1982], pp. 124-25).

31. Thomas Aquinas, *Summa* III.1, 2 ad 2.

32. Ibid., I. 45. 3.

33. Ibid., I.8.3 ad 1.

34. Ian Barbour, *Religion in an Age of Science.* The Gifford Lectures 1989-1991, vol. 1 (San Francisco: Harper & Row, 1990), p. 181.

35. Ibid., p. 145.

36. See David J. Bartholomew, *God of Chance* (London: SCM, 1984).

37. Jacques Monod, *Chance and Necessity* (New York: Vintage Books, 1972), p. 110.

38. John Polkinghorne, "Creation and the Structure of the Physical World," *Theology Today,* vol. 44, no. 1 (April 1987), p. 65.

39. Arthur Peacocke, *Theology for a Scientific Age, Being and Becoming–Natural and Divine* (London: Basil Blackwell, 1990), pp. 118-19.

40. Daly, "Foundations in Systematics for Ecological Theology," p. 44.

41. Peacocke, p. 119.

42. Bartholomew, p. 97.

43. Ibid., p. 107.

44. Polkinghorne, p. 67.

45. Macquarrie, p. 219.

46. William P. Alston writes: "Many people think, and I myself at one time thought, that the belief that God enters into active interaction with his creatures, a belief crucial to the Judeo-Christian tradition, requires us to suppose that God directly intervenes in the world, acting outside the course of nature...Just by virtue of creating and sustaining the natural order God is in as active contact with his creatures as one would wish...If God speaks to me, or guides me, or enlightens me by the use of natural causes, he is as surely in active contact with me as if he had produced the relevant effects by direct fiat...After all, when one human being directly interacts with another...the agent is making use of aspects of the natural order...And surely this does not imply that we are not in active contact with each other in such transactions. However necessary direct intervention may be for the authentication of messengers, it is not required for genuine divine-human interaction" ("God's Action in the World," *Evolution and Creation*, ed. Ernan McMullin [Notre Dame, Ind.: University of Notre Dame Press, 1985], pp. 213-14).

47. David Jenkins writes: "A God who uses the openness of his created universe, the openness and freedom of men and women created in his image and the mystery of his own risky and creative love to insert additional causal events from time to time into that universe to produce particular events or trends by that eventuality alone would be a meddling demigod, a moral monster and a contradiction of himself...God is not an arbitrary meddler nor an occasional fixer. This is morally intolerable, and no appeal to the mysteriousness of particularity or its scandal can overcome this...However he interacts or transacts he cannot intervene as an additional and inserted and occasional historical cause" (*God, Miracle and the Church of England* [London: SCM, 1987], pp. 63-64).

48. Vincent Brummer, *What Are We Doing When We Pray?* (London: SCM, 1984), p. 90.

49. Peacocke, p. 157.

50. Daly, "Foundations in Systematics for Ecological Theology," p. 45.

51. Bartholomew, p. 138.

52. Peacocke, p. 121.

53. Serge Bulgakov, quoted in G. MacGregor, *He Who Lets Us Be: A Theology of Love* (New York: Seabury Press, 1975), p. 104.

54. See Gershon Scholem, *Major Trends in Jewish Mysticism* (New York: Schocken Books, 1961), pp. 260-61.

55. Peacocke, pp. 121-22.

56. Walter Kasper, *Jesus the Christ* (New York: Paulist Press, 1976), p. 95.

57. Jurgen Moltmann, *The Church in the Power of the Spirit* (New York: Harper & Row, 1975), p. 62.

58. Jurgen Moltmann, *The Crucified God* (New York: Harper & Row, 1975), p. 271.

59. Simone Weil, *First and Last Notebooks*, trans. R. Rees (London: Oxford University Press, 1970), p. 297.

60. H. Küng, *On Being a Christian* (Garden City: Doubleday, 1974), pp. 30, 61.

61. D. Dawe, *The Form of a Servant* (Philadelphia: Fortress Press, 1964), p. 189.

62. J. J. O'Donnell, S. J., *Trinity and Temporality* (Oxford: Oxford University Press, 1983), p. 200.

63. K. Rahner, *Foundations of Christian Faith* (New York: Crossroad, 1978), p. 221.

64. Ibid., p. 222.

65. Peter Hodgson, *Jesus—Word and Presence: An Essay in Christology* (Philadelphia: Fortress Press, 1977), p. 128.

66. W. H. Vanstone, *Love's Endeavor, Love's Expense* (London: Darton, Longman, and Todd, 1977), pp. 59-60.

67. MacGregor, p. 25.

68. Vanstone, pp. 62-63.

69. Langdon Gilkey, *Reaping the Whirlwind* (New York: Seabury Press, 1976), p. 113. For other material on process theology see John B. Cobb, Jr., *A Christian Natural Theology* (Philadelphia: Westminster Press, 1965); William Christian, *An Interpretation of Whitehead's Metaphysics* (New Haven: Yale University Press, 1967); Lewis S. Ford, *The Lure of God* (Philadelphia: Fortress Press, 1978); Victor Lowe, *Understanding*

Whitehead (Baltimore: Johns Hopkins, 1966); and Walter Stokes, "A Whiteheadian Reflection on God's Relation to the World," *Process Theology*, ed. Ewert Cousins (New York: Newman, 1971).

70. Gilkey, *Reaping the Whirlwind*, p. 308.

71. Ibid., p. 309.

72. Peacocke, p. 126.

73. Schillebeeckx, p. 810.

74. Daly, "Foundations in Systematics for Ecological Theology," p. 51.

75. Holmes Rolston, "Does Nature Need to Be Redeemed?" *Zygon*, vol. 29, no. 2 (June 1994), p. 219.

76. Ibid., p. 228.

77. A. R. Peacocke, *Creation and the World of Science* (Oxford: Clarendon Press, 1979), p. 296.

78. A. R. Peacocke has written: "Man's role may be conceived as that of *priest of creation*, as a result of whose activity, the sacrament of creation is reverenced; and who, because he is conscious of God, himself, and nature, can mediate between insentient nature and God...Man alone can contemplate and offer the actions of the created world to God. But a priest is also active towards the created world: he alone can consciously seek to further and fulfill God's purposes within it" (ibid.).

79. Alfred North Whitehead, *Process and Reality* (New York: Macmillan, 1929), p. 332.

Chapter Nine

1. Karl Rahner, "Current Problems in Christology," *Theological Investigations*, vol. 1 (New York: Seabury Press, 1974), pp. 149-200.

2. *GS*, no. 3, p. 904. All references to Vatican II documents in this chapter are from Austin P. Flannery, ed., *Documents of Vatican II* (Grand Rapids, Mich.: Eerdmans, 1984).

3. *GS*, no. 40, p. 939.

4. *GS*, no. 13. Cf. *GS*, nos. 10, 22, 38.

5. John P. Meier, "The Historical Jesus: Rethinking Some Concepts," *Theological Studies* 51 (1990), p. 18.

6. John P. Meier, *A Marginal Jew: Rethinking the Historical Jesus* (New York: Doubleday, 1991); John Dominic Crossan, *The Historical Jesus: The Life of a Mediterranean Jewish Peasant* (San Francisco: Harper, 1991).

7. K. Rahner, "Dogmatic Considerations on Knowledge and Consciousness in Christ," in *Dogmatic versus Biblical Theology*, ed. H. Vorgrimler (London: Darton, Longman, and Todd, 1964), pp. 242-43.

8. See R. E. Brown, *Jesus, God and Man: Modern Biblical Reflections* (Milwaukee: Bruce, 1967), pp. 39-103; R. E. Brown, *An Introduction to New Testament Christology* (New York: Paulist Press, 1994), pp. 17-102; E. Gutwenger, "The Problem of Christ's Knowledge," *Concilium*, vol. 1, no. 2 (1966), pp. 48-55.

9. J. Moltmann, *Man: Christian Anthropology in the Conflicts of the Present*, trans. J. Sturdy (London: SPCK, 1974), p. 81.

10. In the exegesis of the New Testament there must be an attempt, to use the words of Leander Keck, to free oneself from the "tyranny" of the negative criterion, according to which that which is "dissimilar to characteristic emphases both of ancient Judaism and of the early Church" is seen as most likely to be from Jesus. To apply this criterion in an absolute way is to isolate Jesus from his social and historical environment (Leander Keck, *A Future for the Historical Jesus* [Nashville: Abingdon Press, 1971], pp. 33-35); see also Gerd Theissen, *Sociology of Early Palestinian Christianity*, trans. J. Bowden (Philadelphia: Fortress Press, 1977).

11. Rahner, "Dogmatic Considerations on Knowledge and Consciousness in Christ," p. 248.

12. Ibid.

13. B. Vawter, *This Man Jesus: An Essay toward a New Testament Christology* (New York: Doubleday, 1973), p. 134.

14. Cf. Rahner, "Dogmatic Considerations on Knowledge and Consciousness in Christ," p. 262.

15. W. Pannenberg, *Jesus—God and Man* (Philadelphia: Westminster, 1968), p. 304.

16. Cf. Rahner, "Dogmatic Reflections on the Knowledge and Self-Consciousness of Christ," *Theological Investigations*, vol. 5 (Baltimore: Helicon Press, 1966), p. 206.

17. Rudolph Pesch, "Jesus: A Free Man," *Concilium*, vol. 3, no. 13 (1974), p. 68.

18. P. C. Hodgson, *New Birth of Freedom. A Theory of Bondage and Liberation* (Philadelphia: Fortress Press, 1976), p. 217.

19. Vawter, p. 213.

20. On this question see J. A. T. Robinson, *The Human Face of God* (Philadelphia: Westminster Press, 1973), pp. 68-98; R. Niebuhr, *The*

Nature and Destiny of Man, vol. 2 (New York: Charles Scribner's Sons, 1966), pp. 53-59.

21. J. Macquarrie, *Principles of Christian Theology* (New York: Charles Scribner's Sons, 1966), pp. 53-59.

22. Cf. Rahner, "Dogmatic Reflections on the Knowledge and Self-Consciousness of Christ," p. 206.

23. Pesch, p. 68.

24. Hodgson, p. 217.

25. Kasper, p. 213.

26. See Robinson, pp. 68-98.

27. Macquarrie, pp. 53-59.

28. Hodgson, p. 171.

29. Moltmann, p. 118.

Chapter Ten

1. D. Tracy, *Blessed Rage for Order* (New York: Seabury Press, 1975), p. 206.

2. *Gaudium et Spes* (Pastoral Constitution on the Church in the Modern World), in *The Conciliar and Post-Conciliar Documents*, A. Flannery, ed. (Northport: Costello Publishing Co., 1975), no. 22, p. 922.

3. G. Baum, *Man Becoming* (New York: Herder and Herder, 1970), p. 37.

4. H. Urs von Balthasar, *A Theological Anthropology* (New York: Sheed and Ward, 1967), p. 85.

5. Ibid., p. 87

6. P. C. Hodgson, *New Birth of Freedom: A Theology of Bondage and Liberation* (Philadelphia: Fortress Press, 1976), p. 103

7. J. M. Laporte, "Kenosis: Old and New," *The Ecumenist*, vol. 12, no. 2 (1974), pp. 17-21.

8. J. Macmurray, *The Form of the Personal*, vol.1: *The Self as Agent* (London: Faber, 1957); *The Form of the Personal*, vol.2: *Persons in Relation* (London: Faber, 1961). There are several other important works by Macmurray, including *Reason and Emotion* (London: Faber and Faber, 1935); *The Structure of Religious Experience* (New Haven: Yale University Press, 1936); *Religion, Art, and Science* (Liverpool: Liverpool University Press, 1961). For a complete bibliography of J. Macmurray's work consult T. E. Wren, ed., *The Personal Universe: Essays in Honor of*

John Macmurray (Atlantic Highlands: Humanities Press, 1975), pp. 109-11.

9. Macmurray, *The Self as Agent*, p. 71.

10. Macmurray, *Persons in Relation*, p. 80.

11. Ibid.

12. Ibid., p. 24

13. Ibid., p. 61.

14. Macmurray, *The Self as Agent*, p. 98.

15. In a dialectic the word *contraplete* is used to refer to one or both of the original terms, suggesting that the terms stand in some sense over each other, yet need each other for a statement of the complete truth (see John W. Buckman, "Contrapletion: The Values of Synthetic Dialectic," *The Personalist*, vol. 26 [1945], pp. 353-66).

16. See Macmurray, *Persons in Relation*, p. 79.

17. Ibid., p. 28.

18. Ibid.

19. Ibid., p. 80.

20. Ibid., p. 169.

21. The identity of a person is relational; it is constituted through interaction with speaking and thinking subjects. Self-identity is mediated through symbolic systems, like language and culture. The attainment of I-identity involves sociolinguistic competence.

22. See Macmurray, *Persons in Relation*, p. 221.

23. Ibid.

24. Macmurray, *The Self as Agent*, p. 148.

25. Macmurray, *Persons in Relation*, p. 223.

26. Ibid.

27. Macmurray, *The Self as Agent*, p. 134.

28. P. Hodgson, *Jesus—Word and Presence, An Essay in Christology* (Philadelphia: Fortress Press, 1971), pp. 123-24.

29. Ibid., p. 126.

30. Macmurray, *Persons in Relation*, p. 66. An analysis of human nature that presupposes the primacy of action rather than of reflection shows that the secular concept of the human person as autonomous could hardly be further from the truth. Individual independence is not appropriate for persons. When Macmurray discusses Freud's view of religion he

agrees that Freud's primary assertion—that religion is a development of the child's experience of family life—must be accepted. But the conclusion that religion is therefore illusory so that the acknowledgment of continuing dependence on God as Father should be outgrown by "man come of age" is quite false. Macmurray writes: "We have seen that the form of the child's experience is dependency on a personal Other, and that this form of experience is never outgrown, but provides the ground plan of all personal experience, which is constituted from start to finish by the relation to the Other and communication with the Other. It is this form which finds expression in religion, no doubt, but there is nothing illusory about this. The adult who endeavors to create or to discover, in the context of mature experience, the form of positive personal relationship which he experienced as a child, is not indulging in phantasy, but seeking to realize his own nature as a person. Phantasy, as Freud recognized, is the result of a failure to grow up properly...The wish to destroy the father and take his place is one of the common phantasies of childhood. Would it be as good an argument as Freud's then if we were to conclude that adult atheism was the projection upon the universe of this childish phantasy?" (*Persons in Relation*, pp. 154ff.).

31. Ibid., p. 211.

32. Ibid.

33. G. W. F. Hegel, *Lectures on the Philosophy of Religion*, vol. 3 (London: Routledge & K. Paul, 1962), pp. 24-25.

34. Cf. K. Rahner, "Is the Church Sent to Humanize the World?" *Theological Digest* (1973), p. 20.

35. Søren Kierkegaard, *Works of Love*, trans. Howard and Edna Hong (New York: Harper & Row, 1962), p. 63.

36. Ibid., p. 79.

37. Ibid., p. 76.

38. G. Outka, *Agape: An Ethical Analysis* (New Haven: Yale University Press, 1972), p. 13.

39. L. Lavelle, *Evil and Suffering*, trans. B. Murchland (New York: Macmillan, 1963), p. 32.

40. See B. Wolf, *Living with Pain* (New York: Seabury Press, 1978); F. J. Buytendijk, *Pain and Experience* (Chicago: University of Chicago Press, 1962); W. J. De Sauvage Nolting, "The Meaning of Suffering," *Existential Psychology* 6:28 (1970), pp. 75-86.

41. Lavelle, p. 65.

42. D. Soelle, *Suffering*, trans. E. R. Kalin (Philadelphia: Fortress Press, 1973), p. 68.

43. All suffering, even the potentially meaningful, seems to have certain characteristics that the individual alone can experience ("You cannot imagine how I suffer or the nature of my suffering"). Suffering is seen by many of us as a solitary act. In a definite way we are alone in our suffering. Lavelle writes: "The existence revealed to me in suffering is that of the individual self in its unique and most privileged aspect, at the moment when it ceases to communicate with the world which is now felt as an oppression that turns the self back upon itself" (p. 207).

44. M. de Unamuno, *Tragic Sense of Life*, trans. T. E. Crawford Flitch (New York: Dover Publications, 1954), p. 207.

45. Psychiatrists are astonished at the amount of suffering people will bear unnecessarily. We cling to our suffering as guaranteeing our identity. Our sufferings are ourselves. The self wants to hold on to anything that makes self-recognition possible rather than move toward an unknown experience. This is pathological and a misunderstanding of the real nature of self-identity. Suffering is both an identification of present being and the possibility of becoming. And both of these dimensions are simultaneously necessary.

46. Lavelle, p. 33.

47. V. Frankl, *Man's Search for Meaning* (New York: Washington Square Press, 1963), pp. 58-59.

48. G. Marcel, *The Mystery of Being* (Chicago: Regency Press, 1951), p. 28.

49. P. Ricoeur, *Fallible Man* (Chicago: Henry Regnery, 1967), p. 93.

50. H. G. Gadamer writes: "Language has its true being only in conversation, in the exercise of understanding between people. The process of communication is not a mere action, a purposeful activity, a setting-up-of-signs through which I transmit my will to others...It is a living process in which a community of life is lived out...All forms of human community of life are forms of linguistic community; even more they constitute language. For language in its nature is the language of conversation, but it acquires its reality only in the process of communicating (*Truth and Method* [New York: Seabury Press, 1975], p. 404).

51. See J. B. Metz, *Faith in History and Society* (New York: Seabury Press, 1980), pp. 88-136.

Conclusion

1. *Lumen Gentium*, no. 1, p. 350. All references to Vatican II docu-

ments in this chapter are from A. Flannery, ed., *Documents of Vatican II* (Grand Rapids, Mich.: Eerdmans, 1984).

2. *Ad Gentes*, no. 1, p. 815.

3. *Ad Gentes*, no. 6, p. 820.

4. J. Moltmann, *The Church in the Power of the Spirit* (New York: Harper & Row, 1975), p. 10.

5. See Ray Anderson, ed., *Theological Foundations for Ministry* (Grand Rapids, Mich.: Eerdmans, 1979); Bernard Cooke, *Ministry of Word and Sacraments* (Philadelphia: Fortress Press, 1976).

6. Michael Lawler, "Perichoresis: New Theological Wine in an Old Wineskin," *Horizons* 22 (1995).

7. Cf. Robert Kress, "The Church as *Communio Sacra*: Trinity and Incarnation as the Foundation of Ecclesiology," *The Jurist* 36 (1976), pp. 140ff.

8. See M. Lawler and T. Shanahan, *Church: A Spirited Communion* (Collegeville, Minn.: Liturgical Press, 1995).

9. J. Moltmann, *The Spirit of Life: A Universal Affirmation* (Minneapolis: Fortress Press, 1992), p. 118.

10. Brian McDermott, "Power, Powerlessness, and the Mystery of Christ, *Proceedings of CTSA*, vol. 37 (1982), p. 27. The reference to Karl Rahner is to "The Theology of Power," *Theological Investigations*, vol. 4 (New York: Seabury Press, 1974), pp. 391-409.

11. Cf. Anna Case Winters, *God's Power: Traditional Understandings and Contemporary Challenges* (Louisville: Westminster/John Knox Press, 1990); David Griffin, *God, Power, and Evil: A Process Theodicy* (Lanham, Md.: University Press of America, 1990).

12. Rahner, p. 406.

13. Abraham Heschel, *The Prophets* (New York: Harper & Row, 1962), p. 114.

14. See Bengt Holmberg, *Paul and Power: The Structure of Authority in the Primitive Church as Reflected in the Pauline Epistles* (Philadelphia: Fortress Press, 1980), pp. 70-73.

15. F. J. Van Beeck, "This Weakness of God Is Stronger," *Toronto Journal of Theology* 9 (1993), pp. 9-26; also, Elizabeth Janeway, *Powers of the Weak* (New York: Alfred Knopf, 1980).

16. Dorothy Lee-Pollard, "Powerlessness as Power: A Key to Emphasis in the Gospel of Mark," *Scot J of Theology*, vol. 40 (1987), p. 185.

17. Rollo May, *Power and Innocence* (New York: Norton, 1972), pp. 105-21.

18. Bernard Loomer, PR Scharpe Lectureship on Social Ethics, quoted in J. Coleman, "Power, the Powers and a Higher Power," *TSA*, vol. 37 (1982), p. 4.

19. Ibid., p. 5.

20. See W. H. Vanstone, *The Stature of Waiting* (London: Darton, Longman, and Todd, 1982).

21. J. Moltmann, *Man: Christian Anthropology in the Conflicts of the Present*, trans. J. Sturdy (London: SPCK, 1974), p. 81; cf. Steven Lukes, *Power: A Radical View* (New York: Macmillan, 1974).

22. Paula Cooey, "The Power of Transformation and the Transformation of Power," *Journal of Feminist Study in Religion*, 1 (1985), pp. 23-30.

23. See Thomas Merton's insightful interpretation of the parable of the Good Samaritan in *A Thomas Merton Reader* (Garden City, N.Y.: Image Books, 1974), pp. 348-56.

24. Moltmann, *The Church in the Power of the Spirit*, p. 97.

25. Rosemary Radford Ruether, *To Change the World: Christology and Cultural Criticism* (New York: Crossroad, 1983), p. 54.

26. Liberation theology in Latin America has emphasized this aspect of the church. See Leonardo Boff, *Ecclesiogenesis: The Base Communities Reinvent the Church*, trans. Robert Barr (Maryknoll, N.Y.: Orbis Books, 1986); G. Gutiérrez, *The Power of the Poor in History* (Maryknoll, N.Y.: Orbis Books, 1983); and Jon Sobrino, *The Church and the Poor* (Maryknoll, N.Y.: Orbis Books, 1984).

27. On the ecumenicity of the church see David Lochhead, *The Dialogical Imperative: A Christian Reflection on Interfaith Encounter* (London: SCM, 1988); John Hick, *God Has Many Names: Britain's New Religious Pluralism* (London: Macmillan, 1990); Alan Race, *Christians and Religious Pluralism: Patterns in the Christian Theology of Religions* (London: SCM, 1983); and Paul Knitter, *No Other Name? A Critical Survey of Christian Attitudes toward the World Religions* (Maryknoll, N.Y.: Orbis Books, 1984).

28. B. Lonergan, *Metaphor in Theology* (New York: Herder and Herder, 1979), p. 361.

29. John V. Taylor writes: "A third aspect of the Spirit's creative activity is his continuous substitution of the principle of the self-sacrifice on behalf of another for the natural drive of self-interest and dominance. He

urges all creatures to live by this principle not as an act of virtue or martyrdom but as the only way to life that is real. This, of course, finds its culmination in Jesus Christ, without whom we could never have suspected the centrality of this principle in the whole scheme of things. Life through dying. Life for others. This is the ethos of the new community, the sheep among wolves. And by this presence of the Spirit will be known: 'If Christ's name is flung in your teeth as an insult, count yourselves happy, because then that glorious Spirit which is the Spirit of God is resting upon you' (I Peter 1:14)" (*Go-Between God: The Holy Spirit and the Christian Mission* [Philadelphia: Fortress Press, 1972], p. 104). Again John Taylor writes: "Life in the Spirit is our foretaste of the new world, not its final fulfillment. His indwelling is the seal with which God stamps us with the mark of his ownership, to ensure that we shall be known as his when finally he enters into his own. Our possession by the Spirit is also called by St. Paul the pledge of our coming inheritance. Both are metaphors of a guaranteed future and an unfulfilled present. So the gift of the Spirit, like the Resurrection of Jesus, frees us from the past to live in that which is flowing to meet us" (p. 116).

30. Douglas J. Hall, *Lighten Our Darkness: Toward an Indigenous Theology of the Cross* (Philadelphia: Westminster, 1976), p. 151.

31. Anthony Russell, *The Clerical Profession* (London: SPCK, 1984), pp. 302-3.

32. Christopher Moody, *Eccentric Ministry* (London: Darton, Longman, and Todd, 1987), p. 132.

33. Ibid.

Appendix

1. Karl Rahner, *Theological Writings,* Vol. IV, translated by K. Smyth, Baltimore and London, 1966, 221-52.

2. Ibid., 357-67.

3. Ibid., 229.

4. Aristotle, *The Nicomachean Ethics: A Commentary by...H. H. Joachim,* Oxford, (1951) 1955, 205 and n. 4.

5. Rahner, 365.

6. Ralph Waldo Emerson, *Essays and Lectures,* edited by J. Porte, New York, 1983, 259-82 (Essay II of *Essays: First Series,* 1841).

7. Ibid., 268-69.

8. John Stuart Mill, *On Liberty,* London, 1859.

9. *On Liberty,* edited by G. Himmelfarb, London (1974) 1988, 132.

10. See Friedrich Nietzsche, *Unmodern Observations,* edited by W. Arrowsmith, New Haven, 1990, 245 n. 55; and Gertrude Himmelfarb, *On Looking Into the Abyss: Untimely Thoughts on Culture and Society,* New York, 1994, 4-5.

11. John McDade, "Beauty's Ghost in the Body," *The Way,* no. 66, Autumn 1989: Supplement, Spirituality and the Artist: Essays in Honor of Gerard Manley Hopkins: 1844-1889, 14-25 (at 14).

12. Karl Barth, *The Resurrection of the Dead,* translated by H. J. Stenning, London, 1933, 1934.

13. Emerson, 410: from "Circles" (Essay X of *Essays: First Series*).

14. Himmelfarb, 118.

15. Paul Tillich, *The Courage to Be,* New Haven, 1960.

16. Rahner, 222 ff.

17. Ibid., 224.

18. A. P. Martinich, *A Hobbes Dictionary,* Oxford, 1995, 28-29, 306.

19. Rahner, 251.

20. The New Testament, MDXXVI, reprinted verbatim, edited by G. Offor, London, 1836, Fo. clxiii: Which beynge in the shape off god/[and] thought it not robbery to be equall [*sic*] with god. Nevertheless he made hym silfe of no reputacion/and toke on hym the shape of a servaunte/and becam lyke vnto men/ and was founde in his aparell as a man. He humbled hym silfe and becam obedient vnto the deeth/even the deeth of the crosse. Wherefore God bath exalted hym/and geven hym a name ahove all names: that in the name off Jesus shulde every knee bowe/both of thynges in heven/and thynges in erth and thynges under erth/and that all tonges shulde confesse that Jesus Christ is the lorde vnto the prayse of god the father.

21. Isaac Walton, *The Life of Mr. George Herbert,* London, 1670. *Walton's Lives,* edited by S. B. Carter, London, 1951, 252.

Subject Index